Numen, Old Men
Contemporary Masculine Spiritualities and the Problem of Patriarchy

Gender, Theology and Spirituality

Series Editor
Lisa Isherwood, University of Winchester
Marcella Althaus-Reid, University of Edinburgh

Gender, Theology and Spirituality explores the notion that theology and spirituality are gendered activities. It offers the opportunity for analysis of that situation as well as provides space for alternative readings. In addition it questions the notion of gender itself and in so doing pushes the theological boundaries to more materialist and radical readings. The series opens the theological and spiritual floodgates through an honest engagement with embodied knowing and critical praxis.

Gender, Theology and Spirituality brings together international scholars from a range of theological areas who offer cutting edge insights and open up exciting and challenging possibilities and futures in theology.

Published:

Resurrecting Erotic Transgression: Subjecting Ambiguity in Theology
Anita Monro

Patriarchs, Prophets and Other Villains
Edited by Lisa Isherwood

Unconventional Wisdom
June Boyce-Tillman

Women and Reiki: Energetic/Holistic Healing in Practice
Judith Macpherson

Forthcoming in the series:

Telling the Stories of Han: A Korean, Feminist Theology of Subjectivity
Jeong-Sook Kim

Ritual Making Women: Shaping Rites for Changing Lives
Jan Berry

Through Eros to Agape: The Radical Embodiment of Faith
Timothy R. Koch

For What Sin was She Slain? A Muslim Feminist Theology
Zayn R. Kassam

Our Cultic Foremothers: Sacred Sexuality and Sexual Hospitality in the Biblical and Related Exegetic Texts
Thalia Gur Klein

Baby, You are My Religion: Theory, Praxis and Possible Theology of Mid-20th Century Urban Butch Femme Community
Marie Cartier

Radical Otherness: A Socio/theological Investigation
Dave Harris and Lisa Isherwood

Catholics, Conflicts and Choices
Angela Coco

Numen, Old Men
Contemporary Masculine Spiritualities and the Problem of Patriarchy

Joseph Gelfer

LONDON   OAKVILLE

Published by Equinox Publishing Ltd.
Unit 6, The Village, 101 Amies St., London SW11 2JW, UK
DBBC, 28 Main Street, Oakville, CT 06779, USA

www.equinoxpub.com

First published 2009

British Library Cataloguing-in-Publication Data
A catalogue record for this book is available from the British Library.

ISBN   978 1 84553 418 9   (hardback)
         978 1 84553 419 6   (paperback)

Library of Congress Cataloging-in-Publication Data

Gelfer, Joseph.
Numen, old men : contemporary masculine spiritualities and the problem
of patriarchy / Joseph Gelfer.
     p. cm. — (Gender, theology, and spirituality)
Includes bibliographical references (p.   ) and index.
ISBN 978-1-84553-418-9 (hb) — ISBN 978-1-84553-419-6 (pb)
1. Men — Religious life. 2. Masculinity — Religious aspects. 3. Homosexuality — Religious
aspects. 4. Wilber, Ken. Sex, ecology, spirituality. 5. Patriarchy — Religious aspects.
I. Title.
BL625.65.G46 2009
204'.4081 — dc22
                              2008023971

Typeset by S.J.I. Services, New Delhi
Printed and bound in Great Britain by Lightning Source, Milton Keynes, UK

CONTENTS

ACKNOWLEDGEMENTS

Numen, Old Men is a product of my doctoral research at Victoria University of Wellington in New Zealand. As such, thanks go to my principal supervisor, Marion Maddox, and secondary supervisor Chris Marshall, who provided valuable feedback and support. I would also like to thank Philip Culbertson, Björn Krondorfer and Harry Brod: while they have not specifically been involved with the book, I have benefited greatly by being warmly welcomed by them into the field of study they helped create. Thanks also to my wife Amanda Thompson and children — Benedict, Ivy and Magnus — who have been as accommodating as possible during the whole process. Thanks to Men's Studies Press for permission to reprint 'Identifying the Catholic Men's Movement' from *Journal of Men's Studies* (16.1, 2008: 41-56), which comprises a significant percentage of chapter 4.

Preface

This work takes its inspiration from feminist and queer theologians. In the past I had always been rather envious of these folks, whose identity and personal experience was so tightly interwoven with their research. This combination appeared to me to produce an unusual level of commitment which often resulted in not just interesting theology but exciting theology. I wanted some of that excitement, but as a straight man it seemed somewhat elusive, as that feminist and queer commitment was forged in resistance to the inequalities imposed by a system of which I was arguably a part. However, I felt strongly that my experience as a straight man was not fully comparable with the structures of patriarchy and homophobia so eloquently identified and critiqued by feminists and queers. I had a deep, intuitive feeling that I could identify a masculine spirituality that did not perpetuate patriarchy and homophobia, and that once I did, I could commit to it with results as exciting as any feminist or queer theology. And this is how this work started out, as a rediscovery, or even a discovery for this first time of a positive masculine spirituality. I wanted to find a non-patriarchal spirituality that was not just lived by men, but also had something to do with being masculine.

As I began to speak with people about my intentions I met with a common question: The whole history of religion and spirituality has been by and about men, so why seek out a masculine spirituality? These people assumed, with some reasonable cause, that such an exploration was about turning back the clock and undoing the good work of feminists and queers. But, following my intuition, I nevertheless began to search for a positive masculine spirituality that would lay to rest such assumptions. I knew that the popular image of masculine spirituality derived mostly from the men's movement, either in the form of the mythopoetic or Christian men's movement. I knew that these movements had come under some sustained criticism from political and ideological positions with which I aligned myself, but felt that if I dug deep enough something new could be uncovered. More than this, I assumed there must be sizable manifestations of masculine spirituality out there that had not come to popular attention and which could be the source of the positive spirituality I sought. However, the evidence suggested otherwise.

As I immersed myself into the literature it became clear to me that much of the criticism of masculine spirituality in the men's movement was perfectly justified, however deep one goes. In fact, much of the criticism was rather generous as it spoke less to the movement's spirituality than its politics. And those manifestations of masculine spirituality I began to identify that had not yet come to such popular attention were equally unfortunate. All but a few mostly academic individuals who articulated a 'masculine spirituality' were actually articulating a patriarchal spirituality. So it became evident to me that before I could even begin to attempt a positive treatment of masculine spirituality I had to further unpack the negative. The following work is part of this unpacking process.

Chapter One

INTRODUCTION

'When you make the male and the female one and the same, so that the male not be male nor the female female...then will you enter the kingdom' (Gospel of Thomas: 22)

'Let us remember here that the Genderfucker may also be straight' (Althaus-Reid 2003: 68)

On its own terms, masculine spirituality is concerned with articulations of masculinity and spirituality that are appropriate for and resonate with men. This is a reasonable enough assertion, especially given the general familiarity with and appreciation of feminist or women's spirituality and theology. In an ideal world, expressions of masculine spirituality would complement feminine spirituality resulting in a holism which bears witness to the beauty and variety of human experiences. This, I believe, is the intention of many men involved with masculine spirituality. The success of this intention lies solely in *how* masculine spirituality is articulated, because as a manifestation of gender, masculine spirituality is not some stable ontological category, rather a social construction. In the following chapters, numerous voices will disagree with this position, suggesting there are essences to masculine spirituality which are innate rather than constructed. Whichever way, we have a problem if the net effect of masculine spirituality does *not* bear witness to the beauty and variety of human experiences: if, for example, it simply perpetuates the patriarchal norm. In fact, we have one of two problems: either the social construction of masculine spirituality is faulty, or the innate reality of masculine spirituality is faulty (perhaps, even, a combination of the two).

In this book I will argue that most manifestations of masculine spirituality are, in fact, manifestations of patriarchal spirituality. A following section will examine exactly what these words mean. In particular, I look at various manifestations of what is commonly referred to as the 'men's movement': the mythopoetic movement, the evangelical men's movement and the Catholic men's movement. I also examine Ken Wilber's brand of integral spirituality, not because it markets itself as a masculine spirituality, but because as a popular new trend it (perhaps unwittingly) repeats many of the mistakes in regard to gender it claims to transcend. From these I conclude that spiritualities which resonate with a heteronormative understanding of masculinity, whatever their actual intentions, perpetuate and rely upon patriarchy. I then look at gay spirituality as a form of spirituality which, for the most part, resists perpetuating patriarchy by encouraging more diverse ways of understanding and performing masculinities. This suggests queerness has a liberating potential, whatever a person's sexual 'orientation'.

Framing Masculine Spirituality

It is common today to hear about the 'crisis in masculinity' whether from the intense urge to rediscover God's image within men of Leanne Payne's *Crisis in Masculinity* (1985) or the more psychiatric musings of Anthony Clare's *On Men: Masculinity in Crisis* (2000).[1] A common concern can be heard within a religious context:

> For some time past it has been noted in the United States that the Churches are falling more and more into the hands of women. They say that on an average there are three women Church members to one male. To arrest this tendency and to restore the requisite masculine element to popular religion in the States, a syndicate was formed for the purpose of uniting evangelical Churches in America, and of combining efforts to bring men and boys into the Church.[2]

The above passage could have appeared in any one of numerous contemporary articles, but it was actually written nearly a century ago by W. T. Stead who was describing an early incarnation of the Christian men's movement, the predominantly Protestant Men and Religion Forward Movement (Bederman 1989; Allen 2002) that focused on the social gospel around the time of the other key

---

1. Other popular crisis titles include Roger Horrocks' (1994) *Masculinity in Crisis: Myths, Fantasies and Realities* and Susan Faludi's (1999) *Stiffed: The Betrayal of the American Man*.

2. From 'Men and Religion Forward Movement' in *The Review of Reviews*, April 1912, reprinted in Frederick Whyte (1925: 312-13).

masculine revival, Muscular Christianity (Hall 1994; Ladd and Mathisen 1999; Putney 2003).[3] More generally, Michael Kimmel (1987) demonstrates the historical nature of the crisis in masculinity via examples in Restoration England (1688-1714) and later in the United States (1880-1914). The contemporary crisis in masculinity clearly exemplifies Walter Benjamin's famous thesis, 'the "state of emergency" in which we live is not the exception but the rule' (1992: 248). Some people reject the whole notion out of hand, such as James Heartfield's insightfully titled paper, *There is No Masculinity Crisis* (2002); however, its perception remains strong. Two intertwining themes behind a popular understanding of the crisis are the disappearance of traditional masculine characteristics and the pathologizing of those characteristics, both at the mercy of an increasingly feminized society. The response to the perceived crisis has been to reclaim the 'authentically masculine'.

In a contemporary context this process of reclamation is most notably connected with the poet Robert Bly whose book *Iron John* lamented the prevalence of the 'soft male' (1990: 2). Bly urged men to embrace their authentic masculinity by engaging with various neo-Jungian archetypes, of which Iron John, the Wild Man, was one. Bly spearheaded the mythopoetic movement during the 1990s, which garnered much media attention due to its promotion of men's retreats in woodlands and wilderness. A key theme Bly promoted was that men suffer from a 'father wound' due to physically or emotionally absent fathers. This absence means boys have no role models to follow or to initiate them into mature masculinity, resulting in grown men who are essentially still boys. Bly's neo-Jungian archetypes take on a spiritual dimension: as Patrick Arnold notes, 'the Wildman is the spiritual archetype that connects men

3. Even back then this masculine focus was relatively widespread. Bederman highlights ten denominational brotherhoods which supported the Men and Religion Forward Movement: Baptist Brotherhood; Brotherhood of Andrew and Philip (Presbyterian); Brotherhood of Disciples of Christ; Brotherhood of Saint Andrew (Episcopalian); Congregational Brotherhood of America; Lutheran Brotherhood; Methodist Brotherhood; Otterbein Brotherhood (United Brethren); Presbyterian Brotherhood of America; United Presbyterian Brotherhood (1989: 459). The cause was also popularized by evangelist Billy Sunday who stated in 1916, 'Lord save us from off-handed, flabby-cheeked, brittle-boned, weak-kneed, thin-skinned, pliable, plastic, spineless, effeminate, ossified three-karat Christianity' (quoted in Culbertson and Krondorfer 2005).

affectively to God as they experience nature in all its sheer wildness' (1991: 124).[4] Initiation also has a spiritual dimension, drawing on tribal customs and Native American aesthetics. These two themes of archetypes and initiation, coupled with an extensive use of myth, led to the movement often being considered the 'spiritual men's movement'.

Similar concerns were expressed in Christian circles, finding masculine archetypes of a Christian nature to which men could aspire. Arnold (1991) identified a wide array of archetypal qualities in Old Testament characters. Richard Rohr and Joseph Martos (1992) also identified the archetypal masculine qualities of John the Baptist, and of course a good number of writers spoke of Jesus in similar terms. Speaking less of the archetypal masculine, but equally of the authentic masculine, men's ministries such as Promise Keepers suggested men follow biblical values to fully live their natural role as men. In particular, men were urged to step up and lead their families rather than leaving this task to their wives. More recently, John Eldredge's hugely popular *Wild at Heart* (2001) argues that men's lives thrive upon three needs: a battle to fight; a beauty to rescue; an adventure to live.

What these various individuals and groups had in common was the idea that there is a certain way of being a man. Arnold saw the masculine spirit as being a blend of four 'primary colours': 'competition, vulnerability, independence, and responsibility' (Arnold 1991: 31). Similarly, Rohr and Martos saw the masculine spirit as being formed by 'the left-brain powers of logic and language, clarity and distinctness, thinking and deciding, organization and order' (Rohr and Martos 1992: 15). These masculine elements translate into a particular type of spirituality: 'in contrast to feminine spirituality, which is inward and interior and rooted in Mother Earth, male spirituality is outwardly orientated and spatial' (Arnold 1991: 39). This expression of a masculine/feminine binary is common. For example, discussing the Center for Action and Contemplation which Rohr directs, Rohr and Martos suggest, 'the center is geared toward action, which is on the masculine side of spirituality, but it is also a place for contemplation, which is on the feminine side' (Rohr and Martos 1992: 5). Masculine spirituality is

4. Different writers refer to 'Wild Man' or 'Wildman': I change my usage with the context.

about celebrating these masculine values and relocating them at the heart of Christianity, to resist what Arnold sees as the emasculation and neutering of God (Arnold 1991: 201).

Such a celebration looks upon the meek and mild presentations of Jesus, for example, and revisions Him as having 'a sword in His mouth and a rod of iron in His hand' (Weber 1993: 41). Similarly, the average Christian man must revision himself and chant, in tune with the title of one book, *No More Christian Nice Guy* (Coughlin 2005). In the end, proponents of masculine spirituality often feel under siege, as if their very essence was being denied. In one appeal to feminist critics, Rohr and Martos conclude their book with, 'Today, God's sons are without dignity, self-confidence, true power. We look like the oppressors, dear sisters, but have no doubt we are really the oppressed' (1992: 225). This is the context in which masculine spirituality operates.

Discussion of Terms

Contemporary

The period of time examined by *Numen, Old Men* is roughly 1990 to the time of writing in 2007. As to whether 1990 is contemporary nearly two decades later is open to debate, but the fact remains that many of the themes around masculine spirituality that came to public attention in 1990 are still relevant today. The year 1990 was a crucial time for masculine spirituality, and men's studies in general. 1990 was the year Bill McCartney founded Promise Keepers. 1990 was also the year Bly's *Iron John: A Book About Men* was published in the United States (it was published a year later in the UK). Thanks to these two phenomena, the early nineties saw an explosion of interest in men and masculinities.[5] While less visible outside the gay community, the early 1990s also saw an increase in popularity surrounding gay spirituality. Gay liberation is historically aligned with the Stonewall riots of 1969 (Carter 2004; Duberman 1993), but popular gay spirituality gained significant momentum in this later

---

5. While not discussed due to space constraints, this period also significantly saw the Million Man March in 1995, organized by Nation of Islam leader Louis Farrakhan; see LaRon D. Bennett (1996), Devon W. Carbado (1999), Michael H. Cottman (1995), Garth Kasimu Baker-Fletcher (1998), Haki R. Madhubuti and Maulana Karenga (1996), Kim Martin Sadler (1996) and Michael O. West (1999).

period with books such as Mark Thompson's (1994) *Gay Soul* and Toby Johnson's (2000) *Gay Spirituality*.

The time frame of 1990 to 2007 also allows for the revisiting of these themes. While it appeared in the late 1990s and early 2000s that Promise Keepers and the mythopoetic movement were on the decline, more recent years have seen a return in interest if not specifically in these groups then at least the issues they explored. In particular, men's ministries and the re-realization that there are fewer men in churches than women returned to the popular agenda as manifest by best-selling books such as David Murrow's (2005) *Why Men Hate Going to Church*. The recent end of this time frame has also seen a spike in interest in Ken Wilber's integral spirituality with its revisiting of certain familiar gender essentialisms. In short, the time frame is brief enough to explore in some useful depth, and long enough to be able to identify the shifting attitudes to, and fortunes of themes pertinent to masculine spirituality.

Masculine

Whether they know it or not, many proponents of masculine spirituality are engaging in a discourse of sex role theory which argues that in order to reach maturity individuals must take on character traits appropriate to their sex. Joseph Pleck (1987) argues that the history of male sex-role identity has revolved around one basic question: 'what makes men less masculine than they should be, and what can be done about it?' (1987: 22). In this theory, a certain type of masculinity is considered the norm and individuals can either possess too much or (more likely) too little of it. In general, masculine spirituality suggests there is too little male sex role identity happening in the spiritual environment and therefore seeks to boost those appropriate male character traits, despite the fact that most sex/gender researchers have long since moved on from sex role theory which 'is now an event in psychology's history' (Pleck 1987: 38).

Sex role theory's claim that there are certain characteristics appropriate to biological sex has largely been replaced with understanding gender as a social construction which, while it may be related, is distinct from biology. In this equation *male* relates to biological sex and *masculine* to gender construction. While this distinction is widely accepted it is interesting to note that it is generally lost within most articulations of masculine spirituality:

the terms *masculine spirituality, male spirituality* and *men's spirituality* are all largely used interchangeably within the literature, an issue I will explore in chapter 7. In this book I use the phrase masculine spirituality unless directly quoting.

In tandem with the demise of sex role theory in the 1970s was the ascendancy of feminism which showed not just how men had come to dominate women in many social, economic and political ways, but also that the whole default mode of scholarship is masculine: mainstream scholarship becomes what Mary O'Brien (1981) called *malestream*. O'Brien is correct inasmuch as women's experiences were largely absent from scholarship, but the universality of the masculine experience does not necessarily bear witness to the particularity of the masculine experience. In one of the early accounts of the study of men and masculinities, *The Making of Masculinities*, Harry Brod (1987a) suggests, 'while *seemingly* about men, traditional scholarship's treatment of generic man as the human norm in fact systematically excludes from consideration what is unique to men *qua* men'; men's studies then becomes, 'the study of masculinities and male experiences as specific and varying social-historical-cultural formations' (1987a: 2).

Brod's title indicates the need for masculinity to be conceived of as masculinities, accommodating the plurality of men's experiences via race, sexuality, class, physical ability and so forth. That masculinities are multiple and diverse is the one key and almost uncontested issue in the study of men and masculinities. Since these early formulations the scholarship surrounding men and masculinities has proliferated to an extraordinary degree.[6] The expansion of masculinities has recently gained particular momentum with a turn to understanding them within a global context (Cleaver 2002; Connell 1998; Jones 2006; Kimmel 2003; Morrell 2001; Ouzgane 2006; Ouzgane and Morrell 2005; Pease and Pringle 2006; Seidler 2006).

Of the many theories of masculinity, one particularly useful concept is hegemonic masculinity, popularized by Tim Carrigan, Bob Connell and John Lee (1987), which built on Antonio Gramsci's modelling of class hegemony. Following the necessity for accommodating multiple masculinities, hegemonic masculinity is 'a

6. For an indicator of the volume of published research in the area see Michael Flood's excellent online *The Men's Bibliography*: http://mensbiblio.xyonline.net

particular variety of masculinity to which others—among them young and effeminate as well as homosexual men—are subordinated' (Carrigan, Connell and Lee 1987: 86). While an early theory of masculinity, some two decades later the concept of hegemony continues to be used and refined in useful ways (Connell and Messerschmidt 2005; Hearn 2004). Hegemony and patriarchy (discussed below) are intimate bedfellows inasmuch as both promote a domineering order, but hegemonic masculinity is particularly useful in highlighting how men operate against other men, a theme less obvious within the single formulation of patriarchy. When I use the term patriarchy I generally intend to include the suppression not just of women, but also of subordinate men.

Spirituality

Spirituality is a complicated word, clearly meaning many things to many people. It is tempting to conclude that the definition of spirituality has become more vague in recent times, although this conclusion may confuse *vague* with *diverse*. Consider Rudolph Otto's (1952) feelings of the *numinous*, the *mysterium tremendum*, which arguably served our concept of spirituality before its common usage. Otto refers to feelings of awefulness, majestas, urgency, the wholly other, and fascination (Otto 1952: 13-31). Otto's spirituality is like peeking through our fingers at the face of God and thrilling at our not being annihilated in the process. Consider then the definition of two proponents of masculine spirituality, Rohr and Martos, who define spirituality as, 'a matter of having a source of energy within which is a motivating and directing force for living' (1992: 97). Otto's spirituality can be fulfilled only by an omnipotent God; Rohr and Martos' perhaps by gardening or an energy drink. This highlights a particular issue highlighted by David Wulff, 'What is conspicuously new in today's spirituality is the frequent absence of an explicit transcendent object outside the self' (1997: 7).

Sandra Schneiders' useful treatment of the academic study of spirituality offers two ways of approaching these differences: the dogmatic and the anthropological. The former dictates that spirituality must refer to the life of the Christian and their relationship with the Divine, and the latter refers to experience that is wider than Christianity and even religion itself (1989: 682-83). I prefer a combination of these two approaches. Certainly the anthropological approach appropriately honours the diverse experiences of the spiritual. However, I am inclined to impose a small amount of dogma on to the equation and suggest that in whichever context the experience takes place it must refer to some actual Divine Other rather than vague feelings of the hard-to-define. This means moving beyond (or stepping back from) Schneiders' contemporary definition of spirituality as 'the experience of consciously striving to integrate one's life in terms not of isolation and self-absorption but of self-transcendence towards the ultimate value one perceives' (1989: 684), because self-transcendence and ultimate value both fall well within the bounds of atheism.

Robert Forman surveyed what he describes as 'Grassroots Spirituality' in North America, which is spirituality in its most inclusive sense: it incorporates faiths of numerous traditions, men and women's movements, ecology and so forth, it works within and without institutions, in short anything which anyone describes as spirituality on their own terms. Forman expected to find diverse opinions to the point that no single useful understanding of the word 'spirituality' could be found. While he found diversity he also identified a startling commonality and concluded the following definition: 'Grassroots Spirituality involves a vaguely pantheistic ultimate that is indwelling, sometimes bodily, as the deepest self and accessed through not-strictly-rational means of self transformation and group process that becomes the holistic organization for all life' (Forman 2004: 51).

I find Forman's definition perfectly acceptable thanks to the 'vaguely pantheistic ultimate' and also a useful complement to the defining aspect of the contemporary 'spirituality revolution' which appears to be about the 'subjective turn' away from transcendent sources of significance and authority towards the internal (Heelas and Woodhead 2005: 6). It is possible to read the 'vaguely pantheistic ultimate' as almost reversely dogmatic, inasmuch as it could exclude Christianity by its monotheism, but I believe 'vaguely pantheistic' can accommodate monotheism. This distinction is crucial and dates back to what Schneiders identifies as the very beginning of the word spirituality: Paul's use of the phrase in 1 Corinthians 2:14-15 'spiritual person' (*pneumatikos*) as opposed to 'natural person' (*psychikos anthropôs*), indicating the former was under the influence of God and the latter was not (Schneiders 1989: 680-81). It is not that spirituality must reflect a Pauline understanding of God, simply a clear theistic element to Schneiders' broader definition of spirituality as 'the horizon of ultimate value' (1989: 684). This distinction will prove to be of particular importance in chapter 2 when distinguishing between the spiritual and psychic aspects of the mythopoetic movement.

Patriarchy

Sylvia Walby defines patriarchy as 'a system of social structures and practices in which men dominate, oppress and exploit women' (Walby 1990: 20). Chief among the interpretations of patriarchy Walby examines are: radical feminism, in which gender inequality is based upon men benefiting from the dominance of women; Marxist feminism, in which gender inequality derives from capitalism; liberal feminism, which locates gender inequality in numerous small-scale deprivations rather than overarching analyses; dual-systems theory, which synthesizes radical and Marxist feminist approaches (Walby 1990: 3-5). Walby suggests there are six aspects to patriarchy: paid work, housework, sexuality, culture, violence and the state (Walby 1990: 16). Throughout this book, some of these aspects, such as sexuality and violence, can be identified quite clearly. Other themes are implicit, but not necessarily articulated in these terms. For example, the evangelical call to 'servant leadership' and its distinct roles within the family clearly feeds in to paid work and housework. Again, I want to also include hegemonic masculinity with its subordination of other masculinities, even if this may be of a different order of domination. As Brod notes, the study of men and masculinities should demonstrate 'the connections between the pursuit of patriarchal power and various sorts of male self-denials' (1987a: 9).

Walby (1990: 173-202) also chronicles the shift from private to public patriarchy in which the family is no longer the main site of patriarchal power and influence, rather the public domain. As Jeff Hearn (1992) argues with special emphasis on men and masculinities, this does not mean a reduction of patriarchy, rather a restructuring of it, a shift which is 'integrally related to or even reproducing private patriarchy' (Hearn 1992: 64). The notion of private and public patriarchy is particularly intriguing in dialogue with masculine spirituality which can be seen as a retreat back from public into private patriarchy, and not just in the obvious reassertion of patriarchal family dynamics, but also a focus on defining the masculine self in interior and psychic terms rather than simply those public manifestations of patriarchy such as the workplace. I do not mean to suggest public patriarchies are being abandoned, simply that there is a partial rediscovery of private patriarchies in articulations of masculine spirituality. If it is possible to argue that 'men's public lives in an important sense represent a retreat and escape from their personal lives, a shrinkage rather than an enlargement of their spheres' (Brod 1987a: 3), then masculine spirituality with its refocus on the personal can be seen as an expansion of men's spheres which requires special attention if this results in an expansion of patriarchy, whether public or private.

When I describe a masculine spirituality as being patriarchal I am making the basic point that the spirituality in question relies on patriarchal themes, or that it appeals to men by promoting masculinities that by a secondary or unwitting order perpetuate or tend towards patriarchal themes. This step of removal is of crucial importance and it underpins a significant theme that reoccurs on a number of occasions in this book: the difference between intention and effect. For example, members of the mythopoetic and various Christian men's movements can be puzzled when they are charged with being patriarchal because it is not necessarily their intention for their projects to manifest any of those six aspects of patriarchy. However, the net effect of building masculinity around, for example, archetypes or servant leadership is a tendency towards those six aspects of patriarchy. We are asked by these men, in all sincerity, to accept their warrior identification and claims to servant leadership with the gentlemanliness with which it is intended, not the despotism to which it can succumb.

There is an obvious and profound ethical impetus for resisting patriarchy, suppressing as it does the experiences of women and subordinated men. But I want also to frame a resistance to patriarchy within the terms of even normative masculine spirituality. According to mythopoets Robert Moore and Douglas Gillette (1992a: 51), archetypes are hardwired in the deepest reptilian parts of the human brain. If we are to appeal to such biological desires in men, why not to the most fundamental desire to survive? One recent study shows there to be 'a substantial and significant association between nations' levels of patriarchy and men's higher mortality' (Stanistreet, Bambra and Scott-Samuel 2005: 874). Hopefully, by clearly identifying some of these patriarchal variables, *Numen, Old Men* will add to the survival of the species: a primal goal that should resonate with even the most hirsute of archetypal wild men.

Men's Studies in Religion

My work is located in what can loosely be described as the field of 'men's studies in religion'. Philip Culbertson and Björn Krondorfer (2005) offer a concise introduction to the field, providing a trajectory dating back to secular feminism of the 1960s. Rather than simply providing an umbrella for 'men writing about religion', men's studies in religion is concerned with the critical examination of how men function within religion; it is distinct from what is perceived as the 'men's movement' due to appreciating the shifting nature of culturally constructed gender identities, as opposed to biologically determined and essentialist models of masculinity.

Culbertson and Krondorfer identify four main themes which occur in men's studies of religion: men reclaiming religion and faith, spiritual and confessional writings, theological and biblical investigations, and gay and queer studies in religion. Men reclaiming religion and faith is concerned with movements which have sought to (re)strengthen the relationships between masculine identity and religion, whether historical such as Muscular Christianity or contemporary such as Promise Keepers. Spiritual and confessional writings refer to the vast wealth of spiritual writings by men throughout history from various traditions which can be re-read with an awareness of how gender functions to gain new insights into men's experiences of the religious. Theological and biblical investigations examine how scripture and heritage place various restrictions on the construction of masculinities which prove problematic for men living their full spiritual potential, as well as promoting a patriarchal dynamic which excludes women. Gay and queer studies in religion, while often considered distinct from men's studies in religion, adds to the field by providing a critique of heteronormativity. This book intersects with most of these concerns, analysing various manifestations of men reclaiming faith, the theological heritages which inform them, and the gay/queer manifestations of spirituality which offer them some resistance.

The interest in men's studies in religion that flowered in the 1990s was aided by various books such as James Nelson's popular *The Intimate Connection: Male Sexuality, Masculine Spirituality* (1988).

Nelson argued that men are largely characterized by separation, a separation between parts of themselves, other people, and also God. What men needed was to regain a familiarity with intimacy. *Regain* is the word, as Nelson identifies the period of the Reformation as one in which 'feminine' aspects of the Christian tradition were abandoned in favour of what were to be understood as 'masculine': transcendence, redemption, otherness, and physicality (Nelson 1988: 36). In stark contrast to the reclaiming men who populate much of this book, Nelson urges that 'masculine spirituality now deeply needs to recognize, name, express, and experience the dimensions of God that have lain so underdeveloped in male theology' (Nelson 1988: 46). Nelson's conclusion, which still has a freshness about it two decades later, is a call for a rediscovery of sexuality and the erotic within men's experiences and presentations of the spiritual. Another important voice in the subject's early years was Harry Brod who edited the insightful collection *A Mensch Among Men: Explorations in Jewish Masculinity* (Brod 1988), which offered a range of articles about Jewish masculinities from a profeminist and gay-affirmative perspective which are quite distinct to the political mood of the various men's movements brewing elsewhere at the same time. Brod has also been instrumental in the development of men's studies beyond religion (Brod 1987b; Brod and Kaufman 1994).

A number of other books framed men's studies in religion in admirable terms, mostly within a Christian context. Culbertson finds hope in what he describes as the New Adam who 'emerges in community between vulnerable human beings in transition and in turn is the fullest expression of the proper relationship between humanity and God' (1992: 39). Culbertson reserves masculine spirituality for 'those males who have taken seriously the opportunity for their own liberation from gender stereotypes and have in the process begun to seek a new and more sensitive self-understanding in light of the feminist critique' (1992: 110-11). Howard Eilberg-Schwartz (1994) discusses the problematic nature of 'God's phallus', unpacking the homoerotic issues at play for heterosexual (and homophobic) Judeo-Christian men who devote themselves to a male God, rendering them, in heterosexist logic, as feminine. Stephen Boyd's *The Men We Long to Be* (1995) highlights six 'sins' which most Christian men must overcome in order to engage a more useful masculine spirituality: classism, anti-Semitism, racism, homophobia, sexism, and femiphobia. Krondorfer's (1996) collection of essays raises a host of topics including: the problematic nature of masculinity as a category; black men; gay men; masturbation; friendship; male bodies. A further collection (Boyd, Longwood and Meusse 1996) explores the following themes: dynamics of power in masculine identity; how religion shapes masculine identity; how masculinity shapes religion; resources for reconstructing manhood; theology and ethics. Identifying the seeming impasse between the mythopoetic and profeminist men's movements, David Tacey attempted to produce a synthesis of the two with his *Remaking Men: Jung, Spirituality, and Social Change* (1997). These, coupled with significant pieces of gay theology (Cleaver 1995; Comstock 1993; Goss 1993; McNeill 1995), were some of the key texts and themes which shaped the subject during the 1990s.

Certainly in the late 1990s one could be forgiven for thinking men's studies in religion was gaining some momentum and would soon be complementing women's studies in a fully-fledged gender studies, but after this promising start a certain quietude surrounded the subject. Part of this may be to do with the perceived decline in the men's movement. The popularity of the mythopoetic movement and Promise Keepers provided a focus for men's studies in religion, even if it was simply something to counter. As these movements began to decrease in visibility, so too the need to counter them (although as the following chapters show, this perceived decline was not entirely accurate). But more than this, men's studies in religion has not always managed to define itself with ease. The field's theoretical, hermeneutical and methodological framework is not as clear as some other disciplines. And there can also be a resistance to men's studies in religion from some feminists which, while perfectly understandable and in various ways necessary, is also unfortunate as the two share many of the same goals, namely how gender identities are constructed and the power dynamics between them in a religious context. These two factors have not helped the development of the field.

This lacking in definition can even be identified when men's studies in religion is put in dialogue with the wider study of men and masculinities. I use the term 'men's studies in religion' for this section because the one small identifiable collective of researchers in the subject area is the 'Men's Studies in Religion Group' of the American Academy of Religion, but I use it with some caution. Jeff Hearn (1997) introduced the concept of Critical Studies on Men which takes an explicitly feminist/profeminist approach to the study of men and masculinities. This is often put in opposition to men's studies with what some feel are its 'much more ambiguous and sometimes even anti-feminist activities ... which can become defined in a much less critical way as "by men, on men, for men" (Hearn and Pringle 2006: 5). Certainly the general study of men, masculinities and religion is perceived to belong more to 'men's studies' than 'critical studies on men'. More papers appear to have been published on the subject in *Journal of Men's Studies*, for example, than *Men and Masculinities*, the academic journals that can be seen to represent the two approaches respectively.

I fully appreciate Hearn and Pringle's comments about the ambiguous nature of men's studies, and tend to employ their reasoning as my own default position, but it is not necessarily the case. Speculating from my own experience, it may be that people studying men, masculinities and religion feel compelled to 'choose a side' and, while their political allegiances may lie with critical studies on men, they find there a certain resistance to the religious and an assumption that it is inevitably rather conservative and backward, and thus opt for men's studies where at least such conversations are common. The majority of researchers I have communicated with in 'men's studies in religion' are explicitly feminist/profeminist, which may come as a surprise to some proponents of critical studies on men.

Take, for example, Boyd's (1999) understanding of the function of the Men's Studies in Religion Group which is to include, among other things, critical theorizing of patriarchy, hegemonic and subordinated masculinities, and the intersection with feminist, mujerista, womanist and queer theories. Certainly the theoretical and hermeneutical foundation of this book is explicitly feminist and queer. It seems difficult to locate this in opposition to critical studies on men. A loosening of this binary would inevitably be productive for everyone involved. Men's studies would be enriched by pursuing a more transparently critical and political agenda: this means parting company with men's rights/men's movement individuals who are responsible for the 'men's studies is men's work' attitude. Critical studies on men would be enriched by a more subtle (read less suspicious) treatment of the religious. However, critical studies on men is in excellent shape as a discipline and the ultimate winner would be the general study of men, masculinities and religion which, despite the best efforts of those involved, simply does not attract as much attention as it deserves, due in part to perceptions of it which often do not match the reality of its participants.

As already mentioned, both *Journal of Men's Studies* and *Men and Masculinities* do publish papers which intersect with religion and spirituality, but for reasons ranging from lack of interest in the subject to the physical constraints of printed pages, not as often as theologians and religious studies scholars would hope. As I began to engage more fully with the subject it became apparent that what was needed was its own separate publishing venue, and for this reason I founded the online *Journal of Men, Masculinities and Spirituality*.[7] It was a surprisingly easy task to email the key researchers in the subject and say, 'Hey, what we need here is a new journal!' The immediate and positive responses to someone with no profile in the subject spoke volumes about the need for such a journal. Before long many of the subject's pioneers had signed on to the editorial board, including Stephen Boyd, Harry Brod, Philip Culbertson, Björn Krondorfer and David Tacey. Expanding the immediate parameters of the subject, others signed on whose discipline was more defined by sexuality and religion such as Daniel Boyarin and Virginia Burrus, as well as gay scholars such as Bob Goss. The board now represents a variety of different disciplines, traditions and nationalities. Of course, I say this in part to blow my own trumpet, but also as an indicator that the subject is keen to embrace future expansion. Observant readers will notice that the title *Journal of Men, Masculinities and Spirituality* is a cunning mix of *Journal of Men's Studies* and *Men and Masculinities*, which is a small gesture towards moving beyond the binarity of men's studies and critical studies on men, as is this book: it seems a natural progression.

Chapter Outline

Because this book spans various spiritualities, it necessarily works on a rather broad level. The geographical focus is almost exclusively North American. This is not because it is specifically supposed to examine North American masculinities and spiritualities, rather that the majority of the sources involved happen to be North American.

7. http://www.jmmsweb.org

A good deal of those sources have influenced, or have their counterparts in other Western countries, so the content stretches to some extent beyond North America.

The sources are almost exclusively literary, referring both to texts published by popular advocates of masculine spirituality, and also academic critics who answer directly to them or whose work can be applied to them. I also make a significant number of references to the websites of people who resonate with masculine spirituality, as today these, perhaps even more than books and articles, are the 'site' of interaction between them and their audience.[8]

That certain traditions have not been included is simply a matter of spatial constraint. There are numerous trajectories the book could have benefited from developing: even staying within a North American context, manifestations of masculine spirituality from Judaism and the Nation of Islam immediately spring to mind. The majority of the sources also happen to be articulations of white middle-class men, which provides a further veneer of normativity. However, this book is largely a political, spiritual and sexual critique of these sources, so hopefully those voices I've excluded will find it that bit easier to be heard as a result.

Following this introduction, chapter 2 investigates the mythopoetic movement, typified by Bly's *Iron John*. Various themes that lend themselves to the movement being perceived as spiritual are identified. In particular the mythopoets are keen on employing archetypes to demonstrate manifestations of the 'deep' or 'authentic' masculine. Via Robert Moore and Douglas Gillette's treatments of the King and Warrior archetypes I show how engaging with archetypal energies promotes a singular and rather disturbing form of masculinity which cannot help but perpetuate patriarchal norms, and therefore a patriarchal spirituality. Another important theme explored by the movement is a lack of contemporary initiation. I argue that rather than the assumed value of creating mature

8. It is hard to prove, but I also suspect website content to be of a more 'truthful' nature than traditionally published sources: the ease and immediacy of publishing online offers text which often has sharp edges that might otherwise be smoothed out by the traditional editorial process that is sometimes inclined to sanitize or put a spin on questionable material. Citations of articles available via online publications are treated in the same way as print publications and found in the References section. Citations of general websites are indicated by the URLs contained in a footnote. All website references were accessible in September 2007, unless otherwise stated.

identities, initiation actually erases them, encouraging the perpetuation of the patriarchal status quo. More critically, I question the perception that the mythopoetic movement is somehow the 'spiritual men's movement' suggesting this is the result of a series of mistakes: archetypes are considered spiritual when they are more accurately psychic; initiation is considered spiritual when it is more accurately ancient and/or indigenous; wilderness is considered spiritual when it is more accurately majestic.

Chapter 3 examines the evangelical men's movement, identifying its breadth beyond its common alignment with Promise Keepers via a more subtle appreciation of men's ministry. I show how a mythopoetic concern for archetypes and authentic masculinity extends into an evangelical context, resulting in what might be called 'evangelical mythopoeticism' in works such as Gordon Dalbey's *Healing the Masculine Soul* (1988), Stu Weber's *Tender Warrior* (1993) and John Eldredge's *Wild At Heart* (2001). Evangelical men's ministries also perpetuate a patriarchal form of masculinity and spirituality by giving special attention to 'servant leadership' or 'soft patriarchy' in which men are to lead their families in line with biblical values. The type of masculinity encouraged in evangelical men's ministries is also shown to perpetuate a certain form of violence due to a particular fascination with military imagery and combative sports. The violent fantasies explored in evangelical men's ministries extends previous works that establish the connection between Far Right Christian ministries and the ostensible middle ground of evangelical politics (Kintz 1997; Burlein 2002).

Chapter 4 provides a similar treatment of the Catholic men's movement and ministry with the initial task of differentiating it from the more general Christian men's movement. Like its evangelical counterpart, the mythopoetic concern with archetypes and initiation also results in what might be called 'Catholic mythopoeticism' in works such as Richard Rohr and Joseph Martos' *The Wild Man's Journey* (1992), and Patrick Arnold's *Wildmen, Warriors and Kings* (1991). While Catholic men's ministries were fashioned to provide a Catholic alternative to Promise Keepers, they nevertheless encourage different forms of masculinity. In particular, masculinity in this context is shown to be less invested in concepts of servant leadership and less interested in military and sporting themes. Instead, Catholic men's ministry is influenced by elements of Catholic tradition such as the sacraments and devotion to the saints and

Mary, which results in a less patriarchal and more diverse masculinity. In comparison to evangelical masculinities, Catholic masculinities appear to be more feminine, or even queer. This is framed against historical differences in regard to a Catholic ambivalence surrounding the importance of the family (Ruether 2000) and the assumption that a man should aspire to be its leader.

While not articulated as a 'masculine spirituality', chapter 5 looks at integral spirituality as theorized by Ken Wilber. Integral spirituality seeks to integrate both masculine and feminine ways of being in order to achieve an appropriately balanced spirituality. While sounding initially quite reasonable I show how Wilber in his book *Sex, Ecology, Spirituality* (2000) privileges the masculine in this equation and goes so far as to deny the historical realities of patriarchy. Wilber also makes some thematic and personal alliances with the mythopoetic men's movement as well as seeking a revisioning of patriarchy that bears some commonality with the evangelical men's movement. Further masculine-oriented spirituality is identified in the work of Wilber's colleague David Deida and his book, *The Way of the Superior Man* (2004). These themes, coupled with a presentation of Wilber's almost hyper-masculine style result in integral spirituality being not just a form of masculine spirituality, but a 'muscular' spirituality, which I compare with the historical and contemporary waves of Muscular Christianity (Ladd and Mathisen 1999).

Having then given a good deal of attention to how masculine spirituality perpetuates patriarchy I turn in chapter 6 to gay spirituality. While gay spirituality tends not to describe itself as masculine spirituality, it is a spirituality performed exclusively by men.[9] In its popular manifestation, gay spirituality also shares significant commonality with the mythopoetic movement, appropriating neo-Jungian archetypes, albeit of a more androgynous nature than the Warrior or King. I argue that gay spirituality is a valuable form of masculine spirituality that encourages different types of masculinity, rather than the hegemonic, heteronormative and patriarchal masculinities of the previous chapters, which can provide inspiration for all men, gay or straight. Gay liberation

---

9. Clearly, I present gay spirituality as not including lesbian women, although as chapter 6 progresses I draw upon more generally queer themes that are not exclusively about men.

theology is also highlighted as an example of a masculine spirituality with an explicit political conscience which again can serve as inspiration for all masculine spiritualities. Finally, I look at queer theory and theology that troubles many of the categories on which patriarchy relies.

Stepping back from these performed spiritualities, chapter 7 engages the more theoretical debate of gender and sexual difference that underpins masculine spirituality. First, the sex role theory employed by most advocates of masculine spirituality is compared to the version of sexual difference articulated by Luce Irigaray (1993a, 1993b and 2004), and then to the loosening of gender binaries sought by Judith Butler (1999 and 2004b) and Bracha Ettinger (1992, 1996 and 2004). These different understandings of sexual difference are then reapplied to masculine spirituality, highlighting its poorly developed understanding of sex and gender, resulting in confusions such as the interchangeable use of the terms 'male spirituality' and 'masculine spirituality'. I then explore how sexual difference functions in spirituality in regard to spatiality: that the 'up' and 'out' are masculine and the 'down' and 'in' are feminine. While 'orientational metaphors' such as up and down are a crucial part of how we understand our experiences (Lakoff and Johnson 2003), I show how within spiritual space they repeat certain patriarchal values. This confirms the argument that both physical and spiritual (or 'absolute') spaces are socially produced (Lefebvre 1991) and extends into the spiritual realms the gendered nature of physical spaces (Massey 1994; Spain 1992). In search of an alternative to the axial and gendered nature of spiritual space I turn to Gilles Deleuze and Félix Guattari's (1987) concept of smooth and rhizomatic space, as well as revisiting Ettinger's matrixial borderspace.

Naturally, in the concluding chapter I will draw together some of the key themes, in particular how masculine spirituality encourages a patriarchal spirituality by crafting mono-dimensional and oppressive masculinities through neo-Jungian archetypes, and also how it seeks to conceal patriarchy via its revisioning and depoliticization. I will reiterate the value of queer theory for the full spectrum of masculinities, shedding light on the above epigraphic notes about why the author of the Gospel of Thomas is a Genderfucker. And finally, I will close with some suggestions for the immediate progression of the relationship between men and spirituality.

Chapter Two

THE MYTHOPOETIC MOVEMENT: GETTING IT WRONG
FROM THE START

When most people think of the men's movement, the image they conjure in their minds is actually of the mythopoetic men's movement. It is an image of partially clothed, bearded men, smeared with mud in the woods. It is an image of men getting in touch with their feelings, weeping in the company of brothers or releasing a primal scream. It is an image of storytelling, sweat lodges, drumming and talking sticks. It is also an image of a backlash against feminism. The word 'mythopoetic' is a curious choice to describe a popular movement. Christopher Harding, editor of the mythopoetic men's journal *Wingspan*, says the word originated with Shepherd Bliss who was uncomfortable with the phrase 'New Age men's movement', employing instead 'mythopoetic' to mean 'creating or making myth' (Harding 1992: xx). For many, the mythopoetic movement is synonymous with Robert Bly's *Iron John: A Book About Men* (1990), which recreates a (some say spurious[1]) Grimm Brothers' tale about a wild, hairy man, 'Iron John' who becomes a mentor to a young boy. The experiences shared by Iron John and the boy are intended to reflect the stages of masculine development.

Bly claims Iron John, the Wild Man, is a Jungian archetype, which is an integral element of a man's psychological make-up. Archetypes are a key mythopoetic theme and are referred to throughout the movement's literature, including the King, Warrior, Magician, Lover, Trickster, Wild Man and Grief Man.[2] Men are encouraged to reengage with these archetypes to come into full, mature masculinity. Another key theme of the movement is fatherlessness

---

1. See Adrienne Burgess (1997: 27), Bob Connell (1995: 82-85) and chiefly Jack Zipes' (1992) scathing treatment of *Iron John*.

2. The capitalization of these words suggests the *gravitas* assumed to be inherent in archetypes.

(Bly 1990: 21), which has left men incomplete and without inspirational models of mature masculinity. Another theme connected with fatherlessness is a lack of initiation in contemporary society (Meade 1993; Moore and Gillette 1996: 187-96), that there are no longer any rituals to aid boys in their transition to manhood. Another theme is wilderness, which is the theatre or *mis-en-scene* of the movement, in which men come together to explore their archetypal energies via initiatory ritual and male bonding.[3] The mythopoetic movement is typically perceived as the 'spiritual men's movement' due to the transcendental character of archetypal energy, the pagan echoes of wild(er)ness, and the glimpses of indigenous (mainly Native American) spirituality contained within initiatory ritual. In short, the movement's critics charged it with rigid gender stereotyping, misogyny, androcentrism, homophobia and political, racial and economic naïvety (Brod 1992; Hagan 1992; Ross 1992; Kimmel 1995c; Schwalbe 1996; Messner 1997).

This chapter examines these key themes of the mythopoetic movement in order to identify what kind of masculinity and spirituality it promotes. In particular, the mythopoetic movement is shown to perpetuate a heteropatriarchal masculinity. The main vehicle for such masculinity is the adoption by the movement of archetypes as models on which to base men's behaviour. Archetypes are shown to promote a caricatured and one-dimensional masculinity that derives much of its identity from violence and domination. The themes of fatherlessness and initiation continue this masculine model, both of which have less to do with their intention of guiding boys into men and more to do with reinstilling identifiable hierarchies of authority and the erasure of individual identity. These masculine performances are unlikely to produce anything other than a patriarchal spirituality. But more than this, the idea of the mythopoetic movement being the 'spiritual men's movement' is itself brought into question, suggesting there is very little within the movement that can accurately be defined as spiritual, a misperception unwittingly promoted both by the movement and its critics. Throughout the following chapters we will see examples of men's spiritual movements repeating the mistakes of the

---

3. For an insightful treatment of community within the mythopoetic movement see Michael Schwalbe (1996: 71-100).

mythopoetic movement, in particular ideas of gender essentialism and an employment of archetypal models of masculinity.

Archetypes

Bly popularized the idea that Jungian archetypes are sources of energy for modern men to draw upon. In particular, Bly notes seven archetypal beings within man: King; Warrior; Lover; Wild Man; Trickster; Mythologist or Cook; Grief Man. In *Iron John*, Bly gives special attention to the first four of these archetypes, and it is these that have been explored with most enthusiasm within the wider mythopoetic literature.[4] Moore and Gillette (1990) identified four archetypes within man: King; Warrior; Magician; Lover. These four archetypes were each developed in separate follow-up volumes (Moore and Gillette: 1992a, 1992b, 1993a and 1993b). It is interesting to note that while Moore and Gillette's archetypal foursome gives a superficial impression of balance (the patriarchal King and Warrior offset by the Magician and Lover), significantly more attention has been devoted in the use of their work to the King and Warrior archetypes than the Magician and Lover,[5] lending some support to the suggestion that, 'Jungian style archetypes that still idealize "heroic" male violence do not reflect the human psyche, but rather the dominator male psyche' (Eisler 1992: 49).

Within the mythopoetic movement archetypes are considered as part of our 'hard-wiring,' inescapable energies originating from our reptilian brain (Moore and Gillette 1992a: 51). Moore and Gillette, in particular, like to look at animals as an exemplar of archetypal behaviour (1990: 75; 1992a: 53). Following Jung (we are told), the archetypes dwell in the collective unconscious and exist whether we like it or not. Indeed, many of society's ills can be attributed to the ignoring or misuse of archetypal energy. What society needs, and what men need in particular, is to reconnect with these archetypal (read animal) instincts, thus re-establishing the natural order which the mythopoetic movement believes to be so sadly denied. It is not the present concern to deduce exactly how Jungian the mythopoetic movement actually is, although Jungian scholar

4. With some exceptions, such as Glen Mazis (1993).
   5. A casual survey of library holdings also suggests less interest in the Magician and Lover volumes.

David Tacey has charged it with 'conservative and simplistic appropriation of Jungian theory' (1997: ix), rather what kind of masculinity such Jungian appropriation encourages. Within this context Tacey equates archetypes with stereotypes (1997: 4) and Moore and Gillette's treatment of the King and Warrior certainly falls foul of this criticism.

For Moore and Gillette the King archetype 'is primal in all men' and 'comes first in importance' (1990: 49). The King is both sacred and creative: '"World" is defined as that part of reality that is organised and ordered by the King. What is outside the boundaries of his influence is noncreation, chaos, the demonic, and nonworld' (1990: 52). From the very beginning the King is obviously going to be patriarchal, by his very definition, but Moore and Gillette clearly spell out to what extent the King is patriarchal. The King does not only engage in an authoritarian relationship with his kingdom, he actually denies the existence of that which he does not 'create'. To the individuals who reject the King's world he says to them, 'you are chaos, demonic,' and more than this, 'you are noncreation, nonworld'. This is an oft-employed patriarchal device used to exclude and deny the reality of the Other, and falls far short of the 'generative' aspects of the King which Moore and Gillette attempt to establish in order to offset his otherwise unsavoury nature (1992a: 147).

Perhaps Moore and Gillette can be forgiven for not initially noticing the disturbing elements to their treatment of the King archetype, however even when they spell them out they fail to draw the appropriate conclusions. The following example discusses the Shadow King (the archetypal Dark Side), which should be the ideal opportunity to nail down the problematic nature of Kingship:

> In the story of King David and Bathsheba, Bathsheba was the wife of another man, Uriah the Hittite. One day David was walking on the roof of his palace when he spotted Bathsheba bathing. He was so aroused by this sight that he sent for her and forced her to have sex with him. In theory, remember, all the women of the realm were the king's. But they belonged to the *archetype* of the king, not to the mortal king. David unconsciously identified himself with the King energy and not only took Bathsheba but also had her husband, Uriah, killed. Fortunately for the kingdom, David had a conscience in the form of Nathan the prophet, who came to him and indicted him. David, much to his credit, accepted the truth of the indictment and repented (Moore and Gillette 1990: 66).

Let us unpack this paragraph. Moore and Gillette's point is that if a man identifies with the shadow aspect of the King archetype he will become tyrannical. They state that, 'as is the case with all archetypes, the King displays an active-passive bipolar shadow structure' (1990: 63), yet their example of such shows David identifying not with the shadow but the *archetype itself*: 'David unconsciously identified himself with the King energy'. The shadow is the net effect of the identification, not part of 'an active-passive bipolar shadow structure'. This represents one of the least practical elements in the whole mythopoetic call to archetypes: identify with the archetype to find your wholeness but do not identify too much. One must wonder that if King David found this process tricky, with all his experience navigating kingly energy, what hope is there for the average man? Let us give Moore and Gillette the benefit of the doubt on this confusion.

Moore and Gillette say, 'In theory, remember, all the women of the realm were the king's'. Here we see more mythopoetic political naïvety: the women belong to the King, so it is understandable that David should feel some ownership of Bathsheba. 'But,' say Moore and Gillette, anticipating the feminist outcry, 'they belonged to the *archetype* of the king, not to the mortal king'. One must therefore assume that belonging to an archetypal dominating structure is considered less oppressive than a real one. 'David unconsciously identified himself with the King energy and not only took Bathsheba but also had her husband, Uriah, killed'. In short, by being a rapist and a murderer David bears witness to King energy, not just in its shadow form, but its full archetypal form. 'Fortunately for the kingdom, David had a conscience in the form of Nathan the prophet, who came to him and indicted him'. In other words, David did not have a personal conscience, rather an external conscience which was enforced upon him in the same way that fairness must be enforced upon patriarchal/kingly models of power, for it does not eventuate of its own accord. Even then, David is removed from the equation, as the indictment is not fortunate for David personally (though one assumes he had some desire to redeem himself before God) but 'the kingdom'. 'David, much to his credit, accepted the truth of the indictment and repented'. So, King David is an archetypal-delusional murdering rapist who requires external pressure to awaken his conscience for the sake of the supposed greater good, but 'much to his credit' he repents.[6] It is as if Moore and Gillette have unconsciously identified *themselves* with David and are in need of their own prophet Nathan to point out the deeply disturbing nature of the King. At best the King is a benevolent dictator, at worst a despot. Moore and Gillette's kingly energy shares much in common with Bly's Zeus energy, the 'male authority accepted for the sake of the community' (Bly 1990: 22): let us not forget the questionable behaviour often attributed to Zeus.

The call for the return of the King, this 'intuition of holiness…both dreadful and wonderful by virtue of its power,' becomes quite absurd: 'It drops us to our knees with the force of its holiness' (Moore and Gillette 1992a: 209), they shudder, missing the grandiosity, the inflation, the hint of sexual violence.[7] Should readers require music for this drama, they are amusingly directed towards, 'soundtracks from "sword and sandals" movies like *Spartacus* or *Ben Hur*' (1992a: 217). But such daftness undermines the fact that there is a deeply political problem with employing these monarchist images. It suggests to the working- and middle-class man that if he is having trouble reaching spiritual completeness he should try and transcend his lowly nature and identify with the dominator structure. Tired of being a minion of the kingdom (i.e. the patriarchal status quo)? Try fantasizing about being the King! It's rather like saying to a black man that he could find spiritual completeness by transcending his blackness and fantasizing about being white: this self-help volume might be entitled *The Whiteness Within: Accessing the Caucasian in the Male Psyche*.[8]

6. Despite his repentance, David's identification with the archetypal king brings further death in the form of his son who dies in retribution for his sins.

7. Marion Maddox notes 'the sexual overtones to the act of kneeling are never explicit in a liturgical context; but once seen they are hard to ignore' (1994: 50). Marcella Althaus-Reid (2003: 10-12) similarly describes kneeling as revolving around a 'genital axis'.

8. Rosemary Radford Ruether starts this idea but stops short of the real point. Ruether extrapolates the dangers of mythopoetic rhetoric to, 'what is needed is to restore white people's confidence in whiteness as a manifestation of strong and positive psychic traits. Journeys to regions of pure white sands and skies are recommended' (1992: 16-17). This goes only half way because white people are indeed white and encouraging them to reengage with their whiteness is a project within the realms of reality, albeit politically corrupt. Moore and Gillette are asking men to transcend reality, for the 'commoner' to engage with the King, with all its power and value implications, which is why it is more appropriate to liken the call to asking a black man to access his Whiteness.

It is interesting that in the whole volume attributed to the King, which picks up on a multiplicity of kingly myths from many cultures, one of the most insightful is ignored: King Canute on the Seashore. In this story, it is said that Canute stood at the waterside at Southampton[9] and employed all his kingly energy in commanding the waves to turn back, which of course they did not. There are two main interpretations of this story, both of which are useful. First, the King was so deluded as to the capacity of his power that he thought he could turn back the waves, which is a prime example that there is indeed creation, world and order outside of the King's power, and that to deny it is absurd. Second, the King was demonstrating that despite all his kingly power, he could *not* turn back the waves, that despite being the King he was simply a man (albeit a great one). This is precisely the most attractive kind of King in popular culture, such as J.R.R. Tolkien's (1955) Aragorn. No doubt Moore and Gillette purposely ignore the story of Canute (for it can be no accident that it is left out of such a well-researched volume) because neither the option of absurdity nor humbleness fits their King model: both these options are too real, which suggests that Moore and Gillette's King is a fantasy and that they themselves stand at the seashore, barking at the elements to turn on their command.

Moore and Gillette's location of the Warrior archetype seems equally bizarre, noting firstly Jane Goodall's study of chimpanzees, who initially were thought to be peaceful but ended up being Warrior-like (brutal): clearly if the chimpanzees cannot remain peaceful, how can men? They then ask,

> What accounts for the popularity of Rambo, or Arnold Schwarzenegger, of war movies like *Apocalypse Now*, *Platoon*, *Full Metal Jacket* and many, many more? We can deplore the violence in these movies, as well as on our television screens, but, obviously, the Warrior still remains very much alive in us (Moore and Gillette 1990: 76).

It seems incredible that Moore and Gillette are unaware of the different handlings of the Warrior in characters like Rambo or Arnold Schwarzenegger compared to movies like *Apocalypse Now*, *Platoon*, and *Full Metal Jacket* — that one glorifies and the other laments — but there is no mention of this. Moore and Gillette go on

9. The author hereby claims his indigenous rights to pass on this myth having been born and raised in Southampton.

to offer various, rather excitable, examples of the positive Warrior including the shifting tactics of fencers and guerrilla soldiers (1990: 81-82) and the split-second decision making of 'a good Marine' (1990: 83). There are even three references to Carlos Castaneda's Don Juan (1990: 80; 82; 85-86), which one would think more suitable for the Trickster treatment than the Warrior. Moore and Gillette also map the Warrior onto Jesus and Buddha, as they both had to endure temptation, and Islam which, 'as a whole is built on Warrior energy' (1990: 85), citing *jihad* as Islam's defining characteristic rather than its literal meaning of *submission*. Moore and Gillette's examples of Warriors whose alliance with the Lover archetype produced 'humane influences' include Winston Churchill, Yukio Mishima, and General Patton (1990: 87)! Should the reader miss the exciting 'swords and sandals' cinematic references with the Warrior treatment, some consolation can be found with the exemplar of Yul Brenner in *The Magnificent Seven* who, 'says little, moves with the physical control of a predator, attacks only the enemy and has absolute mastery over the technology of his trade' (1990: 82).

Out of the full spectrum of archetypes offered within the mythopoetic movement, most attention is given to the patriarchal and domineering, namely the King and the Warrior, lending support to Tacey that, 'contact with primordial archetypes produces conformity, gender rigidity, and social-political conservatism' (1997: 17). Philip Culbertson is of a similar opinion, suggesting that archetypes are 'calcifications of a patriarchal world view' (1993: 222). If the mythopoetic movement *must* engage with archetypal energies in the spiritual process, then it must start looking at the less patriarchal and oppressive archetypes, such as the Magician, Healer/Shaman and Grief Man, however this assumes that the patriarchal tendency within the mythopoetic movement is in some way accidental and that, having been shown the light, it will seek a different focus.

Aaron Kipnis begins this process with his exploration of the Green Man archetype, 'a creative, fecund, nurturing, protective, and compassionate male, existing in harmony with the earth and the feminine, yet also erotic, free, wild, playful, energetic, and fierce. This is a far cry from the patriarchal, hypermasculine war-making hero'; this sounds quite positive until the sentence is completed and we return to familiar gynophobic territory, 'or the feminized, deenergized, hypomasculine male who is subservient to the

Goddess' (Kipnis 1992: 161). Should readers of Kipnis feel insecure about their attraction to this less-typical masculine archetype they are reminded that Green Man energy also envelopes carving a phallic staff, copulating on the 30-foot-long penis of the Cerne Giant and having the power of massive erect trees (Kipnis 1992: 165). The reader is stirred in the knowledge that he can be simultaneously nurturing *and* hard, in every way.[10] Even when seeking to escape the patriarchal, the mythopoetic movement cannot escape an almost comical phallocentricity.[11]

The focus on archetypes is the main reason why the mythopoetic movement is considered spiritual, yet this equation is problematic. Eugene Pascal defines archetypes as, 'psychological realities of a biological, psycho-biological or image producing character that are typical, stereotypical, and universal' (Pascal 1992: 79-80). This is perfectly consistent with Moore and Gillette's argument that the archetypal origin is located within the reptilian brain (1990: 49-51). However, even if one accepts the biological reality of archetypes, this is a long way from being spiritual, remembering that spirituality must refer to some transcendent Divine Other. Bly makes it clear that the Wild Man has no spiritual aspect but rather dwells 'at the bottom of [the] psyche' (Bly 1990: 6), among 'other interior beings' (Bly 1990: 227). This is the fatal flaw in mythopoetic spirituality: the confusion between the psychological/psychic and the spiritual. Exploration of a biologically-centred psyche may well share some commonality with spirituality, but it is not the same thing. Such an exploration can take place with no reference at all to the spiritual: in this way atheists can do a good job of contemplating their interiority. Spirituality must progress from this interior contemplation and include a transpersonal dimension that has properties of the Divine, as outlined in even Robert Forman's widely-inclusive definition: 'a vaguely pantheistic ultimate' (Forman 2004: 51). Exactly the same confusion takes place in some movements around the term 'consciousness raising': consciousness is interior, and its exploration can lead to spirituality, but it is not the same thing.

10. For a more thorough presentation of the Green Man archetype see William Anderson (1990).
11. See Eugene Monick (1987) for a full frontal presentation of the mytho-Jungian phallus.

This confusion is perpetuated by a loose understanding of the term 'myth' on which the movement is based. Of the mythopoetic psychologist Robert Johnson, Tacey claims, 'he has a way of making the banal and ordinary appear miraculous by adorning conventional attitudes with the mantle of myth' (Tacey 1997: 9). Most mythopoetic writers follow this path, sprinkling their prose with mythical fairy dust with the generally unspoken assumption that the mythical is spiritual, but it is not. Michael Schwalbe illuminates this by quoting James Hillman, the archetypal psychologist who was highly influential on the movement, 'The Gods of psychology are not believed in, not taken literally, not imagined theologically. ...They are formulated ambiguously as metaphors for modes of experience' (Schwalbe 1996: 45). Even the 'priests' of the movement suggest archetypes, the mythopoetic gods, are nothing but stories: powerful and useful stories, perhaps, but not spiritual.

Schwalbe refers to what he calls a 'religious attitude' in the Jungian ideas appropriated by the movement, suggesting that while they do not constitute religion they invoke the 'transcendent meaning of things' (Schwalbe 1996: 49), and also powers greater than ourselves, among which archetypes are included. There is some truth to this statement as long as we acknowledge that a 'religious attitude' falls short of spirituality, and that if the powers of archetypes are indeed 'greater than ourselves' it is only because they work at some unconscious interior level, like the beating of the heart muscle. The only exterior (much less spiritual) reality we can derive from the mythopoetic archetypal treatment is the self-made, which Kenneth Clatterbaugh describes as the reification game:

> Find a human behaviour, label it, invent a psychic thing that is said to cause that behaviour, name it or find a metaphor for it, and pretend you have an explanation of the behaviour in terms of the psychic thing you posited (Clatterbaugh 1995: 52).

Wild(er)ness

Bly's Wild Man is, alongside the King and Warrior, at the heart of the mythopoetic movement. In short, men are told the Wild Man represents the deep masculine, the antidote to Bly's famous description of the contemporary 'soft male' (Bly 1992: 2). The Wild Man is the *essence* of man. The Wild Man is also responsible for some of the misrepresenting of the mythopoetic movement as spiritual. He inhabits, mostly unwittingly, a zone of confusion. In part, the Wild Man is considered spiritual in exactly the same way that all mythopoetic archetypes are considered spiritual, and this has already been shown to be problematic. But there are several other strands that feed into the pseudo-spiritual status of the Wild Man.

Somewhat paradoxically, the Wild Man is considered spiritual because he is not Christian or, more accurately, because he is *pre-Christian*. As we shall see in the proceeding two chapters, the Christian men's movement shares a concern with the mythopoetic movement that both the Church and society have become over-feminized. A retreat from Christianity (and society) is therefore seen as a retreat into the more authentically masculine (Kimmel 1995a: 115-17). Indeed, Bly overtly resists locating the Wild Man within Christianity: 'I'm not so sure that it's right for the New Testament church to claim the Wild Man. The Wild Man seems to me profoundly pagan' (Foreward to Arnold 1991: x). This statement of Bly's helps us further understand the pseudo-spiritual nature of the movement: the appeal to the ancient with the assumption that the ancient is more authentically spiritual. First, Bly refers to the 'New Testament church' as if the newfangled church since the death of Christ has been losing the Old Testament plot: clearly Bly preferred the wrath and wildness of this long-bearded period. Second, Bly refers to the pagan, and a significant part of the mythopoetic project is about appropriating (often inaccurately) ancient and/or indigenous spiritualities (Bonnett 1996; Connell 1995: 82-85) with the assumption that these are less organized, less feminine, wilder, and more authentic.

Folklorist Jack Zipes' blistering deconstruction of *Iron John* offers some particular insights in respect to the Wild Man. The Wild Man folklore type was originally a demonic figure and not a mentor (Zipes 1992: 12), which sits neatly with the above suggestion regarding Moore and Gillette that the shadow (demon) is the net effect of the identification with an archetype. Zipes argues that Wilhelm Grimm (who in 1850 published *Der Eisenhans* or *Iron Hans*, on which *Iron John* is allegedly based) changed the Wild Man type from demon to mentor as part of his falling into line with the 'bourgeois ideology of his time in Germany' (Zipes 1992: 13). Also of importance is the initiatory context of the original *Iron Hans*, which rather than being 'ancient' and 'tribal' can more likely be sourced to a tradition in the Middle Ages of initiating young aristocrats into the role of warrior or king (Zipes 1992: 11). So, far from presenting some kind of authentic 'wildness', Bly actually perpetuates a demonic force which acts out through history among the upper echelons of the class system: the aristocrats of the Middle Ages, the German bourgeoisie of the 1800s, and lately the middle-class attendees of mythopoetic retreats.

Wildness in the mythopoetic movement enables participants to have their cake and eat it. The Wild Man is both spiritual (in an ancient sense) and intensely physical. The Wild Man is simultaneously macho hero pitting himself against the elements and cerebral priest serving at the altar of nature: a final meeting of the previously irreconcilable poles of an adolescent boy's fantasy adulthood. Of course, all such games require a playground and all these wild strands feed into an overarching confusion: that of wilderness *as* spirituality.[12]

It is in the presentation of wilderness that most mythopoetic writers come nearest to being spiritual, in creating mood if not meaning: the 'religious attitude'. Bly writes of the, 'glory of oaks, mountains, glaciers, horses, lions, grasses, waterfalls, deer. We need wilderness and extravagance. Whatever shuts a human being away from the waterfall and the tiger will kill him' (Bly 1990: 55). Bliss (1987: para. 27) offers as ancestors of the mythopoetic approach Francis of Assisi and Henry David Thoreau. We are told of how these two 'nature mystics' communed with the land and exuded wildness.[13] But the wilderness/spirituality connection is incomplete:

12. The mapping of wildness onto the land and the creation of wilderness allows for further patriarchal tendencies. Despite the fact that mythopoetic wilderness is considered a masculine space, Annette Kolodny (1975) shows how pioneers perceived the American landscape as feminine, suggesting a conquering of wilderness is analogous to a conquering of women. This theme is extended by Val Plumwood who shows how a master form of rationality reduces women (and the colonized) to nature and the irrational, to '*terra nullius*, a resource empty of its own purposes or meanings' (1993: 4).

13. For actual references to God in a wilderness context one really needs to shift to the Christian mythopoets who are examined in the proceeding two chapters. For example, Patrick Arnold writes of the men he witnessed growing up in the Black Hills of South Dakota who 'almost always had a very appealing air of wisdom and spiritual strength about them, a sense of belonging to the earth and relatedness to its creatures. They said wise things about life. They were respectful of God' (1991: 4).

there is a gap in reasoning between wilderness reality and divine reality that cannot be filled by the mythopoetic argument which says little more than, 'wilderness is bigger than me and must therefore be spiritual'. Bliss (1987: para. 29) argues that wilderness brings men into touch with what Thoreau called the 'higher laws' of life and death, growth and decay. Why are these higher laws? Thoreau is describing biology, not theology. This, again, is the confusion.

In much the same way as mythopoetic writers identify as spiritual those machinations of their interiority (such as archetypes) which are slightly beyond their ability to manipulate, so too exteriority. Wilderness is seen as spiritual because it is out there and beyond the control of the individual. Viewing wilderness may result in echoes of Rudolph Otto's (1958) *mysterium tremendum*, but that does not actually make wilderness *mysterium tremendum*, rather an approximation of it. In some indigenous and ecological spiritualities, the land may well be *mysterium tremendum*, but this is likely to be because there is a distinct awareness that the land contains (or is) God, that there is a creational dynamic between humanity and the land. While there may be some remnants of this thinking in mythopoetic theologians who see the land as God's creation manifest, this is unlikely to represent the meaning behind most mythopoetic treatments of wilderness. Rather, these epic contemplations feed in to an American romantic myth of wilderness and adventure (Nash 2001; Rosenthal 1980), which is itself a masculine project (Phillips 1997). This continues even when a Christian mythopoet engages the topic. Patrick Arnold (1991: 40) reminds us of Psalm 121 to demonstrate the *gravitas* of nature and the source of Wildness, but in doing so actually shows the basis of the wilderness/spirituality confusion: 'I lift up my eyes to the mountains/ From whence comes my help' (Ps. 121:1). Yes, this is what the mythopoetic movement does, but it forgets to bear witness to the second verse, 'My help is from Yahweh/ The Creator of heaven and earth' (Ps. 121:2). The mountain is *not* the source of 'my help,' the source is Yahweh.

Ultimately, mythopoetic spirituality is little more than that which is beyond the control of the individual, whether it be the archetypal energies dwelling in the reptilian brain or the untameable wilderness. This is harmless enough in itself, albeit faulty, but the flipside of this equation is potentially dangerous: that which is controllable is real/verifiable (as opposed to spiritual). This is getting very close to Moore and Gillette's (1990) disturbing conclusions about the King: "World" is defined as that part of reality that is organised and ordered by the King. What is outside the boundaries of his influence is noncreation, chaos, the demonic, and nonworld' (1990: 52). And so reality or 'world' is continually defined within an economy of control and domination.[14]

Before the *Iron John* phenomenon, Bly spoke more precisely about spirituality in such venues as the Great Mother Conference. And after *Iron John* his co-authored book *The Maiden King: The Reunion of Masculine and Feminine* (Bly and Woodman 1998) again spoke more precisely about spirituality. But within *Iron John* and the wider movement it inspired, there is little that can precisely be described as spirituality, rather incessant plumbing of psychic depths. Perhaps instead of being the 'spiritual men's movement' the mythopoets should have been dubbed the 'introspective men's movement'. While the two share some commonality, they are not the same. Even then, such continued psychic investigation of the wild interior does not result in anything positive. Ultimately, the Wild Man leads us back to violence and domination: 'Both *Iron Hans* and *Iron John* are *warrior* tales, and both celebrate violence and killing as the means to establish male identity' (Zipes 1992: 16).

Fatherlessness

Another key theme erroneously assigned spiritual status is the absence of fathers, which is dubbed 'father hunger' or 'the father wound'. Bly says fathers are absent, either physically or emotionally: perhaps they are even scared to be present, 'When we walk into a contemporary house, it is often the mother who comes forward confidently. The father is somewhere else in the back, being inarticulate' (Bly 1990: 21). Bly tells us the void between boys (he doesn't refer much to girls) and their fathers is filled by suspicious demons which make young men wary of older men and, at the same time, naïve about men their own age and women (Bly 1990: 95), which in turn perpetuates the 'soft male'. Bly also sees the essence of fatherhood as being undermined by fathers and sons

14. Later in chapter 5 we will see how David Deida conflates 'world' with 'woman' in a comparable project of control.

not being able to share work together as in ancient times in which, 'a substance almost like food passes from the older body to the younger' (Bly 1990: 93). This situation (in fact even patriarchy itself, which Bly considers a kind of benign social order of the past) is suppressed by a regime of 'industrial domination' (Bly 1990: 98).

But why is father hunger (assuming it is indeed valid) a spiritual issue? Again, as with numerous 'spiritual' themes in the mythopoetic movement there is nothing essentially spiritual about father hunger: it is another example of confusing the contemplative for the spiritual. Further still, it seems puzzling that while being a 'spiritual' theme there is little mention of God the Father in the mythopoetic jeremiads about fatherlessness. In a way, there need not be any mention of it, because the reader's natural following of this trajectory is enough to inject a spiritual dimension into fatherlessness, even if it remains unspoken: it succeeds in adding to the 'religious attitude', if not actual religiosity. Even if we assign fatherlessness a spiritual dimension we find ourselves in questionable territory. Who actually is 'the father'? The father is actually a micro King. What we are actually reading about is King hunger on behalf of mythopoetic men who would like to see some 'world defining' energy flowing in their own family lives, with themselves at its source. The mythopoetic movement has no framework to articulate the need for King energy within the home that does not appear explicitly patriarchal, hence the downgrade to father, with its more domestic connotations. In the next chapter we will see how the Christian men's movement *does* have such a framework and how kingly behaviour is more transparently adopted via 'servant leadership' and 'soft patriarchy'.

Harry Brod (1992) provides one of the most insightful critiques of father hunger, turning the whole equation of fatherlessness on its head, suggesting men have abandoned their fathers for social success. Noting a high proportion of mythopoetic group participants are the middle-class sons of working-class men, Brod questions,

> how much of the quest for the mythic father is fuelled by guilt over this venal betrayal of our real fathers, the banishing from sight, sound, and sense of their work and sacrifices, their accents and their smells, in order for the next generation to "make it" and "pass" in these WASP, non-class conscious United States (Brod 1992: 233).

This goes some way to highlighting one of the key weaknesses of the mythopoetic movement: a victim mentality. 'Why am I in emotional pain?' asks the generic mythopoetic text; 'because your father was absent,' 'because society is overly-feminised,' 'because industrialisation has taken you away from the land,' are the replies. Brod shows us that instead of being a victim of external pressures, we are in fact often the source of those pressures: we reject our fathers, we fear loss of unjustly held power in society, we perpetuate and reap the rewards of industrialization. This can be seen as part of a mythopoetic 'strategic anti-intellectualism' (Schwalbe 1996: 148), which chooses to ignore real-world political and economic issues in favour of a retreat into mythic fantasy, thus avoiding the need to assume any responsibility.

Given the ostensible mythopoetic concern for the viability of the family, and given that male bonding is a crucial aspect of the movement, it is surprising more emphasis is not laid on *brother hunger* alongside the loss of the father. It is in *fraternal* relations that man finds his centre, in consultation rather than rule. Addressing brother hunger aligns a man as one among equals: he doesn't seek co-power with his brothers but co-support, simultaneously undermining typical homosocial dynamics. Most importantly, addressing brother hunger bypasses the mythopoetic requirement for space-time travel, finding solutions not in a past which may not have existed, nor in a biological father who may be dead and/or misunderstood, but in the here and now with one's fellow men. Given the mythopoetic habit of alluding to the spiritual, one could imagine such a focus on brotherhood appealing to Jesus' disciples or monastic orders. Of course, brother hunger trades upon the gender separatism of the mythopoetic movement: it should more accurately be described as *sibling hunger*, for the co-support can come from men *and* women. Interestingly it is precisely the sibling dynamic that Bly went on to attack in his follow-up to *Iron John*, in *The Sibling Society* (1996). In this book Bly claims that the societal status quo is built on sibling relations, which he interprets as being inherently adolescent, because there are no fathers to initiate the siblings into adults. So here is the reason why brother hunger would not work in the mythopoetic movement: it operates via mutuality, which is fundamentally at odds with a mythopoetic discourse of authority.

Mythopoetic storyteller Michael Meade (1993: 306-18) sees more value in brotherhood than Bly, but within his initiatory framework. For Meade, brothers (whether physical brothers or fraternal aspects of the psyche) are employed in a hierarchical framework and assist via initiation in the transitioning from one life phase to another. But Meade's brothers are lacking the real beauty of the fraternal dynamic because each is stuck in a rigid framework: younger brother, middle brother, elder brother, each with his own unique tasks. More than this it is the elder brother who is clearly the preferred brother: the 'youngest brother [is] part of the shadow of the individual psyche...the shadow of a culture' (1993: 315). It is the elder brother who creates the initiatory space and benign guidance. The elder brother is less of a brother and actually more a mini-father, or even a King. So in much the same way as Bly rejects the sibling society, so too does Meade by stripping the mutuality from the sibling dynamic and replacing it with an authority structure where the authority is derived from nothing more than age.

Initiation

In the mythopoetic movement the main function of our absent fathers (alongside other missing manly men) is to initiate boys into the mysteries of male society. Clatterbaugh locates initiation at the very centre of the movement, 'logically speaking, the goal of the mythopoetic perspective must be the restoration of appropriate male initiation rites' (1997: 200). Initiation is another theme from which the movement derives its status as spiritual. But again, this is questionable. Initiation is seen as spiritual simply because it is 'tribal', 'primitive' and 'ancient' rather than having anything to do with an actual spiritual process. Initiation is another expedition into fantasy realms: they refer to such societies in which boys are initiated into manhood and who then allegedly have a strong sense of identity, and conclude that a lack of social and spiritual identity within contemporary society is the result of a lack of contemporary initiation.

Even if we accept that these conclusions about tribal initiation are founded on something more than a very rudimentary knowledge of tribal societies, and that those initiations are good things within those societies, we are left with a fundamental problem: the assumption that what works in one context works in another. It is quite ridiculous to apply romanticized notions of Australian Aboriginal or Kalahari Bushman initiations on to the streets of London or Los Angeles. Such a blunt instrument may actually prove an obstacle to finding ways of facilitating the emergence of young people's identities within Western contexts.

Again, Brod gets to the heart of the matter suggesting another reason why the initiation of boys by fathers and mentors holds little weight in the West: 'individual manhood is no longer the fundamental site of the exercise of male power. Initiation is always initiation into authority. Today, the most important game in town, the club worth joining is the depersonalised, institutional recognition of one's manhood' (1992: 234). Brod connects initiation with power and authority rather than social and spiritual identity. A further dimension needs to be added to this: initiation in a mythopoetic context is a medium of conformity. Initiation encourages conformist behaviour not in order to *bestow* authority, but in order for the initiate to *adhere to* authority, while all the time duping him into thinking he is part of an exclusive club. The ironic truth is that by operating as a medium of conformity, initiation does not, as is claimed, bestow identity on a boy; rather, it erases it. Similarly, by liberating the young from their position as subordinated masculinities, initiation provides a passage to hegemonic masculinity.

The call to initiation has echoes of what Clatterbaugh referred to as the 'reification game'. One answer is to simply reject the game, the call to initiation, the trial by fire. Meade anticipates this by referring to what he describes as the 'fuck you group'. Faced with the options Meade provides of exile or dangerous/heroic initiation he says, 'some won't even play the game of chess because it is rigged. One of these men says, "Fuck you. I'm not doing it. I'm tired of being forced into bad choices"…Several others join him. They form a "fuck you" group' (Meade 1993: 145). Meade says that being in the fuck you group leads to 'lonely exile' (Meade 1993: 145), that death is inevitable and that refusing to choose can only ever be a 'temporary position'. But this is simply a bluff. Clearly, there are other paths in life which are certainly more than temporary, so Meade's workshop attendees do indeed have the prerogative to turn to him and say, 'fuck you'.

The false options provided by Meade of exile or initiation feel more like a way of elevating himself to the privileged position of initiator. Zipes' comments about Bly also suggest this strategy: 'his eclectic reconstruction of putative initiation rituals has more to do with his…desire to become a male guru than with providing a rigorous analysis of the problems facing men in contemporary America' (Zipes 1992: 8). By creating a need for initiation, Bly and the other mythopoetic elders position themselves in a powerful position within the spiritual marketplace, reaping both 'gerontocratic power' (Ross 1992: 212) and workshop dollars.

Once archetypes and initiation are rejected as spiritual, it becomes hard to understand why *Iron John* ever catalysed the 'spiritual men's movement'. There is a curious anomaly with Bly's book as it both opens and closes on a spiritual note, but does not pursue it in the main text. In the preface Bly refers to the Zen priest, shaman and even George Ivanovitch Gurdjieff (Bly 1990: x; xi); he concludes his epilogue referring to the need for a hairy Christ, a new religious figure who can combine God and sexuality (Bly 1990: 249). But the main text is a curiously anti-spiritual crusade. Nearly all the references to Greek, Egyptian and Hindu gods cannot be considered spiritual, because their readings are almost exclusively mythical. Then Bly is critical of Christianity (Bly 1990: 8), claims engaging with the Wild Man is not about 'spirit' or 'higher consciousness' (Bly 1990: 9), bemoans the abandonment of physical labour as being part of an attempt towards more 'spiritual' work (Bly 1990: 20), attempts to strip religion of both faith and belief (Bly 1990: 38), criticizes on several occasions New Agers, including 'ashram habitués' (Bly 1990: 58), suggests 'spiritual work' should be restricted to those over 35 years old (Bly 1990: 59), claims the 'spiritual man' is 'entirely numb' (Bly 1990: 68), and even has a snipe at the Dalai Lama (Bly 1990: 103). The overriding message of *Iron John* is anti-spiritual, seeking instead salvation in the dark waters of the psyche.[15] Revisiting Sandra Schneiders' historical sourcing of the term

15. Eric Magnuson's (2007) recent treatment of the mythopoetic movement presents it in a more spiritual light, referring to spirituality (in particular Buddhist meditation) on numerous occasions. Magnuson argues that previous examinations of the movement have missed its subtlety by focusing on the leaders (Bly *et al*) rather than the men themselves. This seems a fair enough criticism, but Magnuson's data comes from only one mythopoetic men's group (albeit over a long period of time) rather than the movement as a whole, so suffers its own problems of representation. The leader of the group Magnuson follows repeatedly uses material written by Bly et al and only lets men into the group who are already in line with mythopoetic values, which presumably have come from exposure to such leaders; focusing on them is therefore only sensible. The presence of the (under defined) spiritual in Magnuson's group is really a reflection of the interests of the individual group leader which are brought to the table *alongside* the mythopoetic preoccupation with the psychic, rather than being representative of a mythopoetic spirituality.

'spirituality' in Paul's distinction between the 'spiritual person' (*pneumatikos*) under the influence of God and the 'natural person' (*psychikos anthropôs*), such mythopoetic meditations are clearly *psychikos*. Even engaging Schneiders' broad contemporary definition of spirituality as pertaining to 'the horizon of ultimate value' (Schneiders 1989: 684), in a mythopoetic context that horizon is often a literal one, framing the wilderness playground rather than some preternatural aspiration.

The theme of initiation, along with archetypes, wild(er)ness and fatherlessness were all instrumental as to why the mythopoetic movement was perceived to be the spiritual men's movement. But this was not solely the result of how it presented itself. Crucially, the perception of its critics aided to this misperception. While highlighting many important issues, some feminist and particularly profeminist critics missed the problematic nature of the movement's 'spiritual mantel', thus perpetuating it and unwittingly attributing the movement more *gravitas* than it deserved. The reason for this is that much of the criticism came from the social sciences, whose engagement with masculinity can suffer from a 'spiritual hollowness' (Tacey 1997: ix), has 'for the most part ignored the spiritual side of the male psyche' (Harris 1997: 29) and more generally, men's 'connections to the nonhuman world' (Allister 2004: 9). So while there was much excellent analysis of the mythopoetic movement's political and gender problems, there remained, with a few exceptions such as Schwalbe (1996) and Nonn (1995), a spiritual lacuna.[16] When spirituality was mentioned it tended to be in regard to the appropriation of indigenous culture (which is really a political criticism) or simply scoffed at.[17] This is unfortunate as the

16. As already noted, Schwalbe (1996) identified the 'religious attitude' of the movement, and also the largely unacknowledged influence of Sufi poetry, of which Bly is rather fond. Looking for other spiritual masculinities the movement could use, Nonn (1995: 176-79) argues that Moses and Jesus were usefully atypical men. Charles Upton's (1993) *Hammering Hot Iron: A Spiritual Critique of Iron John*, identifies the spiritual absence of the movement from a different direction: he shows how it *could be* genuinely spiritual rather than psychological if it chose.

17. Michael Kimmel and Michael Kaufman write, 'As Joseph Conwell wrote, in Manhood's Morning... "rot is rot, and it is never more rotten than when it is sandwiched between religious quotations and antiquated poetry"' (1995: 30). Clatterbaugh chides Bly for creating in the mythopoetic movement an 'old time religion' (1995: 57-58) a movement with founding fathers, sacred texts and special language; the irrational nature of religion is implicit.

mythopoetic movement would have been exposed as wanting far quicker had the perception of it being the spiritual men's movement been quashed. In the other direction, if the profeminist men's movement, which Clatterbaugh says 'has almost no life outside the university' (2000: 887), was more open to the spiritual, its numbers would no doubt swell.[18] In the absence of this the left-leaning man with a spiritual conscience finds himself torn between the 'spiritual' mythopoetic movement with no real sense of the political, and the profeminist movement with no real sense of the spiritual.

Sam Keen: The Exception to the Rule?

Quite anomalous in mythopoetic literature, and which needs to be examined separately is Sam Keen's (1991) *Fire in the Belly*, which is often considered to be second only to Bly's *Iron John* in the mythopoetic cannon. From the start the title certainly sounds mythopoetic[19] and there are some common mythopoetic themes. For example, Keen says man must separate from woman, but woman on an absolute level rather than a physical level; this distinction is made by referring to WOMAN in the absolute sense in uppercase letters. WOMEN, 'these archetypal creatures — goddesses, bitches, angels, Madonnas, castrators, witches, Gypsy maidens, earth mothers — must be exorcised from our hearts before we can love women' (Keen 1991: 16). For Keen, the three aspects of WOMAN are goddess and creatrix, mother and matrix, and erotic-spiritual power (Keen 1991: 16): 'she is the magnet, and men the iron filings that lie within her field' (Keen 1991: 21). We are also presented with familiar treatments of men's father wounds and the need for male bonding. However, after this Keen begins to sound rather different to the other mythopoetic writers.

---

18. The National Organization for Men Against Sexism (NOMAS), the main profeminist organization, does possess a 'men and spirituality' task group, although it does not appear to do much. The group's convenor says at one point it had an active campaign which has since quietened (Allen Corben, Personal Communication, October 2005). Since these comments, the NOMAS website has included a full position statement regarding the group noting the often dominating nature of religion, and that 'nevertheless, energy and intellectual support to do the work of ending oppression and injustice flow out of those spiritual convictions' [http://www.nomas.org/node/83].

19. A dismissive stance is encouraged by lampoonery such as Alfred Gingold's (1991) *Fire in the John*, which plays on Keen's title and Bly's *Iron John*.

Keen deviates from two key mythopoetic themes. He is suspicious of tribal initiation rites that 'prevented the development of individuality. Tribal societies ensured conformity by eliminating any time in the life cycle during which freedom could develop' (Keen 1991: 32). And Keen writes of the supposed warrior archetype within man, 'all deterministic explanations ignore the obvious: men are systematically conditioned to endure pain, to kill, and to die in the service of the tribe, nation or state' (Keen 1991: 37). Indeed, Keen makes very little reference to archetypes at all. As if in stubborn refusal to stand in Bly's shadow (excuse the Jungian pun), it takes Keen 100 pages to refer to the Wildman and a further 81 to enter into the 'virtue of wildness' (Keen 1991: 181).

Keen makes much reference to sexuality in daily life. It is interesting to note that apart from a highly abstract and pseudo-mystical fascination with the phallus, and the occasional token nod to the Lover archetype to fulfil the fourth quadrant of Moore and Gillette's archetypal system, mythopoetic literature is curiously asexual. This mythopoetic asexuality can be seen as a further retreat into fantasy. Mature sexuality requires engaging the complex task of relationships with other individuals, whereas the mythopoets have a habit of shying away from the complexity of real world issues, preferring instead the simple dynamics of myth. Or if not asexual, there is a kind of psychosexual adolescence about the movement: it knows it has sexual feelings but is incapable, or too embarrassed, to name them. Ironically, despite the fact that the movement has a tendency to homophobia[20] it simultaneously bristles with homoerotic energy,[21] which is, of course, a perfectly natural element in the full spectrum of male sexuality, especially within

20. See Gordon Murray (1995). Even Jed Diamond from within the movement says that homophobia is 'a major failing of the mythopoetic work' (Diamond 1995: 318).

21. Mark Simpson writes, 'The end of the Iron John story shows that, just as in the Western, the overriding romance was homosexual' (1995: 266). Andrew Ross claims, 'the meeting with the Wild Man capitalizes on the fantasy of a same-sex encounter that dare not speak its name. Too much of this stuff mimics standard exotic gay male narratives and fantasy sexual types to pass itself off as hetero male bonding, no matter how deep or courageous' (1992: 213). Martin Amis' bizarre review of *Iron John* includes his outlining why he could never take even the title seriously: '*iron* is rhyming slang for "male homosexual". Just as *ginger* (ginger beer) means "queer", so, I'm afraid, *iron* (iron hoof) means "poof"' (quoted in Zipes 1992: 3).

childhood and adolescent years on the path to sexual maturation.[22] This is not to say the mythopoetic movement is full of closeted gay men (although there are no doubt some), nor that being gay is inherently adolescent, rather that a form of adolescent homoeroticism seems prevalent in the movement, suggesting its psychic immaturity. By referring to mature sexuality, Keen (1991: 68-79) forces mythopoetic literature (no doubt reluctantly) into the real world.

Keen is also the only major mythopoet who speaks in any useful way about spirituality. In the opening pages of *Fire in the Belly* Keen says he is following a pattern set by Paul Tillich[23] who asks that we,

> must ask three fundamental questions: (1) What is wrong with us? With men? Women? Society? What is the nature of our alienation? Our dis-ease? (2) What would we be like if we were whole? Healed? Actualized? If our potentiality was fulfilled? (3) How do we move from our condition of brokenness to wholeness? What are the means of healing? (Keen 1991: 7)

On numerous occasions Keen interprets masculinity via spirituality, in particular his 'Prophetic Man' and 'Man as Image of God' passages (1991: 100-103). 'A man finds fulfilment (spiritual and sexual) only when he turns aside from willfulness and surrenders to something beyond self' (1991: 102), writes Keen, which seems far more in line with Forman's notion of spirituality than anything in the mythopoetic literature so far discussed. Entering into eco-theology Keen says, 'first and foremost, the vocation of now and future men is to become gentle and earthy' (1991: 120). Consider:

> I suggest the time has come to cease using gendered metaphors for God or nature. It is more confusing than helpful to speak now of God as "Father" or the Earth as "Mother". We need to find metaphors that do not build a genderal claim of superiority into our way of theological thinking and spiritual practice (Keen 1991: 202).

22. Psychoanalyst Joyce McDougall (1995) suggests there are bi-sexual fantasies and desires in all childhood development. The American Academy of Pediatrics (1993) suggests 'homosexual' experimentation among otherwise heterosexual people is common in adolescence. Archconservative clinicians Joseph Nicolosi and Linda Nicolosi (2002) recognize this adolescent habit and even suggest that reparative therapy can be employed if it subsists.

23. Keen describes Tillich as, 'perhaps the greatest philosopher-theologian of our time' (1991: 7). Just how much Tillich would have honored WOMAN is open to debate given his ambiguous opinions about feminism (Irwin 1991: 116-20).

Statements such as these sound more like theology than mythopoetic apology, yet Keen is second only to Bly in the mythopoetic leaders' hierarchy. While Keen is still subject to certain mythopoetic habits of gender essentialism, such as his painting of WOMAN, he nevertheless is free of much of the criticism levelled against his mythopoetic brothers.

Conclusion

The mythopoetic men's movement focuses on the key themes of archetypes, wildness/wilderness, fatherlessness and initiation. The movement suggests men need to engage with these themes in order to free themselves from being what Bly describes as a 'soft male'. The mythopoetic movement was, and continues to be, attractive to many men due to a wide agreement that the current ways of doing masculinity are unsatisfactory, and a good deal of mythopoetic writing can sound quite plausible when taken at face value. Even Moore and Gillette, who are responsible for 'the worst' of mythopoetic texts (Kimmel 1995b: 5), can sound like they are on to a good thing:

> Masculinity is not in its essence abusive. We have within us the innate potential to use our masculine power for blessing, stewardship, and servant leadership. Our ancient longings may yet be fulfilled — not through one messianic person, but through an inner revolution in the maturation of masculine consciousness in which millions of men may participate (Moore and Gillette 1992a: 254).

But what these new and/or reclaimed models of masculinity actually look like is largely problematic.

Archetypes, as Culbertson argued, are 'calcifications of a patriarchal world view'. Identifying with archetypes does not conclude, as suggested by the mythopoetic writers, with the discovery of the mature masculine, rather the rediscovery of the hetereopatriarchal masculine. Moore and Gillette claim men need to access their King energy, but in doing so set up a model of masculinity to which men must aspire based on despotism. Moore and Gillette go on to claim men must reclaim their Warrior energy, which results in a masculinity stained with blood; even when their Warriors are calmed by the Lover archetype the result is Mishima and General Patton. The Wild Man is the archetype favoured by

Bly, which again suggests men must trawl their psychic depths to find the mature masculine, only to discover, as Zipes said, a celebration of 'violence and killing as the means to establish male identity'.

The continued belief in archetypal ontology results in an almost fascistic certainty within the mythopoetic movement, but one which ultimately remains silent due to the movement's fear of really telling it as they perceive it to be, knowing full well their critics would be even more plentiful. It therefore seems appropriate to see where Julius Evola took his proto-mythopoeticism, with all his characteristic transparency:

> The only true problem is to what extent in a given society and epoch man can be himself and woman can be herself in an accurate approximation of their respective archetypes, and also to what extent the relationships of man and woman reflect the natural and unchangeable law rooted in the very metaphysics of male and female. The law is "reciprocal integration and completion together with a subordination of the female principle to the male". Everything else, as Nietzsche would say, is nonsense (Evola 1991: 171).

The real unfairness here might not be to connect mythopoeticism to fascism, rather to connect Evola to mythopoeticism, for despite his many questionable opinions (Goodrick-Clarke 2002: 52-71), he did at least have a complex understanding of the spiritual. The same cannot be said for the mythopoetic movement, which repeatedly mistook psychological realities for spiritual ones. In respect to archetypes, setting aside the unsavoury model of masculinity they encourage, the movement mistook for gods that which its own elders described either as biologically innate or metaphorical. A similar mistake was performed in the movement's appreciation of wilderness, which was transformed from something merely bigger than the individual into the spiritual. Mythopoetic thinking had a tendency to transform much of what was beyond the individual's immediate control into the spiritual. In respect to fatherlessness the spiritual was also misappropriated, confusing a psychological wound with a spiritual one, and also trading upon an unspoken, yet clear connection with God the Father. Lastly, initiation was assumed to be spiritual because of its ancient and tribal origins. This spiritual misperception was perpetuated both by the movement itself and its critics. The anomaly to all this spiritual misuse was

Sam Keen, who did ask some real theological questions in his interpretation of mythopoetic masculinity.

Above all, the mythopoetic movement mistook myth to be spiritual. Roland Barthes claims 'the function of myth is to empty reality; it is, literally, a ceaseless flowing out, a haemorrhage, or perhaps an evaporation, in short a perceptible absence. ...*myth is depoliticised speech*' (quoted in Zipes 1992: 19). Schwalbe argues that the mythopoetic understanding of gender as simply complementary ways of being, obscured obvious gender injustices: 'Jungian psychology, ironically, kept the men from seeing and facing the shadow of patriarchy' (1996: 223). This, in the end, is the result of the mythopoetic movement: not providing a spiritual model for masculinity, but the depoliticization of gender discourses under the guise of a spiritually derived authentic masculinity.

It would be premature to consider the mythopoetic movement as a thing of the past. Yes, it is now well over a decade since Moore and Gillette published *King, Warrior, Magician, Lover*, but their following quartet is currently being reprinted.[24] Numerous mythopoetic organizations still exist such as The ManKind Project, which operates in a number of countries offering the New Warrior Training Adventure, which offers men a form of adult initiation.[25] Younger men who missed the movement in its original glory are rediscovering Bly: Jess Row (2006), who understandably bemoans the archaic models of masculinity promoted in Harvey Mansfield's (2006) *Manliness*, claims 'we need ... more books like *Iron John*...[and to] find a way of emulating Bly's generosity of spirit and willingness to risk truth-telling' (paras. 4-11). The most recent scholarly examination of the movement (Magnuson 2007) is arguably the most favourable there has ever been.[26] Most notably, mythopoetic themes

---

24. http://robertmoore-phd.com/Quartet.cfm

25. http://www.mkp.org

26. It is noteworthy that the two most generous scholarly treatments of the movement (Magnuson 2007; Schwalbe 1996) are those which have engaged the movement at a personal level, where the author has embarked upon a relationship with the movement as a participant observer. This suggests there are some clearly good intentions among members that shine through its problems. However, intentions are not enough, what is most important is the net effect, which in a mythopoetic context is ultimately a retreat to a patriarchal masculinity. A similar process unfolds in the following chapters concerning the Christian men's movements.

live on in the Christian men's movement, both in texts written around the time of *Iron John* (Arnold 1991; Dalbey 1988; Hicks 1993; Rohr and Martos 1992; Rohr 1994; Weber 1993) and also later (Coughlin 2005; Eldredge 2001; Galli 2006; McManus 2005; Murrow 2005; Rohr 2004), as well as a proliferation of men's ministries which echo mythopoetic themes. It is to this subject that the next two chapters turn.

Chapter Three

THE EVANGELICAL MEN'S MOVEMENT: NETWORKING, VIOLENCE AND SPORT

The Christian men's movement, and its articulation of masculine spirituality, is often equated squarely with Promise Keepers, but this is a mistake. Promise Keepers is but one manifestation of the contemporary Christian men's movement that comprises various strands. Kenneth Clatterbaugh's (1990 and 1997) *Contemporary Perspectives on Masculinity* charts the different components of the general men's movement. In the second edition, Clatterbaugh included the evangelical men's movement, exemplified by Promise Keepers, as a significant new strand of men's movement not present on publication of the first edition. While Promise Keepers did not exist at that time, there was a Christian men's movement, but it went by a different name. What Clatterbaugh failed to identify was that the Christian men's movement is indistinguishable from men's ministry, the current form of which can be traced back to the early 1980s. Also, 'the evangelical men's movement' does not acknowledge those strands of Christian men's movement and ministry that are not evangelical. Catholic manifestations of the Christian men's movement, for example, have gone largely unnoticed, and will be discussed separately in the next chapter.

While the exemplar of the Christian men's movement, this chapter does not dwell long on Promise Keepers, which has been the subject of a large body of existing scholarship. Instead, Promise Keepers is located within a wider context of evangelical men's movement and ministry which is shown to perpetuate a masculine spirituality that is overtly patriarchal. There are two key elements to the evangelical men's movement that predate Promise Keepers, one thematic, the other organizational. Acting as a thematic backdrop for much of the evangelical men's movement and ministry is a set of concerns similar to that of the secular men's movement, in particular the feminization of men and society. What we might call 'evangelical mythopoeticism' extends this concern to the feminization of Jesus and the Church, and is subject to all the critiques of mythopoeticism outlined in the previous chapter. A second crucial element predating Promise Keepers is the Christian Men's Network, a network of men's ministries established by Edwin Louis Cole who sought a model of masculinity based on biblical principles, encouraging male leadership within the Church and home.

Both these strands are unusually concerned with the notion of what constitutes authentic masculinity. Indeed, Andrew Singleton argues, 'Christian men devote more time to examining and interrogating their masculinity than most other groups of men' (2004: 154). James Dittes sees five possible reasons for such interrogation: rescuing God the Father; the liberating of men through God the Father; biblical figures taking on new vitality; better use of men's energies for both other men and God; the rescuing of ministry from narrow maleness (1991: 590). The single overriding reason for the Christian men's movement is an anxiety about the fading of men within the Church: either an anxiety about men losing power in the Church as a result of increasing feminine influence, or a missiological anxiety that fewer men are being brought to Christ. Christian concern about masculinity is nothing new: in the introduction we saw how this dates back to movements such as Muscular Christianity and the Men and Religion Forward Movement. This chapter shows how such concerns today result in not only a masculine-patriarchal spirituality in terms of gender dynamics, but also a disturbing propensity to violence. Lastly, this chapter examines how the evangelical men's movement intersects with what can be described as a contemporary Muscular Christianity in the form of ministries and missions which use sport as an evangelizing tool to the general public, and also ministering to sporting people. The net effect of contemporary Muscular Christianity and sports ministries in terms of their gender focus, and sometimes even their administrative structure, is that both are arguably an extension of the evangelical men's movement, further perpetuating a masculine-patriarchal spirituality.

This chapter extends previous observations by Linda Kintz (1996) and Ann Burlein (2004). Both Kintz and Burlein identify some commonality between the Christian Far Right and conservative middle ground politics. Aside from highlighting the prevalence of American warrior masculinity, Kintz shows how extreme positions are accepted as quite reasonable when articulated by clean-cut American men and women. Picking up from Kintz's examination of Stu Weber's popular Christian men's movement book *Tender Warrior* (1993) a range of other extreme voices in men's ministry are identified. These same voices also strengthen the connection made by Burlein between the 'soft' and the 'hard' Christian Right, offering plentiful examples of how ostensibly middle-ground family-focused men's ministries veer alarmingly towards paramilitary themes. Kintz's words resonate throughout this examination of men's ministries: 'The military version of Jesus has to be re-established if men are to be drawn back to spirituality' (1996: 122).

Promise Keepers: Neither the First nor the Last

It is often thought that the Christian men's movement and Promise Keepers are the same thing, but this is not true. Promise Keepers is a non-denominational men's movement alongside other denominational movements such as National Fellowship of Catholic Men, United Methodist Men or Lutheran Men in Mission. Nor is it accurate to make the more narrow equation that the evangelical men's movement and Promise Keepers are the same thing: the next section shows how the evangelical men's movement as we know it was founded nearly a decade before Promise Keepers. Promise Keepers is nevertheless the prime example of the Christian men's movement, or men's ministry, and an awareness of the issues surrounding them is an awareness of the Christian men's movement in general.

Promise Keepers was started in 1990 by American football coach Bill McCartney, and is typified by large gatherings of men worshipping in sports stadia. At its peak in 1996, Promise Keepers events drew well over a million attendees. The name comes from the seven promises the movement's men are to uphold, which provide a useful insight into the general themes of men's ministry: honouring Jesus Christ; pursuing vital relationships with other men; practicing spiritual, moral, ethical, and sexual purity; building families through biblical values; supporting the mission of the church by honouring and praying for the pastor; reaching beyond any racial and denominational barriers to demonstrate the power of biblical unity; and commitment to influencing the world, being obedient to the Great Commandment and the Great Commission (Janssen and Weeden 1994).

There has been considerable research published on the subject of Promise Keepers, the attitude to which has generally softened over time. Michael Messner's (1997) account of the movement is a good example of how early writing on Promise Keepers located it at the heart of an anti-feminist backlash, a New Patriarchy located firmly in the Christian Right. These initial responses inevitably suffered from certain generalizations and were primarily political in their critique, ignoring the more personal and spiritual aspects of the movement. Dane Claussen's two edited volumes (1999 and 2000) began to take a more objective view of Promise Keepers, containing both critical and sympathetic contributions. Rhys Williams' (2001) edited volume swung further towards a generous interpretation of the movement, in particular highlighting a personal (if not political) commitment to racial conciliation (Allen 2001), a keen awareness for the need for therapeutic self-help (Bloch 2001), emotional intimacy within prayer groups (Bartkowski 2001), differing gender ideologies (Lockhart 2001) and varying support for Promise Keepers within the general public (Johnson 2001). One could argue that this literature concentrated on personal intention at the expense of political consequence. Judith Newton (2005) can be read as one attempt to address both the personal and the political which, while written from a feminist position, remains surprisingly sympathetic to Promise Keepers. Many other studies offered findings along this spectrum. If it is possible to draw a single conclusion from the large volume of literature it would be: Promise Keepers is a generally well-meaning movement of men who seek a better world through Christ, but who fail to appreciate the essentially patriarchal implications and consequences of their own project.

Equating the Christian men's movement with Promise Keepers has also led to another significant misperception: as Promise Keepers appears to decline in popularity, so too does the Christian men's movement. It is noteworthy that the apparent decline of Promise Keepers has in part to do with visibility and a change in strategy away from stadium events towards smaller church-based evangelism (Morley 2000: para. 20). But more than this, when the Christian men's movement is appreciated for what it is—namely men's ministry that pre-dates Promise Keepers—instead of decline one sees expansion. The proliferation of men's ministries is quite extraordinary. Patrick Morley, 'Chairman and CEO' of the popular ministry Man in the Mirror, identifies over 34,000 men's ministries in America alone (Morley 2000: para. 17) which are clearly not all Promise Keepers. These numbers highlight a vast network of ministries based on a model established by self-professed 'father of the Christian men's movement' Edwin Louis Cole and his Christian Men's Network.[1] As well as Cole's organizational model, Promise Keepers had the mythopoetic movement to draw upon: both its secular manifestation addressed in the previous chapter, and also an evangelical mythopoeticism, outlined below. Promise Keepers built on these two strands and their success resulted in a synergistic partnership, each one influencing the other. For a while in the 1990s Promise Keepers eclipsed both the ministry networks and evangelical mythopoeticism, but as its visibility decreased, these originating influences once again became more apparent.

Evangelical Mythopoeticism

Evangelical mythopoeticism is not a recognized category, but it is a useful one.[2] In the previous chapter the key themes of 'secular' mythopoeticism were highlighted: archetypes; fatherlessness; initiation; wildness/wilderness; male bonding. Evangelical mythopoeticism picks up these themes and frames them within an evangelical worldview. Men's ministries, which are examined in a following section, draw deeply on this tradition. There also exists a parallel Catholic mythopoeticism, which is discussed in the next chapter. Three of the key evangelical mythopoetic texts referred to here are Gordon Dalbey's *Healing the Masculine Soul* (1988), Stu Weber's *Tender Warrior* (1993), and John Eldredge's *Wild at*

---

1. Ed Cole is singled out due to his modelling men's networks, but his was not the only significant voice to influence the Christian men's movement. Another example is Gene Getz, whose book *The Measure of a Man* (1974) has sold over a million copies. Getz promotes a biblical model of masculinity as outlined by Paul's letters to Timothy and Titus. To elaborate on this model, in the (2004) revised edition he likens appropriate masculinity to middle management, in particular to that of a steel mill (17-19). The back cover of the revised edition carries a testimonial from Bill McCartney, 'a classic that continues to be the basis for men's bible studies around the world'.

2. William Lockhart (2001) notes Promise Keepers' appreciation of mythopoetic literature. This section presents evangelical mythopoeticism as a wider phenomenon.

Heart (2001).[3] These are among the most widely read evangelical mythopoetic books, and are roughly representative of the period of time we are looking at, having been published between 1988 and 2001.[4]

Robert Bly is at the heart of evangelical mythopoeticism in much the same way as secular mythopoeticism. Although Dalbey predates the publication of *Iron John* by two years, he was significantly influenced by an earlier interview of Bly with Keith Thompson entitled *What Men Really Want* (Bly and Thompson 1982). This interview is basically an 8,000-word summary of *Iron John* and Dalbey quotes it extensively. Weber also acknowledges Bly as an influence, and Eldredge refers to Bly on 13 separate occasions. The relationship between secular and evangelical mythopoeticism is, however, probably two-directional. Dalbey, for example, develops the warrior archetype that is absent in the early Bly interview, and which went on to be a crucial motif within secular mythopoeticism (Moore and Gillette 1990 and 1992). While started by Bly, one can speculate that the many secular, evangelical and Catholic mythopoetic books written throughout the 1990s and 2000s influenced each other in complex ways.

Dalbey does not employ the term 'archetypes' in the mantra-like way of other mythopoetic texts, but he means the same thing, referring to 'the four basic roles by which most of us judge our masculinity: son of the father, warrior, lover of a woman, and provider' (1988: 15). There are immediate echoes here of Moore and Gillette's later quadratic archetypal model. Weber's masculinity also comprises four similar aspects: king, warrior, mentor and friend (1993: 38). Eldredge uses the word 'archetype' only once (2001: 115) but holds the warrior up as the central theme of 'authentic masculinity' (2001: 13).

Like Bly, Dalbey is concerned with the effeminate nature of contemporary man, repeatedly locating the source of this problem as the father wound, referring to both absentee earthly fathers and an inadequate relationship with the heavenly Father. Dalbey

3. See Sally K. Gallagher and Sabrina L. Wood (2005) for an extended critique of Eldredge.

4. Aside from various similar books by Dalbey and Weber, other typical examples of evangelical mythopoeticism include Robert Lewis' *Raising a Modern-day Knight* (1997), and more recently Erwin McManus' *The Barbarian Way* (2005), and Paul Coughlin's *No More Christian Nice Guy* (2005); see Joseph Gelfer (2006a) for a critique of Coughlin.

recounts numerous stories about how the earthly father wound is healed by accepting the heavenly Father. Contemporary man is also made effeminate by an inability to disengage with the mother, another common theme of Bly. This results in men abdicating their responsibilities to the various women in their lives, and Dalbey begins to promote the necessity of servant leadership (1988: 40-41), a theme central to men's ministries and discussed in a later section. More than just criticizing overly-feminine characteristics within men, Dalbey appears to consider the feminine as fundamentally problematic within a spiritual context: 'all goddess-focused religions ultimately betray roots in such idolatry of the mother/woman and proceed upon natural, earth-bound theologies. Thus, they cannot portray true spirituality, which requires a breaking of the powers of the flesh' (1988: 42). It is in order to reengage effeminate men (indeed to battle idolatry) that Dalbey seeks out wildness.

Dalbey's wildness is typified by the image of the lion (1988: 25-26). The lion represents courage and strength within a man, and also the Lord. The lion is the authentically wild masculine. Weber's model of authentic masculinity derives from a less dramatic source: his favourite childhood TV show, *Wagon Train*, and the character of Flint McCullugh, 'lithe-limbed, cleft-chinned, raven-haired' (1993: 21). Allusions to *Wagon Train* simultaneously indicate a mythopoetic mode of masculinity and also mythopoetic wilderness, and we are also presented with various stories of Weber's delight of outdoorsmanship. The wilderness, for Weber, plays host to a form of natural masculinity, the archetypal basis of which can be discovered in the Bible (1993: 37). Precisely the same theme is presented by Eldredge who opens *Wild at Heart* with a scene of him hunting elk in the Sawatch Range of central Colorado (2001: 2), and he returns to the wilderness repeatedly whether alone, with his buddies, or sons.

Following Bly, Dalbey suggests that in order for men to engage their wildness they need to be initiated into it. Bly and Thompson (1982) refer to initiation of boys into men among the Hopi of North America and Kikuyus of Africa, suggesting similar rituals are necessary within the West. Dalbey has his own initiation stories comparable to Bly, drawing on his Peace Corps years in Nigeria (1988: 49-54). Dalbey suggests on several occasions that Christ can initiate a man, if He is allowed, a method also cited by Eldredge (2001: 102; 148). He presents a vision of what a Christian initiation might look like, in which men from the church arrive at a boy's house singing *Faith of Our Fathers*, encouraging the boy to leave his mother's apron strings, after which he is 'driven to a church campground for a period of discipline and instruction' (1988: 57). Such initiation ritual provides bonding experiences for men and boys, another mythopoetic theme Weber picks up by his use of the word 'tender' (man's emotional outreach). For Weber, it is man's need for tenderness that sees him reach out for other men in sport (1993: 70), military comradery (1993: 171-76), and even mission (1993: 214). Tenderness for Weber also encompasses the mythopoetic theme of the father-son relationship (1993: 77). In the end, these mythopoetic themes of wildness, initiation and bonding enable a man to step up as a warrior: a key focus of evangelical mythopoeticism.

Weber is in total agreement with Bly that modern man is 'soft' but instead of blaming this, as does Bly, on the feminization of modern society or the Industrial Revolution's wrenching of man from the land, Weber locates the problem further back in time: namely the feminization of Jesus. Weber wants to remasculinize Jesus and align Him with the warrior archetype in much the same way as Moore and Gillette (1990: 52). Jesus, for Weber, is to be found, 'on a white horse, in a bloodspattered robe, with a sword in His mouth and a rod of iron in His hand' (1993: 41). Presumably, it is such behaviour to which mortal man should aspire given Jesus is 'the ultimate Man. Maximum manhood. The perfect Model. The complete Hero' (1993: 207). Weber is fascinated with aligning masculinity with violent images, to the point where 'warrior and military metaphors saturate his book' (Kintz 1997: 116). Dalbey also focuses on the Warrior, first attempting to navigate his own warrior potential, having missed out on combat in Korea and Vietnam (1988: 117-20) and also presenting Jesus as the exemplar warrior (1988: 125). Eldredge, too, is keen on repeatedly showing the wrathful side of not only the Old Testament scriptures, but also Jesus, and devotes a full chapter (2001: 157-78) to strategies for spiritual warfare with 'the Evil One'. Eldredge also has more contemporary sources for his warrior masculinity, including extensive visions of Omaha Beach on D-Day (2001: 84-86) and numerous references to battle movies such as *Saving Private Ryan*, *Gladiator* and *Braveheart*. Eldredge takes his movies seriously: at one point God informs him that he is a great warrior akin to Maximus, the gladiator played by

Russell Crowe (2001: 135), and to fuel his *Braveheart* fantasies, for Christmas his wife buys him 'a full-size claymore, a Scottish broadsword exactly like the one used by William Wallace' (2001: 195).

All these mythopoetic themes are picked up within men's ministries. For example, in Band of Brothers men can buy their sons a young warrior pendent, a gift intended to mark a son's rite of passage into manhood.[5] Building Brothers ministry (not to be confused with Band of Brothers) describe issues that stand between man and God that sound distinctly mythopoetic: all men experience a father vacuum; the church lacks a safe masculine environment; men do not trust their leaders.[6] In particular, evangelical men's ministries have focused on the need for Bly's famous soft male to be hardened up for his divinely ordained role as a leader. For this process, men's ministries have appropriated the warrior archetype, and later we will see how this has resulted in a proliferation of violent imagery.

Christian Men's Network

The Christian Men's Network was founded by Ed Cole in 1977. It is the connectivity of the network that enables men's ministry to be seen as a movement. Cole's books and relentless public speaking enabled his message to be widespread. Leaders in men's ministry will often trace their teaching back to Cole, perhaps even received from him in person, akin to apostolic succession. A men's ministry can be anything from one man seeking to minister to a small group of men right through to an organization with a large dedicated staff. The power of the network is in the different parts knowing of one another and being able to draw from each other inspiration, learning and resources. The success of Promise Keepers built on the network concept, working at various levels: small groups, congregations, seminars, conferences and stadium events. Individual men's ministries tend to be affiliated to ministry coalitions, the most significant of which is the National Coalition of Men's Ministries (NCMM), which lists 81 prominent men's ministries among its membership.[7] The relationships between the many men's ministries

5. http://www.bandofbrothers.org/bob/html/GifttoSonRiteofPassage.html
6. http://www.buildingbrothers.org/newsite/index.asp?PG=01&Sub=2
7. http://www.ncmm.org/site.cfm/NCMM-Member-Directory-5

can be complex and bewildering, but whether a one-man outfit in Wyoming or Promise Keepers, they all share an extraordinary commonality, based in the work of Ed Cole.

Cole was an angry man who wrote angry words in numerous books focusing on manhood. In his 'pioneering' *Maximized Manhood*, Cole launched in to what is wrong with modern man: 'lust, idolatry, fornication' (1982: 12). Sat around the breakfast table Cole's own daughter tells him, 'Dad, don't you know that sex sins will be the problem of the Church in the 80s?' (1982: 13). More than two decades later Cole's *Real Man* (2003) was still fighting the battle: 'feminists rage against maleness, creating a new perception of the word *man*, and cry out to replace gender specific terms with neuter terms. Gay-rights activists rage against heterosexuality and parade with "I hate straight" banners' (2003: 7); in order to placate this rage men 'end up castrating their identity, becoming ineffective and sterile' (2003: 7). Cole's anger was fearful of manhood falling apart in the absence of his vision of man in Christ. He was an 'anxious patriarch' (Lienesch 1990). Cole sought to bring men back to Christ by (re)instilling in them an authority he believed was lost. He never compromised on his opinions. In his last interview (Cole and Morley 2003) Cole states, 'One of the pastor's primary responsibilities is to disciple men. Then each man is to disciple his family. ...When women see men taking their rightful place of leadership in the church, they love it' (para. 53). Cole goes on to reflect on this manly role in the household, inferring the rest of the family are akin to loose change, 'if pastors minister to families, they get the tithe on the grocery money. If pastors minister to men, they get the tithe on the gross income' (para. 20).

Cole's message of fear and anger should not be considered an extreme voice in men's ministry that was watered down before becoming popular. Cole is openly recognized as a key influence on many mainstream men's ministries such as Promise Keepers. Bill McCartney said, 'Edwin Louis Cole modelled the key essentials' (quoted in Andrescik 2002, para. 7), and Cole's (1982) *Maximum Manhood* is one of three recommended texts on the Promise Keepers 2006 Unleashed Program.[8]

8. Along with Eldredge's *Wild at Heart* (2001), and McManus' *The Barbarian Way* (2005) https://www.promisekeepers.org/uploads/images/5erCXBXywD_vyHAXhA8BMg/unleashed_prog_summary.pdf, accessed 20 May 2006.

The issue of men being leaders in the home is fundamental to nearly all men's ministries.[9] The primacy of men is sprinkled liberally throughout the contributions to the key handbook *Effective Men's Ministry*. 'The greatest need in the church today is for men to become the leaders that God has called them to be,' writes Chuck Stecker (2001: 107). Consequently, amongst the competing ministry responsibilities within most churches, it should 'focus on building up the men's ministry first' (Sonderman 2001: 25). According to Vince D'Acchioli men are the 'key to a healthy church' (2001: 40). Stecker claims that even women want to put men's ministry first, referring to a woman who 'would be willing to cancel every program in the church that did not relate directly to developing men as leaders' (2001: 107).

Weber writes of man's primacy over woman, 'Accept it and live it. Trust it and obey it. Take the orders and follow them' (1993: 94). Male primacy, we are told by Weber, is not about superiority, 'any more than blue is superior to green' (1993: 128), rather just the way things are. The abdication of leadership stems all the way back to the Fall. In *Effective Men's Ministry* (2001: 63-64), Jack Hayford notes that the Fall was not the responsibility of Eve, rather Adam. Eve was deceived by the serpent, but Adam disobeyed God with his eyes wide open. In the same way Weber says Adam *allowed* Eve to sin, a sin that man must now redress by taking back leadership (1993: 90-91); for Weber, woman is the 'weaker vessel' (1993: 90-120). The call to leadership is exemplified by Tony Evans' now infamous suggestion,

> Sit down with your wife and say something like this "Honey, I've made a terrible mistake. I've given you my role. I gave up leading this family, and I forced you to take my place. Now I must reclaim that role." Don't misunderstand what I'm saying here. I'm not suggesting that you *ask* for your role back, I'm urging you to *take it back* (Evans 1994: 79, original emphases).

There is a growing body of (particularly sociological) scholarship that seeks to justify such leadership within the home. Such

9. Honorbound, for example, emphasize becoming spiritual leaders in the home [http://armensministry.org]. Some ministries employ a supposedly gentler 'servant leadership' position on men and their families, typified by Men of Integrity [http://www.menofintegrity.org]. Servant Leadership is one of the four key values of the most central of all men's ministries, The National Coalition of Men's Ministries [http://www.ncmm.org/site.cfm/Mission,-Vision-and-Values-3].

scholarship does not so much deny that evangelical Christianity is, 'pushing men toward authoritarian and stereotypical forms of masculinity and attempting to renew patriarchal family relations' (McQuillan and Marx Ferree 1998: 223), rather it seeks to reformulate and relocate the meaning of 'patriarchal family relations'.

W. Bradford Wilcox promotes 'soft patriarchs' who have, 'the attributes of the iconic new man—namely, a more egalitarian division of household labour and somewhat higher levels of paternal and marital involvement and emotional engagement' (2004: 14).[10] There are two significant problems with this argument. First, Wilcox claims evangelical men are not patriarchal due to his data indicating they engage in less patriarchal activity than non-evangelical men. But this does not take into account that non-evangelical men are themselves patriarchal, and therefore are not an appropriate yardstick by which to be measured. Second, Wilcox fails to appreciate that an 'egalitarian division of household labour and somewhat higher levels of paternal and marital involvement and emotional engagement' can co-exist quite comfortably within a wider patriarchal order, which is the very crux of 'servant leadership'. Mary Stewart Van Leeuwen (1997) asks the question, 'servanthood or soft patriarchy?' But this is a false binary. Nor does Van Leeuwen's conclusion ring true that the evangelical men's movement is *ambiguously* servanthood *and* soft patriarchy. In reality the movement is *explicitly* servanthood *and* soft patriarchy, because the two happily co-exist in the way that a Monarch 'serves' his or her country: it is a rhetoric afforded by the explicit assumption of an authoritative position. The servant leader does his share of the washing up and plays with his children in full knowledge that he is in charge, that he is the Patriarch. Wilcox knows this, but attempts to relocate the reality of patriarchy:

> conservative Protestant patriarchy is moving in the direction of being more symbolic than practical. Conservative Protestants still overwhelmingly endorse male headship but this headship appears to be more of a salve for men's threatened manhood than a license for them to exercise authority over their wives or demand they stay at home (Wilcox 2004: 143).

This is where the insidious nature of 'soft patriarchy' raises its head. A transaction is suggested: the servant leader will attempt to

10. See John Wall (2007) for an extended critique of Wilcox.

pull his weight around the house and all he asks in return is the 'symbolic' position of patriarch, a salve for his threatened manhood. Patriarchy is redefined in such a way that 'soft patriarchy' is marketed as quite reasonable: presumably soft patriarchy results in soft oppression and soft violence.

As men's ministries proliferate and patriarchy is softened there is a danger that audiences become desensitized to hard patriarchal and separatist tendencies. We begin to see and hear consequences of men's ministries that before would not have seemed very likely, such as the founding of the first 'man church' in Peoria, Illinois. The Grove Church was planted by businessman-turned-Pastor Mark Doebler, who was influenced by David Murrow's book titled *Why Men Hate Going To Church* (2005). The cover of Murrow's book shows a clean-cut, suit-and-tied man asleep in the pews, and it continues with the bemoaning of the feminized space that is the Church, a now familiar mantra. Murrow's website is, tellingly, www. churchformen.com. Murrow criticizes regular models of men's ministry for providing a satellite function, offering men a separate space to worship rather than encouraging them to be integrated throughout church life. Somewhat paradoxically, part of this integration of the masculine and feminine involves creating man-only opportunities within the church, which women are requested to read as non-discriminatory. It is such man-only opportunities that inspired Doebler's planting of The Grove.

Doebler wanted to create a church that was not only friendly to men, but exclusively *for* men. Right from the start Doebler sets out to engage a (rather one-dimensional) masculine atmosphere: he doesn't call himself Pastor or Reverend, but 'Head Coach'. In a Promise Keepers podcast[11] Doebler says, 'Our décor is very masculine. We've set up sod inside with golf tees and flags and golf balls for our refreshment area. We've had sawhorses with doors and paint tins with muffins in them. Everything that you see, all the elements that you see, are very manly and masculine'. The Grove Church's motto is 'Strong Men, Strong Families, Strong Community'.

The manly church service, which 'moves quickly' and is 'challenge-orientated' concludes with 'the huddle'. Doebler says, 'I invite every man in the church to meet me off to the side. No microphones or nothing. We gather just like a football huddle. I stare the men in

11. http://www.promisekeepers.org/may06_enl_b, accessed 18 May 2006.

the eye. I usually have something to hand to them for them to take, put in their pocket, carry with them during the week'. One can only imagine the intensity of the moment. The business of The Grove turns away from an ostensibly amusing environment when the direction of male leadership and information-power becomes evident. Doebler says, 'God called men to be spiritual leaders. And when men are not being the spiritual leaders that God created us to be, then everything else is out of kilter. It's out of place, it's out of line'. Clearly Doebler is not interested in the church Murrow initially describes, in which feminine and masculine spirits are integrated, rather a church in which masculine spirits lead (read dominate). Doebler also makes clear the method by which this process takes place, suggesting that the first thing a man's wife asks him (marriage is presumed in these ministries) on returning to the car after the service (one dreads to think of legions of wives waiting in car parks) is, 'What did you do in the huddle?' Doebler goes on, 'and so for a man who does not know how to minister to his family, for the first time in his life, even without trying, he is beginning to minister to his family in spiritual things'. It is clear that Doebler not only believes that men should lead their families (and churches), but that this is achieved by keeping women at the end of an information-sharing chain: knowledge is power. Men at The Grove are reinstated as a priestly caste, administering spiritual advice to their families who should apparently be prevented from direct access to spiritual information, demoted instead to waiting in the car park while their husbands and fathers bear witness to the truth.

Underpinned by Violence

Building on the Pentecostal preoccupation with spiritual warfare and the apocalyptic imaginary exemplified by the *Left Behind* series (LaHaye 1995), evangelical masculine spirituality has a dark fascination with violence: it revolves around themes of both spiritual and worldly warfare. This fascination locates men's ministries within what James William Gibson (1994) has described as a 'paramilitary culture' which has developed within the popular American masculine psyche in the post-Vietnam era. We have already seen how Dalbey refers to warrior manhood and his later book captures this theme with the title, *Fight Like a Man: Redeeming Manhood for Kingdom Warfare*

(1996). Eldredge also makes ample use of the warrior and claims that 'having a battle to fight' is one of the three key desires in a man's heart (2001: 9). We have also seen how Weber, author of *Tender Warrior*, is keen on militaristic images. Weber is often credited for his military experience within the world of men's ministries, and such military pedigrees are intended to demonstrate authentic masculinity. A 2006 Promise Keepers' news release about the 'Unleashed' conferences introduces Weber as a Vietnam era Green Beret who talks about men's ministry in terms of the Ranger Creed and being a warrior.[12] Similarly, Geoff Gorsuch, Promise Keeper and National Coalition of Men's Ministries leader, and author of the popular *Brothers! Calling Men into Vital Relationships: A Small Group Discussion Guide* (1994) kicks off his biographical profile with reference to his meritorious service as a reconnaissance pilot in Vietnam.[13]

In *Effective Men's Ministry: The Indispensable Toolkit for Your Church* (Downer 2001b), various contributors allude to military action. On the first page of Morley's foreword we read that men's ministry, located in a war zone, is 'trench work' (Downer 2001b: 9). Later in the volume, answering the question, What is men's ministry? Sonderman begins with an image of General Eisenhower, 'walk[ing] the beaches of England, deep in thought' (2001b, 25), planning the Allied push into France. A young Private meets Eisenhower on the beach and the two give each other encouragement: this is what men's ministry, it seems, is all about. Elsewhere, Stacy T. Rinehart (2001: 98-99) swiftly consolidates his credentials by reminding us he served in Vietnam, as does Phil Downer (2001a: 178), Stecker (2001: 108) and Haman Cross and Thomas Fritz (2001: 190). Chuck Brewster (2001: 209-10) perhaps trumps his co-authoring Vietnam vets by parading his twenty years in the United States Secret Service.

Continuing their fascination with violence, three separate contributors to *Effective Men's Ministry* refer to the Columbine High School massacre (D'Acchioli 2001: 37; Stecker 2001: 112; Schaffer 2001: 116). While it is understandable that Columbine would be in the minds of the authors, writing not too long after the event, it perhaps resonates with a certain excitement around violence within men's ministry. Of the three references to Columbine, two

12. http://www.promisekeepers.org/news_070806, accessed 29 May 2006.
13. http://www.lifecoach.org/site.cfm/p/3

(D'Acchioli and Schaffer) suggest the massacre was in some way down to misguided vision and action in the perpetrators' lives, as if such violence is natural within man and all that is needed is an appropriate (masculine) way for it to be channelled.[14]

There are also many explicit allusions to violence within men's ministries. It should be noted that the following ministries are not marginal, but indicate a representative voice within all men's ministry. Top Gun Men's Ministries clearly appeal to a perceived attraction to militaristic violence within the male psyche: participants enter 'basic training,' facilitated by 'men equipping men'.[15] Continuing the use of militaristic language they sell books such as Steve Farrar's *Point Man: How a Man Can Lead His Family* (2003) and Stephen Arterburn, Fred Stoeker and Mike Yorkey's *Every Man's Battle: Winning the War on Sexual Temptation One Victory at a Time* (2000), not to mention other familiar mythopoetic titles referring to warriors and wildness.[16] Man in the Mirror has actually trademarked the phrase, 'The Battle For Men's Souls'.[17] Band of Brothers ministry bases its name on Henry V's speech to rally the troops and they have, 'made the decision to fight'.[18] Being in the Band of Brothers is to answer 'the call to war,'[19] with a distinct eschatological twist. The whole Band of Brothers ministry is built around the theme of war and the enemy, and perhaps they expect casualties for every registration pack comes with a card that includes a Dog Tag number.[20] The International Pentecostal Holiness Church Men's Ministries' DVD set *Intentionally Making Disciples* carries the text, 'six hours of training … marching orders' in a military-style font upon a picture of troops going into battle.[21] The On Target Ministries' logo is the crosshairs of a firearm scope.[22] On the

14. Eldredge also refers to Columbine (2001: 82-83).

15. http://www.topgunministries.org/programs.asp

16. As an indication of just how influential such books can be, in February 2007 a judge who found a man guilty of arranging sexual encounters with two 14 year-olds he met on MySpace.com ordered the offender to read *Every Man's Battle* as part of his sentence (Flanagan 2007).

17. http://www.maninthemirror.org/alm/alm85.htm

18. http://www.bandofbrothers.org/bob/html/AboutUsandourName.html

19. http://www.bandofbrothers.org/bob/html/TheCalltoBattle.html

20. http://www.bandofbrothers.org/bob/html/RegisterYourRing.html

21. http://www.men.iphc.org

22. http://www.ontargetministries.net/Home_Page.html

BattleZone Ministries' website[23] one chooses which battle zone to enter (sexual, addiction, attitude or verbal) via a graphic of a military radar. Encourage Men to Pray Ministries promote the Stealth Fighter Prayer Squadron, complete with a picture of two F-117 Nighthawk Stealth Fighter attack aircraft.[24] Noble Warriors' executive summary[25] lays out its 'Battle Plan' and updates its members with a 'Battle Bulletin' (it has a less technological aesthetic than similar ministries: its logo is an arrow). Battles, wars and other military and violent references are commonplace in men's ministries.

Some men's ministries, such as Grace Chapel[26] and Faith Builders[27] employ the phrase 'G-Men,' which has historical connotations of violent gangsters.[28] Clearly, these ministries do not overtly allude to being gangsters. The 'G' may well stand for God. G. F. Watkins' (of Powerhouse ministry) *G-Men: The Final Strategy* (2001) bases his title on Joel Comiskey's (1999) *Groups of 12* or 'G-12' cell church strategy, but the G-Men reference nevertheless invokes a subliminal shudder of violence-derived excitement. Interestingly, as if by proxy, it takes Watkins just one short page to pick up this theme: evangelizing while helping out in a Houston flood, he notes, 'another older woman claimed she'd been the mistress of a mobster, and had been living in hiding ever since to protect herself...By the time the group was finished ministering to her, she was saved and praying for healing' (Watkins 2001: 10). If the reader wonders about the method of evangelism Watkins tells us, 'the group simply mobilized like a SWAT team, bringing a spiritually-alert answer to a desperate need' (Watkins 2001: 13).

Other men's ministries actually equip their men with weapons. Once men have been released from 'mediocre lives into lives of excellence' by Real Man Ministries, the men receive a Real Man Sword symbolizing the Sword of Truth.[29] A sword is also the emblem of Faithful Men Ministries.[30] Both Faithful Men Ministries' swords and Real Man Ministries' swords are Richard Lionheart

23. http://www.battlezoneministries.org
24. http://www.affinityministries.org/offerings.html
25. http://www.noblewarriors.org/pdf/Executive%20Summary.pdf
26. http://www.grace-chapel.com
27. http://www.faithbuilders.cc/GMEN.php
28. No doubt the men's ministries would be upset to discover *G-Men* is also the name of a Japanese soft-porn magazine for gay men [http://www.gproject.com].
29. http://www.realmanministries.com/about.asp
30. http://www.fm318.com

swords, an aesthetic beloved by extremist right-wingers with a propensity to violence. Honorbound, a significant men's ministry of the Assemblies of God, has a logo of a crusader shield and they continue the theme with their 'Raise an Army' conferences.[31] Honorbound's accompanying music CDs *Raise an Army* and *Take the Nations* again carry graphics of crusader swords. Some Honorbound promotional material is quite fanciful in this respect. Their *Rise Up and Do Battle* poster depicts a clean-cut individual in a battle stance with his sword: he stands upon an apocalyptic scene of ruin, above him ascends a muscular Aryan angel, also carrying a sword.[32] Champions of Honor ministry also use a shield as their logo and their founder, Chuck Brewster (the ex-United States Secret Service Special Agent), is shown wielding a sword.[33]

Men's ministries also intersect with weapons via hunting. Men's Life ministry sells Maury De Young's hunting devotional, *Hunting Season* (2002).[34] Christian Outdoorsmen celebrate their manly faith by hunting and their website contains pictures of both men and children proudly posing with guns and crossbows.[35] Outdoor Connection Ministries, an affiliate member of the National Coalition of Men's Ministries, continues this delight in killing animals. Their *Ultimate Challenge Magazine* contains numerous weapon product reviews and notices such as 'Pistol Club Devotionals: Join us for a weekly devotional that's combined with target practice'.[36] Outdoor

31. http://honorbound.ag.org/raiseanarmy, accessed 15 May 2006.

32. Kintz (1997: 121) picks up another Germanic theme, noting that the cover of Stu Weber's *Tender Warrior* looks like a scene from the *Nibelungenlied*: a muscle-bound knight wielding a sword to protect his family. Dalbey also flirts with these images, 'Jesus, a man on a white horse, carrying a big sword… this guy is muscular, with big broad shoulders' (1998: 77). Eldredge repeats the allusion, describing a drawing his son shows him,

> of an angel with broad shoulders and long hair; his wings are sweeping around him as if just unfurled to reveal that he is holding a large two-handed sword like a Scottish claymore. He holds the blade upright, ready for action; his gaze is steady and fierce. Beneath the drawing are the words, written in the hand of a nine-year-old boy, 'Every man is a warrior inside. But the choice to fight is his own' (Eldredge 2001: 140).

33. http://www.championsofhonor.com/content/view/110/195/

34. http://www.menslife.org/hmml_devotional.htm

35. http://www.christianoutdoorsmen.org

36. http://www.theoutdoorconnection.org/winter%2005%20ult%20challenge.pdf, accessed 19 May 2006. Gibson (1994, ch. 9) identifies pistol shooting as one key aspect of American paramilitary culture.

Connection Ministries' evangelism resources include 'Laser Shot—
a shooting simulation system'.[37] Within the movement's key
literature, Eldredge also naturalizes the use of guns, suggesting
that to prevent a boy from learning about them 'is emasculation'
(2001: 65). It is exactly this type of hyper-masculinity that is promoted
at Doug Giles' Florida-based Clash Church in which he sells videos
of himself killing nilgai antelope, and his congregation carry
camouflage Bibles (Blake 2006: paras. 1-3, 19). His column on the
right-wing Townhall.com[38] contains numerous tirades against
liberals, both secular and Christian, such as the multi-part *Raising
Boys that Feminists Will Hate*. And who is Giles looking for the return
of to save the world from feminized churches? A 'Dirty Harry-like
prophet, patriarch, warrior and wild man returning to the house of
God' (Giles 2004: para. 23). Clearly, it is not just antelope Giles
wishes to target, but perhaps also feminists with a .44 Magnum: 'go
ahead, make my day'.

Ann Burlein (2002) charts the intersection of the Christian Right
and white supremacists, whose strategies share some disturbing
commonality with men's ministries. Burlein looks at two case
studies, one 'hard' and one 'soft': Pete Peters of Christian Identity
and James Dobson of Focus on the Family. Dobson has written
several books about Christian masculinity (Dobson 1975, 2001, 2003
and 2005) and is often referred to within men's ministry material.
We have already seen how men's ministries have a penchant for
swords and knights, and it is possible to identify a similar attraction
with Christian Identity-aligned ministries similar to Peters'. Church
of the Sons of YHVH/Legion of Saints employs the 'sword of
truth'.[39] Kingdom Identity Ministries shows a sword-wielding
knight.[40] The Scriptures For America logo employs a sword,[41] as
does The Church of Jesus Christ Christian/Aryan Nations,[42] not to
mention the crusader aesthetics of those others upholding white
Christian ideals: Stormfront and the Knights of the Ku Klux Klan.

---

37. http://www.theoutdoorconnection.org/outdoorconn.htm, accessed 19 May
2006.
38. For an archive of Giles' columns see http://www.townhall.com/columnists/
douggiles
39. http://www.churchofthesonsofyhvh.org/sword_of_truth.htm
40. http://www.kingidentity.com
41. http://www.scripturesforamerica.org
42. http://www.aryannations.org

Burlein argues that the Christian Right engages in a process of countermemory, (re)creating romantic and imaginary pasts on which to base their unsavoury present. Certainly the recreation of a more 'authentically' masculine past is a preoccupation of evangelical mythopoeticism and men's ministry. Burlein highlights a 'desire for action-adventure heroism. Each [Peters and Dobson] dreams of this land made holy by white Christian men who rise from the ashes of victimization like a phoenix, poised to take a stand and take this country back' (2002: 26-27), which accurately reflects the imagery used by Honorbound. Reflecting the overarching theme of men's ministries, Burlein argues, 'by invoking biblical language of 'spiritual warfare,' he [Peters] can deny violence as he invokes it' (2002: 70). Exactly the same can be said for many men's ministries.

Of course, it would be wrong to suggest that men's ministries are full of white supremacists, far from it. But if it is reasonable to state, as suggested earlier that, 'Promise Keepers is a generally well-meaning movement of men who seek a better world through Christ, but who fail to appreciate the essentially patriarchal implications and consequences of their own project,' we must also consider that men's ministries fail to appreciate the implications and consequences of their fascination with violent and Aryan aesthetics. How can a masculine spirituality that revolves around such images be anything other than patriarchal?

The Sport Factor

Sport, masculinity and Christianity form a powerful trinity, the historical roots of which can be seen most explicitly in the rise of Muscular Christianity (Putney 2003).[43] Men's ministries are riddled

43. There is an interesting tangent to be explored about the intersection of Christian sports, men's ministries and business. As William Connolly notes, subverting the image of the sporting body, 'the right leg of the evangelical movement is joined at the hip to the left leg of the capitalist juggernaut. Neither leg could hop far unless it was joined to the other' (2005: 874). It is commonplace for men's ministry leaders to flaunt their business pedigree to confirm their ministry leadership. Indeed, ministry leadership is often spoken of using business terminology. For example, Patrick Morley is described as 'Chairman and CEO' of Man in the Mirror and his biographical details refer to his past business success [http://www.maninthemirror.org/patrick.htm]. Similarly, Phil Downer boasts of his success in practicing law and for a decade being president of Christian Business Men's Committee [http://www.downer.org/aboutus.html]. The kind of sporting competition apologetics employed by some evangelicals is also mapped

with sporting metaphors: the team, coaches, winning, and competition. Let us not forget that Promise Keepers, the exemplar of the Christian men's movement, was founded by a football coach and continues to be staged in sports stadia. More than this, with a few exceptions[44] the intersection of sport, masculinity and evangelical Christianity promotes a particular political stance which continues to align 'masculine spirituality' with patriarchy.

Muscular Christianity of the late 1800s and early 1900s can be considered a 'first wave'. Ladd and Mathisen (1999) point to a second wave that began after World War II, which provides the roots for contemporary Muscular Christianity. The second wave differs from the first in one crucial aspect, 'while the original Muscular Christianity was focused on sport building character, the modern version focuses on sport spreading the gospel (Ladd and Mathisen 1999: 215).[45] Further differences between the two include a shift in focus from the earlier Social Gospel with its emphasis on reform towards a closer alignment with the later Prosperity Gospel with its more individualistic goals.[46] Ladd and Mathisen

on to the capitalistic pursuit of wealth, thus Ronald H. Nash argues, 'capitalism is denounced because of the mistaken belief that market exchanges are examples of what is called a zero-sum game. ...On the contrary, market exchanges illustrate what is called a positive-sum game...in which both players may win' (1986: 71). It is in this light that the International Men's Network runs the 'Wealth Producer$' seminars which give 'permission' (even IMN put that word in inverted commas) to be wealthy [http://www.imnonline.org/content.asp?id=14]. The precedent of men gathering in a Christian business context goes back a long time, at least since the right-wing Abraham Vereide established the prayer breakfast movement in the 1930s (Lindsay 2006: 391), as well as promoting the theme of servant leadership.

44. One notable exception is Christian Surfers International, a worldwide evangelical network. Christian Surfers has a characteristically relaxed style while pursuing its missiological activities, which include the publication with Australian Bible Society of *The Surfers Bible*, which has since gone on to be published in French, Spanish and Portuguese.

45. It is not possible to assume any historical awareness about Muscular Christianity by its contemporary proponents. In the article, 'This Battle's Been Fought Before...' [http://www.churchformen.com/leadstory.php, accessed 1 August 2006] from his August 2006 newsletter, David Murrow, author of *Why Men Hate Going to Church* (2005), indicates that he had only just discovered that such a thing as Muscular Christianity had ever existed.

46. These differences between first and second wave Muscular Christianity do not always hold, such as Billy Sunday who despite being first wave does not rely theologically upon the Social Gospel and who also used some of the more explosive performance techniques typical of the second wave.

show contemporary sports ministries have been around for some time, since Sports Ambassadors was founded in 1952 and which legitimized using sports as a context for evangelism (1999: 127-28). *Sports Spectrum*, a magazine focused on Christian sports, lists over 130 individual sports ministries currently in operation.[47]

Contemporary Muscular Christianity is, then, widespread and rooted in over 50 years of dedicated sports evangelism. But even before the starting whistle blows there are innate tensions in the world of sport and Christianity that are never adequately answered, the most explicit of which is how to resolve Christianity with competition. Shirl J. Hoffman encapsulates this issue:

> Sport, which celebrates the myth of success, is harnessed to a theology which consistently stresses the importance of losing. Sport, which symbolises the morality of self-reliance and teaches the just rewards of hard work, is used to propagate a theology dominated by the radicalism of grace ("The first shall be the last and the last first"). Sport, a microcosm of meritocracy, is used to celebrate a religion which says all are unworthy and undeserving (Hoffman 1992a: 122).

Christian sportspeople tend not to think so much of the theology and instead focus on the performance. Indeed, 'Total Release Performance' has been an attempt to solve the issue of competition, in which God accepts an athletic performance if the intensity (love for God) behind it is sufficiently high. The Total Release Performance is no doubt a primary focus of The Power Team, which seeks to evangelize by touring churches on 'crusades' and performing spectacular feats of strength include ripping telephone directories and smashing concrete blocks.[48] The Power Team notes that not only are its performances athletic but it has success in converting sporting people including a number of pro-baseball players, entire football teams and even Chuck Norris and his family.[49]

Such is the prestige of sporting personalities that citing their conversion lends special emphasis to their evangelical potency. This is an example of how success on the sports field, coupled with

47. http://www.sportsspectrum.com/links.html
48. http://www.thepowerteam.com/vision.html Other missions explicitly employ similar muscular themes, such as the BodyBuilders [http://www.thebodybuilders.net] which run recruitment seminars called 'Boot Camps'. Team Faith pursues a comparable agenda by focussing on extreme sports, in particular motocross performances [http://www.teamfaithracing.com].
49. http://www.thepowerteam.com/why.html

a devout faith can result in a person (man) wielding influence beyond his position. In this way people like Bill McCartney of Promise Keepers and A. C. Green of Athletes for Abstinence are taken seriously on a range of moral issues in which they have no particular expertise (Ladd and Mathisen 1999: 210).

The battle for hearts and minds starts early with The Power Team which often bypass churches altogether, claiming to have performed in more than 25,000 schools across the United States.[50] As to what politics The Power Team appeals to, and also reminiscent of the presidential endorsement of Muscular Christianity by Theodore Roosevelt, its school assemblies program contains a recommendation from George W. Bush.[51] Team Impact is another extreme sports evangelist similar to The Power Team which bypasses churches altogether evangelizing directly in schools, attending over 700 assemblies each year.[52]

Of course, because The Power Team is so over-the-top in its seemingly steroid-driven evangelism it is tempting to assume it may not be representative of contemporary sporting and Muscular Christians. However, Dalbey draws an explicit connection between masculinity, sports and violence, outlining numerous Christian masculine traits that can all be 'applied to both soldier and sportsman' (1998: 124). Dalbey goes on to quote A. C. Green talking during the 1987 NBA playoffs, 'God wants His people to be Warriors—to be battlers and fighters…I don't think any Christian should be a passive kind of person' (1998: 126).

When not addressing school assemblies, Team Impact also specializes in taking its evangelizing show to military bases.[53] Aside from evangelizing, Ron Waterman, one of Team Impact's members, has a parallel career in 'ultimate fighting,' a mixed martial arts competition that takes place in a large octagonal cage. Waterman sees no conflict between being a preacher and engaging in such a 'sport' viewing it as simply, 'another form of competition… I am not out there to try to hurt my opponent. I don't go out there angry. I don't try to maim him or something. I just go out there and try to win' (quoted in Meachum 2006: para. 7).

50. http://www.powerteamschools.com
51. http://www.thepowerteam.com/rec-gov.html
52. http://www.team-impact.net
53. http://www.team-impact.com/military_bases.cfm

The mainstream Athletes in Action literature perpetuates this disturbingly violent masculinity. In the leaflet, *Spiritual Warfare (Engaging in the Unseen Battle)*, Athletes in Action notes that despite the fact that paintball is a violent game it is perfectly suitable for Christians.[54] In its call to evangelism the leaflet goes on to talk about various types of defensive and offensive weapons: language that seems more fitting for military combat than the Christian life. Athletes in Action also holds some other rather unsavoury positions. Tom Krattenmaker (2006) notes its origins in the religious right with evangelist Bill Bright and also its hard line against employing gay staff (para. 12). Krattenmaker comes to similar conclusions about The Fellowship of Christian Athletes, again representative of the mainstream meeting of sport and Christianity, which has not only awarded Focus on the Family chairman James Dobson, but its previous CEO Dal Shealy is 'listed by Source Watch as a member of the board of the Council for National Policy, a far-right organization, launched in part on the largesse of notorious right-wing magnate Joseph Coors, who also contributed to FCA' (para. 11).

Across the Atlantic Ocean in England, Christians in Sport appears less extreme, but this is down to trying to avoid the 'tough' issues altogether, relegating them to a single resource document, *Answering Tough Questions*, which reminds sporting readers that, amongst other things: evolution is just a theory, non-Christian religions are false, and homosexuality is incompatible with the Bible.[55] All the above discussion confirms sport is indeed aligned with a 'conservative, orthodox position' and, more than this, 'it socializes well its youthful participants to accept society's values as articulated by their coaches and administrators' (Ladd and Mathisen 1999: 204). It is clear those values are patriarchal.

Ladd and Mathisen generously identify modern Muscular Christianity as being defined by: pragmatic utility of sport as a medium of conversion; meritocratic democracy where success in sports reflects success in American society; competitive virtue where winning/succeeding is reconciled with the gospel message; heroic models for youth; therapeutic self-control where improved sporting

54. http://www.aia.com/getinvolved/notebook/SpiritualWarfare.pdf Gibson (1994: ch. 7) identifies paintball as one aspect of American post-Vietnam paramilitary culture.

55. http://www.christiansinsport.org.uk/downloads/files/study_guides/AnsweringToughQuestions.pdf

performance mirrors the self-discipline of a mature Christian (215-18). Hoffman concludes that the sporting performance has darker consequences, a tension derived from considering the body as divine creation and 'the implicit appropriation by the athletic community of athletes' bodies as instruments of destruction, expendable machinery designed and developed to test the limits of expendability of the bodies of those with whom they complete' (Hoffman 1992b: 276).[56] Thus sports, especially contact sports, become a 'cult of Nimrod' which 'blur the distinction between war and recreation' (1992b: 281). Hoffman also notes 'the cult of the Nephilim' which exploits science and technology in the pursuit of athletic excellence: in this context 'bodies become little more than mind-operated machines' (1992b: 282). Hoffman does not believe that sport is inherently incompatible with Christianity, just the variety that focuses on competition, requiring destruction of both the other and self. Instead, Hoffman sees the value of sport as being the reflection of the Creative act, namely play, which does not sit particularly comfortably within the present masculine understanding of sport.

While not innately masculine, sport and Christianity is a predominantly male world: 'Muscular Christianity has been a masculine domain since its inception, perhaps so by definition. Not only are there relatively fewer elite female athletes, but the total population of female sports chaplains might well be counted on one hand' (Ladd and Mathisen 1999: 152). The net effect is that sports ministries are so androcentric as to arguably be a subset of men's ministries (or an exemplar of 'normative' ministry that excludes women). Some sports ministries make this connection explicit, for example, Third Coast Sports is an affiliate member of the National Coalition of Men's Ministries. The Power Team says it is interested in 'family-focused evangelism,'[57] but more accurately it is focused on men. Of the 18 team members only one is a woman and the team is described as 'Godly men'.[58] The 24 members of

---

56. Athletes' bodies are then similar to warrior bodies: Gibson argues, 'while the paramilitary warrior's body remains hard and intact, the ruptured body of the enemy confesses its evil by exposing all its rotten spilled fluids' (1994: 111). See also Michael Messner (1992).

57. http://www.thepowerteam.com/crusades.html

58. http://www.thepowerteam.com/church.html

Team Impact are all men.[59] In The Power Team claim about converting athletes all those referred to are men, and it is noteworthy that Chuck Norris' family fell into line behind his conversion, repeating the mantra of men leading their families.

It appears that women are not welcome in the world of sports and Christianity in much the same way as they are not particularly welcome in the general Christian men's movement. Evidence to this effect is quite explicit. The website, www.thegoal.com, is a repository of testimonials from professional Christian athletes: it has over 530 entries, 35 of which are from women.[60] *Sports Spectrum*, a Christian sports magazine, has had two female cover athletes in its 15-year history.[61] The Fellowship of Christian Athletes publishes the newsletter, *Behind the Bench*, for coaches' wives, clearly assuming coaching to be a man's job. Could it be that 'Behind the Bench' actually means 'Behind Your Man,' falling into line with the traditional family dynamic?

Sports ministries and men's ministries appear, then, to share distinct commonalities. Both perpetuate a conservative form of masculinity. Both allude to violence, whether via military references or destructive competition. Both assume male leadership which leaves women either waiting in the car park or on the sidelines while their husbands undertake the primary business of being godly men. Given that numerous men's ministries employ sport in their rhetoric, and sports ministries clearly focus on men and even affiliate with the National Coalition of Men's Ministries, it is possible to see them as part of the same evangelical men's movement.

Conclusion

Men's ministry in its current form dates back to the early 1980s, and is influenced by the writings of Ed Cole and the organizational structures he promoted in establishing the Christian Men's Network. Men's ministry is also influenced by what we could call 'evangelical mythopoeticism,' typified by the writings of Gordon Dalbey, Stu Weber and John Eldredge. Evangelical mythopoeticism shares many

59. http://www.team-impact.com/team.cfm
60. As of June 2006.
61. Wendy Ward and Betsy King (Sports Spectrum, Personal Communication, June 2006).

of the themes of secular mythopoeticism, namely archetypes, fatherlessness, initiation, wildness/wilderness and male bonding. It extends these concerns to include a perceived feminization of Jesus and the Church. The exemplar of men's ministry is Promise Keepers, but it was by no means the first. As Promise Keepers appears to wane the underlying themes of ministry networks and evangelical mythopoeticism remain as strong as ever, perhaps more so: Morley (2000) identifies over 34,000 men's ministries in the United States, not including those outside evangelical churches. Given the preponderance and influence of these ministries, the types of masculinities they promote represent a significant manifestation of contemporary masculine spirituality.

Cole sought a biblical model of masculinity focused on male leadership in the home and church. Cole's message was popularized in the theme of 'servant leadership'. Leaders within men's ministry encourage men to take control back in their families. Evans suggests men look their wives in the eye saying, 'I've made a terrible mistake. I've given you my role. I gave up leading this family, and I forced you to take my place. Now I must reclaim that role' (1994: 79). Evangelical men are told not to dominate their families through their leadership, but to serve them. Some apologists therefore promote servant leaders in the home as being 'soft patriarchs'. But soft patriarchy is, at best, a benign dictatorship. Far from being symbolic (Wilcox 2004: 143) soft patriarchy retains all the power dynamics of regular patriarchy, but tries to hide this fact by redefining patriarchy as including greater involvement with housework and emotional engagement with the family. Soft patriarchy seeks not only male leadership, but exclusively male environments such as The Grove, America's first 'man church'.

More than just male power, another key patriarchal theme of men's ministries is violence. Evangelical mythopoetic literature is particularly fond of the warrior archetype and pursues a vision of Christ 'in a bloodspattered robe' (Weber 1993: 41). Violent imagery permeates even mainstream men's ministries with incessant references to spiritual warfare and battles, and the military service of ministry leaders is often invoked to confirm the authenticity of their masculinity. Some men's ministries go so far as to equip their members with swords.

Masculinity is also defined via sports ministries. Some ministries use sport as a tool for evangelism to regular people, often the kind of sport used is extreme. These contemporary forms of Muscular Christianity are focused on masculinity defined by extraordinary feats of strength such as ripping telephone directories or smashing bricks. This, we are told, is an appropriate form of masculinity for bearing witness to Christ. Other sports ministries are focused on sporting people and again echo violent and militaristic themes, as well as promoting destructive behaviour in competition and its approach to the body: the cult of Nimrod and Nephilim (Hoffman 1992b). Even mainstream sports ministries such as Fellowship of Christian Athletes have clear right-wing leanings in their leadership and policies. Opinions of sporting personalities hold disproportionate weight in society, so these right-wing opinions are propagated. Such is the androcentric nature of most sports ministries in terms of leadership, audience and administrative affiliation, that in effect sports ministries are men's ministries.

The intentions of many men involved in the various strands of the evangelical men's movement are often good. In their contribution to *Effective Men's Ministry* Dan Erickson and Dan Schaffer state, 'a successful ministry to men will encompass the following key components of a man's life: identity, friendship, God's calling, discipline, marriage and family skills, and stewardship' (2001: 17). Such sentiments are certainly reasonable. However, the way these sentiments manifest must be monitored. This chapter has shown that the net effect of men's ministry is a focus on domination and violence. No doubt the majority of men engaged in these ministries would find this statement puzzling, despite attempting to lead their families whilst wielding a sword. The previous chapter presented a certain naïvety on the part of the mythopoetic movement, which often appeared oblivious to the political implications of its own project. The same can be said for the evangelical men's movement which genuinely desires a better spiritually-engaged world, but fails to appreciate its methods do nothing but perpetuate the patriarchal status quo.

Chapter Four

THE CATHOLIC MEN'S MOVEMENT: SACRAMENTS AND ADORATION

While establishing some granularity to the evangelical men's movement gives us a better understanding of the composition of the general Christian men's movement, it is only a start. The diversity of the Christian men's movement(s) is only recently receiving appropriate attention. Philip Culbertson (2007) identifies various streams of the Christians men's movement which he argues share no common theology, spirituality or goal. This plurality is extended in this chapter by identifying the Catholic men's movement, which has remained largely unnoticed outside its own tradition, yet maintains a significant influence on the Christian men's movement in general. For example, Richard Rohr, who was the most vocal Christian talking about 'wildness' at the height of the mythopoetic years, and who remains arguably the most identifiable proponent of 'male spirituality,'[1] is a Catholic priest. While the intention is to identify the Catholic men's movement, the following sources show there to be a significant interaction with other streams of the Christian men's movement. The aim is more to identify a Catholic 'flavour' rather than engage in an exercise of reification about a singular, distinct Catholic men's movement.

This chapter maps out some of the territory inhabited by the Catholic men's movement. In particular, a Catholic mythopoeticism is identified that, like its evangelical counterpart, arose in response to secular mythopoeticism. We will see how, in 1996, the United States Conference of Catholic Bishops Committee on Marriage and Family identified the success of Promise Keepers and set out a Catholic response. Comparisons will then be drawn between

---

1. Discussion of the interchangeable use of the terms 'male spirituality' and 'masculine spirituality' within popular (and some academic) literature is provided in chapter 7.

evangelical and Catholic men's ministry/movement on those themes identified in the previous chapter, namely, servant leadership, sport and violence. In general, the Catholic men's movement is shown to be more diverse than its evangelical counterpart. While it perpetuates some patriarchal and violent tendencies, the middle ground is more moderate. Finally, some of the unique aspects of the Catholic men's movement will be identified along with some suggestions as to *why* such differences exist. In particular it is suggested that Catholicism has a certain queerness about it, exemplified by defining masculinity not exclusively in terms of heteronormativity but also a theoretically celibate priesthood with a propensity for campness.

Catholic Mythopoeticism

In much the same way as there is an evangelical version of secular mythopoeticism, there is also a Catholic version. Catholic input to the mythopoetic melting pot can be traced back to at least 1985. Dalbey's pioneering evangelical mythopoetic text, *Healing the Masculine Soul* (1988) quotes at some length from an article 'Healing the Tear in the Masculine Soul' by Catholic priest Ted Dobson.[2] Catholic mythopoeticism does not articulate itself as such, appearing on the surface as general Christian mythopoeticism, or even simply 'male spirituality'.[3] Like its secular and evangelical brothers, Catholic mythopoeticism is concerned with the classic themes of archetypes, fatherlessness, initiation, wildness/wilderness, male bonding and the feminization of society and the Church. This chapter refers to two key Catholic mythopoetic texts: Patrick Arnold's *Wildmen, Warriors and Kings: Masculine Spirituality and the Bible* (1991), and Richard Rohr and Joseph Martos' *The Wild Man's Journey: Reflections on Male Spirituality* (1992).[4] These books represent two versions of Catholic mythopoeticism: Arnold's is conservative, Rohr and Martos' more liberal. Rohr, in particular, has remained popular over the

2. Again, the buck probably stops with Bly, as Dobson refers to German psychologist Alexander Mitscherlich's theory of fatherlessness which Bly popularized in his *What Men Really Want* interview (Bly and Thompson 1982).

3. Internet searches on men and spirituality in general will quickly bring researchers to a Catholic viewpoint as www.malespirituality.org belongs to Richard Rohr.

4. Other comparable texts from a Catholic perspective include William J. O'Malley (1999) and Martin W. Pable (1988 and 1996).

years, publishing numerous books, including in 2005 a revised and expanded edition of *The Wild Man's Journey*. Looking at these two texts in isolation, Catholic mythopoeticism looks very similar to its evangelical and secular counterparts, articulating a distinct anxiety about the slipping of men's power and promoting some rather one-dimensional (archetypal) models of masculinity.

Arnold's main concern is the by now familiar mantra, 'Western culture and the Christian church are becoming more feminine and less masculine' (1991: 51). More than this, Arnold says there is an inherent paradox in Christianity that keeps men at arm's length from God, 'we thus arrive at the great oddity of traditional Christian spirituality. While males clearly rule the church patriarchally, they do so with the strong implication that their very power, position and wealth violate the essence of the spiritual life!' (1991: 18). If this feels like questionable territory to the reader, Arnold restates his point: 'it is widely assumed that prayer and spirituality are basically female enterprises, and that all but a few unusual men can relate to religion only in a peripheral way' (1991: 71-72). It seems Arnold believes men are not only subject to the feminization of society, but also some innate problems with religiosity, which is a curious conclusion given the preponderance of men in the leadership roles of all the world's major religious traditions.[5] For Arnold the feminization of the Church is no accident: men are under attack from certain feminist quarters from what he describes at length as 'misandry'[6] at the hand of 'gaialogians' (1991: 56) who not only blame men for society's current ills but also reinvent archaeological history to suit their gaialogical agenda. Arnold says the *National Catholic Reporter*, 'is increasingly allowing itself to become a conduit for this toxic waste-product of *ressentiment*' (1991: 60) and that, 'there is sometimes a vague undercurrent of feeling that resistance to

5. For a more scientific take on this, Dean Hamer noted that women did indeed rate higher on his application of Robert Clonginer's Self-Transcendence Scale (a yardstick for measuring spirituality), but that this may be down to their greater willingness to express their feelings than men (2004: 36). However, when it came to the isolation of VMAT2 (the gene which Hamer connects to perception of the spiritual) he discovered the influence of the variant genotype was the same regardless of gender (2004: 74). See also James R. Mahalik and Hugh D. Lagan (2001), Rodney Stark (2002) and Edward H. Thompson and Kathryn R. Remmes (2002).

6. An earlier incarnation of Arnold's work (1989) focuses more on what he describes as 'feminist Manichaeism'. For a secular treatment of this see 'The New Sexism' in Warren Farrell (1986: 189-236).

feminism is indicative of psycho-sexual problems, which can, in turn, raise questions regarding possible ordination' (1991: 61). Arnold finds feminism rampant even in places where women are forbidden to go.

Arnold fails to appreciate that the misandry of which he speaks is not a hatred of men, but a hatred of patriarchy and a particular way of being a man: he clearly cannot unpack a perception of patriarchy from masculinity, a distinction sought by his mentor Robert Bly (Bly 1990: 98). One of the numerous problems with engaging with an archetypal model of masculinity (for Arnold, the Wild Man, the Warrior and the King) is that it has trouble accommodating real, plural, masculinities. Thus, an attack on one form of masculinity is interpreted by Arnold as an attack on all. Arnold suggests that a young man setting out on a spiritual life and faced with such systematic misandry might start to feel somehow useless and devalued (1991: 61). Perhaps there is a good reason why that young man might start to feel useless or devalued: because he is possibly guilty of that particular way of being a man, of which the supposed misandry is so critical. The reader is left to draw one of two immediate conclusions: either men are subject to a society-wide misandry, or at some level of awareness Arnold is a misogynist. He is transparently dismissive of the feminine, even through a theological cooption of psychic evolution:

> The centrality of God the Father represents human psychic maturation from a feminine matrix of undifferentiated primitive religiosity into a highly masculine, individuated spirituality that values the independence of other beings and appreciates the graciousness of their free and unmerited love. The Father metaphor is an apt symbol for this reality (Arnold 1991: 214).

Arnold here explicitly reworks Dalbey's earlier mutterings, 'all goddess-focused religions ultimately betray roots in such idolatry of the mother/woman and proceed upon natural, earth-bound theologies. Thus, they cannot portray true spirituality, which requires a breaking of the powers of the flesh' (1988: 42), showing both evangelical and Catholic mythopoeticism to be more explicitly resistant to the feminine than its secular counterpart, which kept largely silent on such issues.

Rohr and Martos, Arnold's fellow Catholic mythopoets, seek less to attack women, rather to keep them (and atypical men) at arm's length. 'This book is not for women. Nor is it for softies, wimps or nerds who intend to stay that way for the rest of their lives,' write Rohr and Martos at the beginning of their influential *The Wild Man's Journey* (1992: i). They make much of a supposed male/female polarity, which is described as, 'the male-female antagonism' (1992: 12, 14) falling into the traditional rut of contrasting men as orientated towards action and women towards reflection (1992: 5). In an attempt to perpetuate this distinction Rohr and Martos come to some peculiar conclusions about the nature of Catholic spirituality,

> Believe it or not, this same contrast between the bias toward reflection and the bias toward action has a counterpart in traditional Catholic spirituality. The bias toward reflection is epitomized in the approach of Ignatius of Loyola, or Jesuit spirituality, and the bias toward action is exemplified in the approach of Francis of Assisi or Franciscan spirituality (Rohr and Martos 1992: 6).

It seems counterintuitive to paint Jesuit spirituality as 'feminine' when it is based on Ignatius, a man. Further still, Jesuit spirituality is *not* epitomized by reflection. Even fellow mythopoets document how Jesuit spirituality, 'vibrated with military images' (Arnold 1991: 70) and 'for centuries taught self-negation for the sake of carrying God's message into the most hostile and dangerous areas of the world' (Moore and Gillette 1990: 85). These comments seem to suggest a balance between action and reflection, a bias, even, towards action. Not only, then, do Rohr and Martos present many simplistic gender binaries, they base these on questionable assumptions.

Beyond a concern for the feminization of society and the church and a rather essentialist understanding of gender, Catholic mythopoeticism also intersects with the secular mythopoetic theme of neo-Jungian archetypes. Arnold identifies common masculine archetypes but locates them within the Bible. In particular, Arnold interprets Abraham as Patriarch and Pilgrim, Moses as Warrior and Magician, Solomon as King, Elijah as Wildman, Elisha as Healer, Jeremiah as Prophet, and Jonah as Trickster. Adam, also, is 'the first biblical Wildman' (1991: 124). Arnold complements these more typical archetypes with Jesus as the Christ archetype.[7] Rohr and Martos also locate the Wild Man in God, various Old Testament

7. A similar treatment of these Old Testament figures can be found in William O'Malley (1992). William Thompson (1992) also focuses on archetypal aspects of Jesus in the gospels.

prophets and John the Baptist (1992: 33-9). Rohr and Martos' mixing of their ill-reasoned gender characteristics with the King archetype would make Moore and Gillette proud: 'the feminine virtues are humility, obedience, openness, receptivity, trust, forgiveness, patience and long-suffering. ...They are the kind of qualities a king wants all his subjects to have. If they do, his role is a lot easier' (1992: 132). Here the archetype of the King bears some commonality with the 'soft patriarch' (Wilcox 2004), suggesting our problems could be solved if we were all just a little more reasonable in accepting our God-given hierarchical positions.

The 'father wound,' is another mythopoetic theme common among Catholic writers (Arnold 1991: 65, 94-96; Healy 1992). Rohr and Martos write,

> It is no accident that Jesus addressed God as Abba, Daddy...Jesus understood from within his own soul the emptiness that many people feel. He knew it would be harder and more necessary for most of humanity to say 'Daddy' than 'Mama' (Rohr and Martos 1992: 94).

This points to a fundamental concern among various Christian mythopoets.[8] In the chapter 2 discussion of the mythopoetic movement it was noted that for the 'spiritual men's movement' there is surprisingly little reference to God the Father in its treatment of father hunger/wound. The father wound is, then, especially interesting within a Christian context. Phillip Merdinger, founder of The Brotherhood of Hope, the Catholic order, says, 'one of the reasons men find God the Father so distant often has to do with their relationship with their own father. If this issue is reconciled or healed, then you can open (men) up to a greater imitation of Jesus. It's a gateway issue' (quoted in Ernster 2005: para. 15). Repeatedly, there is an assumption of a direct correlation between worldly and divine father hunger. Merdinger correctly highlights that this is a 'gateway issue' that is going to hook the attention of men. Certainly, a hierarchical relationship between worldly and divine father hunger seems initially plausible, but it is more accurately a literal confusion of two separate themes that no Christian mythopoet appears inclined to untangle. Nevertheless this double father wound remains significant.

8. Chiefly, the reference to 'abba' or 'daddy' is also used by Dalbey (1988: 171). The theme of 'abba' is so central to Dalbey that his website is called 'Abba Father': http://www.abbafather.com.

There are several other secular mythopoetic themes that appear in Catholic mythopoeticism. William J. O'Malley, in his seeking of Catholic renewal, clearly echoes Sam Keen's fiery spirituality: 'every mystic who ever suffered the Spirit's love has been aware of the burning. Love is not always gentle; it is sometimes fierce, challenging, relentless. That is the kind of Christian love men need far more of' (O'Malley 1992: 405). Elsewhere O'Malley draws on the wild and mythic journey metaphors of Bly:

> The male soul thrives on challenge, the heroic, the wild, the individuated—qualities not expected in Catholic males, in the pew or in the pulpit... What Catholic males need to regain is our sense of pilgrimage, of the bloodless crusade: the Grail Quest (O'Malley 1992: 405).

Extending his mythical methodology, Rohr (1994), too, engages in an extended Catholic mythopoetic treatment of the grail quest.

O'Malley picks up the need for initiation for boys, developing Dalbey's idea of modelling a contemporary Christian initiation, for '10 older men who would go away for a weekend with 10 boys who are just undergoing puberty, to explain to them not only their new function in the human family but also their new function in the church' (O'Malley 1992: 407). He argues there should be a monthly mass set aside for the older men who have guided initiation during these retreats alongside the younger men who they initiated (1992: 407). Rohr and Martos also write of the need for initiation, suggesting 'men must be tried, limited, challenged, punished, hazed, circumcised, isolated, starved, stripped and goaded into maturity;' continuing their rigid gender categorization Rohr and Martos note such brutality is just for men as, 'it is almost as if the biological experiences of menstruation and childbirth are enough wisdom for women' (Rohr and Martos 1992: 49). Their vision of initiation again trades on an attraction to violence as seen in the earlier discussion of evangelical men's ministries.

From the opposite direction some Catholics identify elements from their tradition within secular mythopoetic gatherings. Tom McGrath writes of a ManKind Project New Warrior Weekend he attended,

> I couldn't help but seek connections to my own Christian story. They were easy to find: The Paschal Mystery (dying to old life, rising to new); the paradoxical call to both self-love and self-sacrificing love;

the sense of vocation and mission (which had been spoken of in my years in the seminary, but which came alive in the powerful work we did in a sacred circle of men); notions like 'the first shall be last and the last shall be first' (McGrath 2002: para. 62).

There is, then, a Catholic mythopoeticism in much the same way that there is an evangelical mythopoeticism. Arnold, and Rohr and Martos present a similar masculine spirituality to that of Dalbey, Weber and Eldredge, although possibly one that is more contemplative and less focused on the warrior. It should be noted, however, that while in *The Wild Man's Journey* Rohr gives a rather simplistic presentation of what constitutes masculinity and femininity, elsewhere his actions put him quite at odds with nearly every other individual in the Christian men's movement: namely his approach to sexuality in general, and homosexuality in particular. Stephanie Block (1997) writes at some length of Rohr's desire to explore and promote homosexuality within the church and her concern for inappropriate amounts of nudity and sexual content at his men's retreats. In October 2000, Rohr drew further conservative attention to himself by publishing an open letter of endorsement to Soulforce, an organization committed to equality for religious lesbian, gay, bi-sexual and transgendered people.[9] Rohr's activities have even resulted in *Los Pequeños de Cristo*, a Catholic special interest group, compiling an Internet dossier of his conduct alleged to be incompatible with Catholic teaching.[10] Rohr also articulates a centre-left opinion about various current affairs as contributing editor of *Sojourners*, a progressive Christian magazine focusing on social justice.[11]

Catholic mythopoeticism may, then, be slightly more diverse than its evangelical counterpart. Both can be traced back to the secular mythopoeticism of Robert Bly. It must be remembered, however, that the secular mythopoetic movement was not born in a cultural vacuum. All the mythopoetic writers grew up and/or work in Christian environments. Robert Bly is frequently described as a Lutheran. Sam Keen was a professor of religion for many years. Robert Moore was appointed Distinguished Service Professor of Psychology, Psychoanalysis, and Spirituality at the Chicago

9. http://www.soulforce.org/article/464
10. http://www.lospequenos.org/RohrDossier
11. http://www.sojo.net/index.cfm?action=about_us.staff#editors

Theological Seminary. It is tempting to speculate that the Bible stories these mythopoets were exposed to throughout their lives are equally the source of mythopoetic archetypes as Jung. It is equally tempting to speculate that mythopoetic social gathering and ritual in some way emulate the church services, or at least the Christian fellowship, abandoned in droves by the educated classes in the past two generations.

The Origins of the Catholic Men's Movement and Ministry

The Catholic men's movement has significant historical precedent. The Holy Name Society is a fraternal movement dating back to the Council of Lyons in 1274 and continues today with around 500,000 members in America.[12] The Knights of Columbus is another men-only organization founded in 1882 to act as a mutual benefit society and to encourage pride in American Catholicism (Kaufman 1982). It remains an influential organization of 1.7 million members[13] and ranks among 15 groups comprising The International Alliance of Catholic Knights[14] which operates in 27 countries. Another significant member of the Alliance is the Knights of Peter Claver, founded in 1909 and operating in 34 states and constituting America's largest African-American lay Catholic organization.[15] These, and other similar fraternal groups, while having a different brief to what we currently understand as men's movement and ministry, nevertheless indicate a tendency for Catholic men to gather in order to promote their particular interests.

The contemporary Catholic men's movement has close two-directional ties to Promise Keepers. Bill McCartney was raised Catholic and identified himself as such until a conversion experience at the age of 33, after which he remained sympathetic to the Catholic Church. Promise Keepers was always intended to be an ecumenical movement and welcomed Catholic men to its events. Mike Aquilina, editor of the conservative Catholic *Our Sunday Visitor*, notes four key ways Promise Keepers sought out Catholic participation: appointing the Catholic Mike Timmis to its board of directors;

12. http://www.newadvent.org/cathen/07420b.htm
13. http://www.kofc.org/un/about/index.cfm
14. http://www.iack.org/members.htm
15. http://www.kofpc.org/about_us.htm

spotlighting at events Catholic evangelist Jim Berlucchi; hosting a 'Catholic Summit'; amending its statement of faith, revising content deemed to be offensive to Catholics (1997: 10). David W. Cloud, founder of Way Of Life Literature, a 'Fundamental Baptist preaching and publishing ministry' has catalogued at some length the ways in which Promise Keepers has soiled its reputation by encouraging Catholic participation.[16] However, the more noticeable influence is that of Promise Keepers on the Catholic Church.

In June 1996, the United States Conference of Catholic Bishops (USCCB) Committee on Marriage and Family published 'A Perspective on Promise Keepers,' which took note of the evangelical multitudes being attracted by a simple Bible message to stadia across North America. The report states an unknown number of Catholic laymen and clergy had attended Promise Keepers events, and that USCCB had dealt with many queries on the matter. Three reasons why Catholic men in particular might be attracted to Promise Keepers were highlighted: men having experienced Catholic charismatic renewal, thus being comfortable with the Promise Keepers setting; men seeking more traditionalist leanings; men seeking viable men's ministry. While some notes of caution are sounded, the report ultimately sees Promise Keepers as a positive phenomenon, indicating a need to catalyse a similar Catholic revival, concluding that instead of simply reacting to Promise Keepers they should be proactive in offering something distinct from within the Roman Catholic faith tradition.[17]

In July 1999, the USCCB Committee on Marriage and Family published 'Catholic Men's Ministries: An Introductory Report,' that presented what such proactive responses might be. The report aimed to build on Promise Keepers' abilities in reaching and organizing men, yet did not want simply a Catholic version of Promise Keepers.[18] Two specific needs were identified for Catholic men's ministry: sacramental celebration and devotion to the saints, and ministry resources that identified with Catholic history and tradition. This would require a national network of men's ministries with a central clearinghouse for shared information. In other words, a

---

16. See numerous articles listed at http://www.wayoflife.org/special/spec0001.htm

17. http://www.usccb.org/laity/marriage/promise.shtml

18. http://www.usccb.org/laity/marriage/menministry.shtml

Catholic Christian Men's Network. The result was the creation of the National Resource Centre for Catholic Men, now known as the National Fellowship of Catholic Men (NFCM). These concerns were confirmed and expanded in the 2002, 'Catholic Men's Ministries: A Progress Report'[19] and a leadership manual entitled *Hearing Christ's Call: A Resource for the Formation and Spirituality of Catholic Men*. The success of NFCM may not look as extraordinary as evangelical men's ministries, but is nevertheless noteworthy. NFCM lists over 100 affiliated Catholic Men's Fellowships across the Unites States.[20] Each of the fellowships may contain within them many, mostly parish-based men's groups. For example, the Greater Cincinnati Catholic Men's Fellowship lists nearly 200 men's groups within its fold.[21]

Direct and indirect allusions to Promise Keepers can be found in various Catholic men's ministries. The concept of the 'promise' is particularly popular. Catholic Men's Fellowship of California encourages participants to commit to Seven Principles.[22] Catholic Men for Jesus Christ use the same seven promises but call them the Seven Pledges.[23] Rhode Island Men of St. Joseph whittle the promises down to five,[24] and single out Promise Keepers when talking about mutual support with other ministries.[25] Men of St. Joseph (not to be confused with Rhode Island Men of St. Joseph) invite members to accept certain promises which bear a resemblance to Promise Keepers.[26] That Man is You! members commit to Seven Covenants.[27] Promise Keepers are also clearly echoed by the sizeable St. Joseph's Covenant Keepers who adhere to Eight Commitments.[28] There is certainly no shying away from Promise Keepers as a role model in

19. http://www.usccb.org/laity/marriage/mensprogress.shtml
20. http://catholicmensresources.org/fellowships.php
21. http://www.thecall.org/joingroup.htm
22. http://www.catholicmen.org/OurSevenPrinciples.htm
23. http://mywebpages.comcast.net/nugental/pledges.htm
24. http://members.cox.net/rimosjweb/whoarewe.html#pledge
25. 'Rhode Island Men of St. Joseph: Men of St. Joseph Pilgrim's Guide (14): http://members.aol.com/rimosjweb/pilgrims_guide.doc
26. http://www.menofstjoseph.us
27. http://www.paradisusdei.org/tmiy/program_covenants.asp?varyear=1
28. Affirming Christ's lordship over our families; following St. Joseph, the loving leader and head of the Holy Family; loving our wives all our lives; turning our heart toward our children; educating our children in the discipline and instruction of the Lord; protecting our families; providing for our families; building our marriages and families on the 'rock' (Wood 1997).

Catholic men's ministry, nor any hesitance by Promise Keepers in welcoming Catholic men. In this respect men's ministry can be seen as a fine example of ecumenism, even if a cynical interpretation might suggest this is because men have found it easy to identify their commonality when faced with a perceived challenge to their status at the centre of Christian life.

Patriarchs, Warriors and Sport

Servant Leadership or 'soft patriarchy' (Wilcox 2004) was shown in the previous chapter to be a central theme of evangelical men's ministry. It is also present in Catholic men's ministry, but is a good example of how there are a wider variety of positions in Catholic men's ministry than its evangelical counterpart. The 1996 USCCB report highlights servant leadership as a point of caution, noting it contains none of the subtlety of the mutuality of men and women as outlined by Pope John Paul II.[29] His comments on this matter appear in his 1998 Apostolic Letter *Mulieris Dignitatem*, 'On the Dignity and Vocation of Women' which states, 'all the reasons in favour of the "subjection" of woman to man in marriage must be understood in the sense of a "mutual subjection" of both "out of reverence for Christ"' (section 24).[30]

Bill Bawden and Tim Sullivan's *Signposts* (1999) is a workbook recommended by NFCM and is the most widely used text among Catholic men's ministries. Bawden and Sullivan are equally cautious in their references to servant leadership. They note from the start that these are confusing times in which 'many sincere men are trying to reclaim aspects of their lives that in the past have been abdicated: spiritual leadership of the family' (1999: 4). The lesson 'Leading the Family' is, however, reluctant to employ the kind of language of evangelical servant leadership, focusing instead on passages from the Catechism (2202-06; 2223) which refer specifically to the responsibility of parents to children, not husbands to their wives and children. Mutuality is again alluded to, asking the question, 'in what ways might a father's leadership differ or contrast with a wife's leadership in the home?' (1999: 85).

29. http://www.usccb.org/laity/marriage/promise.shtml
30. http://www.vatican.va/holy_father/john_paul_ii/apost_letters/documents/hf_jp-ii_apl_15081988_mulieris-dignitatem_en.html

Catholic Men's Fellowship of Pittsburgh carefully words its intention, referring to men's God-given roles as individuals in families, marriages, and churches.[31] Men of St Joseph talk about servant leadership, but within the context of men's ministry rather than the family.[32] Heading into more traditional territory, Oklahoma Fellowship of Catholic Men talk about men becoming spiritual leaders of their families,[33] as do Catholic Men's Fellowship DFW.[34] At the conservative end of the Catholic spectrum, St. Joseph's Covenant Keepers present a vision of servant leadership that could be drawn from many evangelical ministries.[35] Among their resources are Paul N. Check's *'Wives, Be Subject to Your Husbands' The Authority of the Husband According to the Magisterium*, a 26,000 word document canvassing numerous magisterial texts and theologians which spell out the authority of the husband.[36] St. Joseph's Covenant Keepers is a significant ministry, but its position on servant leadership is not representative of all Catholic ministries. In general, Catholic men's ministry either ignores the subject of servant leadership or treats it far more delicately than its evangelical counterpart.

The difference in focus surrounding servant leadership in evangelical and Catholic men's ministries should not really come as any surprise given their historical theological differences regarding the significance of the family. Rosemary Radford Ruether shows how from the earliest days of the Jesus movement, Christianity was almost anti-family, opting instead for 'a new eschatological family that negates the natural family' (2000: 25). This ambivalence towards the family was continued throughout the Patristic and Medieval periods in which celibacy rather than marriage was upheld as the ideal. It was only during the Reformation that the family began to increase in importance, providing a venue for companionship and procreation, as well as a sinless outlet for lust, which had been raging in humanity since the Fall. While contemporary Catholic men's ministry still expects a layman to have

31. http://www.cmfpitt.org/purpose.aspx
32. http://www.menofstjoseph.us
33. http://www.catholicmen.net/about.html
34. http://www.dfwcatholicmen.org
35. http://www.dads.org/article.asp?artId=71
36. http://www.dads.org/article.asp?artId=185

a regular family, its pre-eminence is problematized by the continuing assumption of a celibate clergy. The supremacy of the family, and of the man's role within it, is therefore more deeply ingrained in the Protestant tradition than the Catholic.

In the previous chapter we saw how evangelical men's ministries are littered with violent imagery. The above discussion of Catholic mythopoeticism would initially suggest a similar preoccupation in Catholic men's ministry. Certainly, this is sometimes the case. True Knights enters familiar territory, showing a crusading knight whose shield bears a George Cross, requiring their members to adhere to a Code of Chivalry which, along with the Seven Steps to Freedom and Purity and 10 Promises, comprise the Daily Combat Prayer. These themes are proliferated by Satan's battle plan, combat training and a large arsenal of other military allusions.[37] Elsewhere The Knights of Divine Mercy equates masculine spirituality with 'heroic virtues' and 'spiritual warriors'.[38] *Catholic Men's Quarterly* columnist Father J. Patrick Serna suggests the 'crisis in Fatherhood and manhood in America' could be solved by more hunting (Serna 2005: para. 21). That Man is You! promotes masculine military leadership in which man battles Satan over the family.[39] *Signposts* contains the lesson 'The Man as a Warrior' (Bawden and Sullivan 1999: 86) but it should be noted it contains only quotes from evangelical sources: Steve Farrah's (2003) *Point Man* and Focus on the Family leader James Dobson. This lesson stands out in tone quite dramatically from the other *Signposts* lessons and one can speculate its inclusion was intended as a concession to the popularity of such images in evangelical men's ministries rather than any particular Catholic resonance. Apart from occasional examples such as these, violent imagery is missing from Catholic men's ministry, in stark contrast to its evangelical counterpart.

Another key theme in evangelical men's ministry is sport. Again, there are instances of sport occurring in Catholic men's ministry. Reminiscent of Promise Keepers' appeal to sport, and actually a Catholic revision of a Promise Keepers title, NFCM resources include Geoff Gorsuch's *Brothers! Calling Catholic Men into Vital Relationship*, which employs the baseball diamond to represent the process of

37. http://www.trueknights.org
38. http://www.knightsofdivinemercy.com
39. http://www.paradisusdei.org/tmiy/program_fall.asp?varyear=1

building relationships with other Catholic men. NFCM also encourages the reading of Danny Abramowicz's *Spiritual Workout of a Former Saint* (2004), which tells of the former All-Pro wide receiver for the New Orleans Saints' battles with alcoholism and his path to Christ. Catholic Men in Action Prayer Group follows the sporting theme: instead of a group meeting it has a 'workout' which follows the 'stretch-out' (prayer), 'warm-up/breathing' (praise and worship), 'team work' (catechism, scripture readings), 'lifting' (prayers and petitions for healing) and the 'huddle' (refreshments and fellowship).[40] While not exactly sporting, but nonetheless what might be called a 'bodily performance,' e5 Men is an organization that focuses on devotion to wives through fasting.[41] But sporting imagery, and an inevitable focus on competition and winning, is nowhere near as present in Catholic men's ministry as evangelical. *Signposts* speaks of men who want 'relationships with other men that don't have to flow from a mutual love of sport' (Bawden and Sullivan 1999: 4). Only one of the 52 *Signposts* lessons (Bawden and Sullivan 1999: 50) appeals to sport to communicate a message. In short, the three themes of servant leadership, violence and sport which go a long way to promoting an unsavoury model of masculinity within evangelical men's ministry are largely absent in Catholic men's ministry.

Underpinning these themes lies a fundamental difference in focus concerning evangelism and fellowship. Evangelical men's ministries by definition seek to evangelize. Catholic men's ministries rarely emphasize evangelism, seeking instead to minister to existing Catholics. Fellowship, being with other men, is a crucial, but secondary focus for evangelical men's ministry, whereas it is of primary importance to Catholics. J. D. Castellini *et al.* (2005) examined the motivations behind male spirituality among Catholic men. Their aim was not to examine specifically Catholic attitudes,

40. http://www.hebert.austin.tx.us/CMIA/Workout.htm, accessed 26 August 2006.

41. http://www.e5men.org. While regular e5 men fast for their wives for one day per month, the testosterone level is raised in e5 Special Forces, whose members take on additional fasting days for other women who may or may not be known to them. Testosterone aside, while e5 focuses primarily on wives, its attention is also to all women sinned against by men which is about as profeminist a statement as one can find in the whole Christian men's movement. e5 also gives special attention to Mary via the e5 Sons of Mary group http://www.e5men.org/docs/e5_consecration_to_mary.htm.

rather 99% of those men questioned happened to be Catholic as the research was undertaken via attendees of NFCM conferences and retreats. Castellini identified the following motivations for men's involvement with spirituality which are here ordered in a way that arguably move from the most spiritual to the least: relationship with God; faith/prayer community; self-awareness, or relationship with self; isolation or existential emptiness; fear or grief; father-son relationships; coping strategies; male bonding, or relationships with other men. The results showed, 'the factor accounting for the largest portion of the shared variances was that of Male Bonding, or relationships with other men' (Castellini *et al* 2005: 52), precisely the least spiritual of all the motivations, and also a defining characteristic of the mythopoetic movement. A relationship with God is relegated to third place in the motivation stakes, second to self-awareness, indicating 'that men have a profound innate need to be affirmed in their masculinity by other males' (Castellini *et al* 2005: 53). This particular focus on male bonding and fellowship suggests the Catholic men's movement is more closely aligned than the evangelical men's movement to the secular men's movement.

The Uniqueness of Catholic Men's Ministry

The 1999 USCCB 'Catholic Men's Ministries: An Introductory Report' makes the primary uniqueness of the movement quite clear. It states that Catholic leaders had laid out various measures that must be developed for a specifically Catholic men's ministry, first of which was what many Catholics find missing in the Promise Keepers, namely, sacramental celebration (Eucharist and Reconciliation) and devotion to the saints.[42] Responses to this need had been identified before the USCCB report. Among others, SacraMentors was operating in 1996 and a previous incarnation (Men of the Upper Room) in 1993.[43] The power of the sacraments in Catholic men's ministry should not be underestimated. Speaking of the Sacrament of Reconciliation, Maurice Blumberg, executive director of NFCM says, 'seventy to eighty percent of the men who go to [NFCM] conferences go to confession there. …What really touches the priests more than anything is the depth of the confessions. Priests tell me, "They are really repenting; I've never heard confessions like this"'

42. http://www.usccb.org/laity/marriage/menministry.shtml
43. http://www.sacramentors.org/History.php

(quoted in Szyszkiewicz 2005: para. 14).[44] While not on the scale of their evangelical counterparts, Catholic conferences are nevertheless significant events. In 2006, there were 40 NFCM conferences[45] including Boston (5,200 men attending), Detroit (3,500 men), Cincinnati (3,200 men), Pittsburgh (1,400 men), and Worcester (1,200 men).[46] This means a significant amount of men are going to confession at NFCM conferences who we can imagine might otherwise fail to do so.

Devotion to the saints and Mary is also common among Catholic men's ministries. Clearly, St. Joseph is a popular figure of worship, with many men's ministries following his name.[47] KEPHA, a fellowship of Catholic fathers and sons, talks at great length of its devotion to the 'Big 3': St. John Bosco, Blessed Mother Teresa of Calcutta, and Blessed Pier Giorgio Frassati.[48] Catholic Men for Jesus Christ dedicates itself to Padre Pio of Pietrelcina.[49] The rosary is also upheld as an important part of Catholic tradition, gaining particular attention from Men of the Upper Room[50] and Men of St. Joseph.[51] This dedication to a wider tradition can be seen in the most immediate link in the chain of authority. Evangelical men's ministries' primary concern is the pastor leading the church in which the ministry takes place (promise five of Promise Keepers). In Catholic men's ministry this focus generally switches to the Bishop of the diocese overseeing the ministry. The importance of tradition alongside scripture is also indicated in the *Signposts* workbook lesson *Sacred Tradition*, 'even before the New Testament was written

44. Confession itself may subvert the hyper-masculinity seen in evangelical men's ministries. Seeking forgiveness through prayer alone between man and God is a typically solitary business, lending itself to a 'go it alone' masculinity. Confession necessarily involves another man and actual vocalization of the perceived sin. This is a type of talking therapy which is, in part, at odds with the rugged individualism of evangelical masculinity.

45. http://catholicmensresources.org/index.php?XCARTSESSID=c43578464d5b3145b21493e0b23bf282andMID=0006, accessed 29 September 2006.

46. http://catholicmensresources.org/index.php?XCARTSESSID=c43578464d5b3145b21493e0b23bf282andMID=0020, accessed 29 September 2006.

47. Including, among others: The St. Joseph Center; Men of St. Joseph; Rhode Island Men of St. Joseph; and St. Joseph Covenant Keepers.

48. http://www.kepharocks.org/bigthree.html

49. http://mywebpages.comcast.net/nugenta1/pio.htm

50. http://www.geocities.com/menoftheupperroom/rosary.htm

51. http://www.menofstjoseph.us/therosary.htm

down and compiled, the gospel was being proclaimed and bishops were teaching new Christians about the truths of their faith' (Bawden and Sullivan 1999: 42).

Another significant differentiating factor between evangelical and Catholic men's ministry is the treatment of money. In an evangelical context the pursuit of the dollar is encouraged as worthy. Across the literature evangelical leaders parade their business pedigree in much the same way as their military history as an indication of authentic manliness. Articles about managing money abound and wealth is often seen as a sign that God is pleased with a man's behaviour. There is a different focus in the Catholic men's movement which is rather suspicious of wealth. Even before engaging with the literature on this matter this theme is obvious. Most of the evangelical websites, even of relatively small men's ministries, have clearly been designed and maintained by professional web designers. These sites are often of unusual quality, sometimes expanded into multi-media resources. The Champions of Honor site, for example, contains a 12-minute promotional video[52] of such impeccable production it views like a Hollywood trailer. Catholic men's ministry websites, in contrast, often have a distinctly homespun appearance, as if maintained by Father Tony. The message of these Catholic websites is no less sophisticated, but clearly there is less money invested in them.

In the *Signposts* workbook, four separate lessons (38; 56; 60; 64) spell out the dangers of money, whether it be seeking more income via promotion at the detriment of the family, profiting off ethically questionable business activities, or placing inappropriate value on material possessions. A further three lessons (112; 114; 117) reiterate a Catholic responsibility to care for the poor and less privileged in explicit ways:

> In his encyclical on social justice, Pope John Paul II called on all Catholics to stand in solidarity with the poor and the oppressed—not just to help them, but to be one of them. …What is your parish doing to stand in solidarity with the poor? (Bawden and Sullivan 1999: 112).

The image of a men's group dedicating their discussion along these lines is a heartening one. If a particular preoccupation with the pursuit of wealth (and the power that comes with it) is another highly masculine trait within the evangelical men's movement, its

---

52. http://www.championsofhonor.com/content/view/81/197/

absence is another example of the Catholic men's movement being less 'masculine'.[53]

The difference in attitude to wealth between Catholic and evangelical ministries, like those regarding the family, has historical roots. Before the Reformation, charitable acts and a general concern for the poor were more commonplace, albeit within an economy of salvation. Ruether shows how the closing of monastic communities saw a reduction in charitable help for the poor, it was 'no longer seen as a "good work" by which one could commend one's soul to God and gain forgiveness of sins, and so benefices for good works fell off in reformed cities' (Ruether 2000: 71). This shift set some Protestant theologies on a different path in regard to the perception of money and social responsibility. While early manifestations of masculine spirituality such as Muscular Christianity embraced the Social Gospel that was sweeping Protestant churches at the time (Putney 2003: 39-44), later evangelical forms, including those today, focus instead on the Prosperity Gospel.

We are faced with a curious paradox. While Catholicism is in some ways more conservative than other Christian orientations (responses to women's ordination and birth control, for example) its men's ministry promotes a broader spectrum masculinity which is generally less patriarchal than that of evangelical men's ministry. Clearly, there is a feminine principle (whatever that means) at the heart of Catholicism. Marian theology at once exalts a woman to the highest mortal position in the Catholic tradition, and also demands a devotion that is in itself perceived as feminine.[54] But there must be more to the paradox than this double femininity.

Mark P. Shea (2002), a conservative evangelical who converted to Catholicism, suggests Catholic and evangelical orientations take on gender differences, that Catholicism 'tends to be feminine, body-centred, eucharistic, and contemplative. Prayer in such a culture is primarily for seeking union with God,' whereas evangelical approaches 'tend to be masculine—centred on Scripture, centred

53. Of course, there are some Catholic exceptions, such as The St. Joseph Center's Marketplace Mentors program that aims to assist young executives in their 'marketplace ministry'. http://www.stjosephcenter.com Catholic capitalists clearly also abound outside men's ministries; see, for example, Michael Novak (1993).

54. However, being *truly* dedicated to a tradition that does not appear masculine can itself be a masculine trait. For example, Jacqueline Murray (2004) argues that in the Middle Ages, monks were able to transform their (feminine) chastity into something inherently masculine: it was not an easy gift, but a hard-won reward (36).

on mission, centred on the Spirit working in power. Prayer in such a culture is primarily for getting things done' (paras. 16-17).[55] From a normative understanding of masculine and feminine, this sounds reasonable enough in light of the evidence, but attempting to attribute this to actual personality differences between Catholics and other men appears problematic. Again, from a normative understanding of masculine and feminine, one study (Louden and Francis 1999) shows that while Catholic clergy exhibit more 'feminine' personality traits than men in general, they are also more tough-minded; another (Francis and Thomas 1996) shows that among Anglican clergy[56] there are no personality differences between those of a Catholic orientation and those who are not.

It could be that aligning evangelical and Catholic differences as masculine and feminine is to miss a further subtlety: that evangelical orientation is straight and Catholicism is slightly queer. The historical connection between Catholicism and homoeroticism is nothing new.[57] Rémy Bethmont, whose concern is contemporary Anglo-Catholicism, decides two main attractions stand out for gay men: 'a spirituality that is more conscious of the body…and their need for a church community life in which the family ideal is not the sole model for structuring relationships' (Bethmont 2006: 235) Several of Bethmont's interviewees were of an evangelical origin, and they saw Catholicism as being inherently more open to a gay perspective, if not a gay lifestyle. One interviewee made the telling point, 'Catholic spirituality is better at handling contradiction. …Evangelicalism is more upset than Catholicism by what disturbs consistency' (Bethmont 2006: 239).[58] Certainly some

55. There is one major consideration which problematizes the equation of evangelicalism as masculine: its emphasis, derived from the exchange between Jesus and Nicodemus in John 3, on being 'born again'. Michael Piazza notes that, 'it is amazing that evangelical Christianity can so emphasize the need to be born again but neglect completely that giving birth is a feminine act' (1997: 79-80).

56. The use of Anglo-Catholic examples is clearly different from the predominantly Roman Catholic discussion of this chapter, but it functions as part of identifying a 'Catholic flavour' to the Christian men's movement rather than a wholly separate Catholic men's movement.

57. See Ellis Hanson (1997) for the correlations with Roman Catholicism, David Hilliard (1982) for English Anglo-Catholicism, and Douglas Shand-Tucci (1996) for American Anglo-Catholicism.

58. Bethmont also reminds us of Evelyn Waugh's famous comments on the subject in *Brideshead Revisited*, 'Beware of the Anglo-Catholics—they're all sodomites with unpleasant accents' (1962: 28).

such contradictions have already been identified in regard to men's ministries. Writing specifically of the priesthood, Mark Jordan (2000) argues that there are disproportionately more gay men in the priesthood than society in general and that the priesthood itself can appear queer:

> The priest who holds the body of Christ is supposed to be an unmarried man who cultivates sexual purity. He is allowed or encouraged to take on certain stereotypically female attributes, such as fancy costume, (ritualized) domestic service, specific luxury goods, and a competence for beautiful furnishings. More cynically, but no less generally, he is suspected of being 'womanish' sexually — that is, of wanting sex with other men (Jordan 2000: 204).

But the queerness seems also to transcend effeminacy. One delightful example can be found in the hunt-loving *Catholic Men's Quarterly* column of Father J. Patrick Serna. Serna is queuing for gas en route to a camping trip with a fellow Father.[59] He feels a tap on his shoulder, 'fearing that a sissie was getting friendly, I quickly turned around with an "unfriendly" and maybe less than priestly look'. Luckily it was his buddy, who was 'admiring my custom tee shirt which has the "Exterminatrix of Heresies" Virgin Mary image on [the] back' (Serna 2006: para. 6). With a tee shirt like that, Serna can rightly expect some sissie attention!

Catholic queerness may be deeper still, and quite separate from a gay orientation. Nikki Sullivan argues that to queer something is 'to make strange, to frustrate, to counteract, to delegitimise, to camp up — heteronormative knowledges and institutions' (Sullivan 2003: vi). In the West, at least, where men's ministry is most active, to be Catholic is inherently a little strange. In regard to Anglo-Catholicism, Hilliard writes of a correlation with 'homosexuality' based on 'an affinity in outlook between a sexual minority and a minority religious movement within the established church' (Hilliard 1982: 209). The Catholic Church may be a heteronormative institution *in itself*, but when located within a greater cultural context it becomes less so. Given this and the historical ambivalence to the family in favour of a celibate and in some ways camp priesthood, it seems

59. From the start, this story sets itself up for a 'queer' ending, given the cinematic image of men in the countryside has been infiltrated by buggery, whether the unwanted attention of hillbillies in *Deliverance* or the poorly articulated love of bisexual shepherds in *Brokeback Mountain*.

reasonable for Catholic men to be less heteronormative, to be slightly queer in accommodating that which 'disturbs consistency'. The importance of queerness to masculine spirituality in general will be explored further in chapter 6.

Conclusion

The Catholic men's movement is largely unknown to non-Catholics, yet it does influence the Christian men's movement as a whole. Richard Rohr, who remains one of the most widely recognized voices of masculine spirituality is a Catholic priest. Rohr also played a significant role in Christian responses to the mythopoetic movement in the early 1990s. In doing so he formed with other Catholics such as Patrick Arnold a Catholic mythopoeticism, which shared many of the concerns of its secular and evangelical counterparts, namely the perceived feminization of society and the church, fatherlessness, archetypal models of masculinity and the need for initiation among boys in their journey to manhood.

Alongside Catholic mythopoeticism is a men's movement and/ or ministry that shares some distinct commonality with its evangelical counterpart. Indeed, the United States Conference of Catholic Bishops identified the success of Promise Keepers and called for a similar vision to meet the needs of Catholic men. This call resulted in the formation of the National Fellowship of Catholic Men, which acted as a central hub for Catholic men's ministries and source of resources in much the same way that Christian Men's Network and National Coalition of Men's Ministries did for the evangelical men's movement. Numerous Catholic men's ministries, fellowships and groups were established which carried direct allusions to Promise Keepers, asking their members to bear witness to various promises or pledges. Other themes predominate in evangelical men's ministry can be identified in a Catholic context, such as servant leadership and allusions to violence and sport. However, the middle ground of Catholic men's ministry is more moderate than its evangelical counterpart.

Various themes were shown to be unique to the Catholic men's movement, such as a dedication to the sacraments, and adoration of Mary and the saints. Certainly one would expect to find such themes within a Catholic environment, but it is noteworthy that these themes, which are generally perceived as feminine, are in no way tempered in the Catholic men's movement. While evangelical men's ministries go to some quite extraordinary lengths to masculinize both their aesthetics and theology, there is no such common practice among Catholic men's ministries. The net effect is that Catholic models of masculinity are less inclined to the hyper-masculine and patriarchal models of their evangelical counterpart. This appears to result from Catholicism being inherently more 'feminine' or perhaps even more 'queer' than non-Catholic Christian traditions. This is a curious paradox indeed given the transparently patriarchal and homophobic nature of Catholicism.

If it is possible, then, to put to one side the fundamentally patriarchal nature of the Catholic Church and focus solely on the gender performances that take place within Catholic men's ministries, it is possible to conclude that Catholic masculinity is focused primarily on fellowship and adoration. Evangelical masculinity, on the other hand, is focused on aggression, whether the aggressive call to evangelize, lead the family, or battle sin. In this respect, Catholic masculinity is preferable to evangelical masculinity, offering as it does a more diverse performance.

However, there is little about Catholic masculinity that actively seeks out more plurality and acceptance. The fact that it is less typically masculine than its evangelical counterpart is more a happy accident reflecting long-held traditions than a proactive campaign to challenge the privileges of heteronormativity. For example, while not such an explicit advocate of servant leadership, Catholic men's ministries still uphold among the laity the traditional family as the exemplar relationship model for society. There is little room for even the heterosexual layman who seeks to pursue a mindful and compassionate sexuality, while remaining single and childless. There is even less room for a gay man, whether he chooses to remain single or committed to a long-term relationship. So despite being less troublesome than its evangelical counterpart, Catholic masculinity is still a bastion of heteronormativity. Any man seeking a masculine spirituality that is more inclusive than exclusive has *no choice* but to look beyond the confines of the Christian men's movements as so far articulated. Chapter six examines one such place in the form of gay spirituality, which has important lessons for both gay and straight men alike. But before this, the next chapter examines integral spirituality, which claims to offer some solutions to the problems of masculine spirituality seen so far.

Chapter Five

INTEGRAL SPIRITUALITY OR MUSCULAR SPIRITUALITY?

In a basic sense, integral spirituality is about bringing together the commonalities of differing belief systems, in particular a fusion of 'Eastern' and 'Western' modes of spirituality. The early example of integral thought generally cited is Sri Aurobindo who combined, among other things, Hindu concepts of the Divine and yoga with evolution to describe an evolution of the Spirit or consciousness (Ghose 1939-40 and 1948). The Bengali philosopher Haridas Chaudhuri, a student of Aurobindo's, helped popularize integral thought via books such as *The Philosophy of Integralism* (1954) and went on in 1968 to found the California Institute of Integral Studies,[1] which today remains the primary seat of integral learning. Other significant integral writers include the Swiss philosopher Jean Gebser, whose *The Ever Present Origin* (1985) placed the integral stage at the end of humanity's evolution of consciousness, and Michael Murphy who founded the trans-disciplinary Esalen Institute at Big Sur, California. More recently, Jorge Ferrer (2002) and John Heron (2006) have articulated an alternative notion of the integral known as 'participatory spirituality'.

But more than any other individual, since the mid-1990s integral spirituality has become synonymous with one man: Ken Wilber, whose particular brand is the subject of this chapter.[2] Wilber aims to construct 'a world philosophy. ...one that would believably weave together the many pluralistic contexts of science, morals, aesthetics, Eastern as well as Western philosophy, and the world's great wisdom traditions' (2000a: xii). Wilber's model of integral spirituality, while combining differing belief systems, also recognizes

1. http://www.ciis.edu/about/history.html
2. Wilber's *One Taste* (1999) is an accessible introduction to his work. For a reasonably balanced overview of Wilber's life and work see Frank Visser (2003). For a more critical take see Geoffrey D. Falk (2006).

that the individual comprises many different aspects, including masculine and feminine, and that all these must be acknowledged and integrated in order to live in fullness.

Wilber has undertaken this lofty exercise in a large body of work. Aside from his writing, in 1998 Wilber also founded Integral Institute,[3] intended to further promote integral thought. At the time of writing, Integral Institute offered a range of training, products and services such as *Integral Life Practice*,[4] a media outlet called *Integral Naked*[5] and had affiliated with two academic institutions to provide certificate- and Masters-level qualifications in integral theory.[6] If the perceived expansion of Integral Institute is anything to go by, coupled with Wilber's continued publishing success,[7] his alignment with popular New Age guru Andrew Cohen and his media outlet *What Is Enlightenment?*[8] and his increasing popularity in spiritually-inclined online communities,[9] then Wilber's brand of integral spirituality is an influential force in the contemporary spiritual marketplace, and consequently his presentation of gender is equally influential.

Two books in particular are here examined to glean an insight into Wilber's treatment of gender: *Sex, Ecology and Spirituality* (2000a) and *Integral Spirituality* (2006) (henceforth known as *SES* and *IS*). These books are selected because *SES* refers more than any other

3. http://www.integralinstitute.org/public/static/abthistory.aspx

4. http://www.myilp.com

5. http://in.integralinstitute.org

6. Fielding Graduate University offers the Certificate in Integral Studies and the Concentration in Integral Studies in Fielding's Master's Program in Organizational Management and Development [http://www.fielding.edu/hod/ce/integral]. John F. Kennedy University offers the Certificate in Integral Theory with an intention of offering the Masters of Integral Theory [http://www.jfku.edu/programs/programs/int_theory].

7. Which now includes his own imprint, Integral Books, at Shambhala Publications.

8. Wilber was first featured in Cohen's *What is Enlightenment?* magazine in Issue 12 (1997). He was featured again in Issue 18 (2000), Issue 20 (2001) and consequently featured in a regular column with Cohen called 'The Guru and the Pandit'. Various other articles in the magazine applaud Wilber's work. Wilber returned this exposure by featuring Cohen numerous times in his *Integral Naked* content.

9. For example, Zaadz, the online community built on 'conscious capitalism' ranks Wilber in its 'our most loved teachers' section alongside Buddha, Jesus and Life [http://www.zaadz.com, accessed 16 January 2007].

to the question of gender and *IS* represents his more recent work.[10] Other material used in this chapter shows how Wilber's flavour of integral thought has influence beyond his books, and includes content produced by Integral Institute and Integral Naked, as well as those closely associated with Wilber and Integral Institute.

The first section provides an introduction to Wilber's integral theory and its basis in the development and evolution of consciousness. Wilber offers a map of integral development known as the 'AQAL matrix' which comprises what he defines as quadrants, levels, lines, states and types. In particular, Wilber suggests there are masculine and feminine 'types'. These types, which might more accurately be called 'stereotypes', are shown to be problematic due to their restrictive nature. More than this, Wilber's masculine and feminine types also have an archetypal quality which shares some commonality with the mythopoetic movement as outlined in chapter 2, and we see how Wilber has attracted some figures previously connected with the men's movement.

Wilber's use of types then filters through to his presentation of the evolution of women's consciousness and position within society throughout history. In particular, Wilber denies that patriarchy operated as a dominating force within history, arguing instead that men and women co-created their circumstances to reflect the best possible outcomes in any given time. Wilber here shares some commonality with the redefining of 'patriarchy' from certain quarters of the evangelical men's movement, as outlined in chapter 3. This results in a reluctance to accept certain types of feminism and some curious conclusions about the differing consciousness of men and women, which privilege the masculine mode as a type and also its position in evolutionary development.

Finally, Wilber is shown to perpetuate a certain 'masculinist style' which enables his flavour of integral spirituality to be interpreted as a form of 'muscular spirituality'. Furthermore, in order to define this muscular spirituality as broader than just one man, another Wilberian writer is considered: David Deida. While Wilber does not present integral spirituality as masculine in any way (indeed he

10. Wilber is often sensitive to criticism of his earlier work, which he claims to have superseded. Wilber's work has gone through various self-identified stages and *IS* represents the first book of 'Wilber 5'. An examination of *IS* should, then, avoid this issue, even if it must refer to what is absent (such as gender), as well as what is present.

argues for the integration of the masculine and feminine), that he clearly privileges the masculine mode is not only another example of the androcentric nature of most spiritual discourse, but also a disturbing contemporary twist where many of the problems of masculine spirituality highlighted in the previous chapters are stealthily perpetuated as Wilber claims they are transcended.

An Introduction to Wilber's Integral Theory

There are numerous aspects to integral theory, a few of which are highlighted below to create a context in which to locate Wilber's treatment of gender. The overarching aim of integral theory is to establish a model that envelops all the world's knowledge, an aim reflected in two of Wilber's book titles, *A Brief History of Everything* (1996b) and *A Theory of Everything: An Integral Vision for Business, Politics, Science, and Spirituality* (2000b). Wilber argues there is a truth claim to most things, subject to where that claim originates. In this way we can honour the truth of, for example, 'the world is flat' by acknowledging that this partial truth claim was made in a time where humanity had evolved to a point where making such a statement was true.

Evolution is the trajectory on which all partial truth claims are located, whether the evolution of humanity from pre-historical times to the present, or the evolution of consciousness within each individual. Wilber categorizes evolution in various ways which echo those of Jean Gebser, who suggested evolution unfolded via the following stages: 'the archaic, magical, mythical, mental, and integral' (1985: 42). This is complemented by various other models including the 'Great Nest of Being' built on the following trajectory: matter/physics, biology/life, psychology/mind, theology/soul, mysticism/spirit (Wilber 2000a: 444); egocentric, ethnocentric and worldcentric (Wilber 2006: 6); and the visually attractive colour stages of spiral dynamics developed by Don Edward Beck and Christopher C. Cowan (1996). Wilber argues each level of evolution 'transcends and includes' the previous level, thus honouring the partial truth claims revealed within them rather than negating them. Wilber's understanding of evolution will prove to be crucial in his treatment of gender and the role of the masculine in the unfolding of integral consciousness.

Wilber aims to compare these multiple truth claims and find points of agreement between them or 'orienting generalizations', combining them into a single model, an integral map. Wilber's integral map is represented by the 'AQAL matrix'. AQAL is an acronym of 'all quadrants, all levels', and shorthand for the five elements of the integral map: quadrants, levels, lines, states and types (Wilber 2006: 18). By adequately addressing these five elements, followers are able to live an integral, fuller life. Of these five elements, 'states' refers to states of consciousness and the subjective realities they suggest including waking, dreaming, meditative, and altered states. 'Levels' refer to stages of consciousness or development, as outlined above in Wilber's understanding of evolution. 'Lines' refer to the development of multiple intelligences via stages, for example an individual may have a more advanced line of logical development than emotional development. States, levels and lines have a masculine or feminine 'type' which also develops through stages, both of which should be integrated and honoured. Within the AQAL matrix, these four elements are located in the final element: the quadrants.

The upper left quadrant refers to the interior-individual, which contains our own sensations and emotions. The upper right refers to the exterior-individual, or how we physically appear from the outside as physical objects. The lower left refers to the interior collective, which contains cultural manifestations and worldviews. The lower right refers to the exterior-collective, which contains social manifestations such as tribes and nations. The quadrants show 'the inside and the outside of the individual and the collective, and the point is that all 4 quadrants need to be included if we want to be as integral as possible' (Wilber 2006: 23). The unfolding of all states, levels, lines and types can be plotted on the four quadrants. The AQAL matrix maps a very large territory, often in useful ways, however, it is Wilber's employment of masculine and feminine 'types' that begins Wilber's problematic presentation of gender.

Ken Wilber and the Problem of Masculine and Feminine

Elements of Wilber's AQAL matrix can be of a masculine or feminine 'type'. Much of Wilber's presentation of masculine and feminine types is based on his reading of Carol Gilligan's *In a Different Voice* (1993) from which he concludes that men and women are different, that men focus on agency and ranking, whereas women focus on communion and linking (Wilber 2000a: 32). Wilber notes that both men and women possess masculine and feminine types, thus instilling some potential distance between sex and gender, however he is quite clear in his general meaning: 'men tend to translate with an emphasis on agency, women tend to translate with an emphasis on communion. And men tend to transform with an emphasis on Eros (transcendence), women tend to transform with an emphasis on Agape (immanence)' (2000a: 759, n. 11). Wilber reminds people that his work evolves and goes through stages, and he is happy to move on from previous positions he has since developed more thoroughly, however gender is not one of them. More than a decade after the first edition of *SES* and six years after the revised edition, Wilber makes no further progress with gender in *IS*: he simply regurgitates for several pages his original reading of Gilligan.

But Wilber misses Gilligan's point, which is not specifically about the differences between men and women. If Wilber had read just the introduction to *In a Different Voice* he would read, 'when I hear my work being cast in terms of whether women and men are really (essentially) different...I know that I have lost my voice, because these are not my questions' (Gilligan 1993: xiii). Or to put it another way, 'I would not label agency "masculine" or communion "feminine"' (Gilligan, Personal Communication, November 2006). Wilber strips much of the subtlety out of Gilligan's argument, which showed 'a different voice' was marked more by theme than gender, and that women's voices are often 'lost' in a patriarchal discourse, in order to bolster his own rather wooden concepts about what constitutes masculine and feminine 'types'. Gilligan, it seems, is quite used to this kind of thing happening, as suggested by the above quote. Just two months after the publication of *IS* she publicly denounced another misrepresentation of her work (see Thacker 2006) after the conservative Christian campaigner James Dobson (2006) cited Gilligan in an editorial arguing against gay families. Interestingly, two of the most popular books in the evangelical men's movement—Dalbey (1988) and Weber (1993)—also employ a similar reading of Gilligan to justify their essentialist treatment of gender, as well as yet another problematic evangelical treatment of masculinity: George Gilder's (1986) *Men and Marriage*.

The most significant critique of Wilber's use of gender is that of Peggy Wright (1995 and 1996). Wright and Wilber agree in essence about what masculine and feminine types actually are: both agree there is a difference marked by agency/communion and transcendence/imminence. Wright's quite reasonable point is that Wilber privileges in various ways the masculine mode, and this will be examined further in the following section. Another critique of Wilber's masculine and feminine types would be to simply reject them out of hand, as they bear no witness to the diversity and fluidity of gender performances (Butler 1999), nor the complex distinction between sex and gender in all our lives (Gatens 1991).

A further criticism can be made in regard to Wilber's treatment of gender using one of his own insightful contributions: the 'pre/trans fallacy'. Wilber states that, 'Spirit is indeed nonrational; but it is trans, not pre. It transcends but includes reason; it does not regress and exclude it' (2000a: 212). The pre/trans fallacy elegantly highlights two common mistakes made in considerations of spiritual matters: the pre-rational can be elevated to the transrational, and the transrational can be reduced to the pre-rational. In this way, flakey New Age advocates can elevate archaic and magical reasoning to the heady heights of Wilberian transrationalism, and scientific rationalists can reduce Wilberian transrationalism to the primeval swamp of archaic and magical pre-rationalism. The pre/trans fallacy highlights why much of the conversation about spiritual matters between different parties can be a frustrating and confusing business.

However, Wilber's whole application of masculine and feminine 'types' falls foul of the pre/trans fallacy. The immediate reasoning is that as Judith Butler (1999) has shown, there is no such thing as a concrete notion of masculine and feminine, certainly not two 'types'. Wilber's simplistic approach to gender, even if we give him credit for removing masculine and feminine one step away from actual men and women (which he does on occasion) is clearly pre-rational. There is nothing transrational about locating masculine and feminine types, of agency and communion, all the way back in to what Wilber himself identifies as pre-rational times such as the beginning of the agricultural era (2000a: 160-63).

More interestingly, masculine and feminine 'types' have a distinctly polar nature. Jean Gebser, whose *The Ever Present Origin* (1985) was a significant influence on Wilber,[11] categorized the

11. Anyone familiar with Gebser will note the pre/trans fallacy has echoes of his model: unperspectival, perspectival, aperspectival.

evolutionary stages of human consciousness as 'the archaic, magical, mythical, mental, and integral' (1985: 42). Gebser states, 'the mythical structure [is] the expression of two-dimensional polarity' (1985: 66). Masculine and feminine types are then, given their polarity, manifestations of mythic consciousness and distinctly pre-rational: they should not fit within an integral understanding of gender, even if just two of numerous elements within the AQAL matrix.

This is a curious anomaly given that Wilber is acutely aware of the danger of the mythic succumbing to the pre/trans fallacy. Wilber correctly argues that Joseph Campbell (and with him Robert Bly and the mythopoetic men's movement) fall into the pre/trans fallacy by elevationism. According to Wilber (2000a: 246), Campbell mistakenly understood a literal understanding of myth, the most common interpretation, as the distortion of myth. For Campbell it was only when the myth was interpreted 'as if' that it operates in accordance with its actual nature, and such an understanding can only come with a more developed level of consciousness, hence locating myth into at least the rational, if not the transrational realms. This was Campbell and Bly's crime of elevationism. As we have seen, archetypes act as characters in myths, and Wilber correctly claims 'Jungian archetypes...are for the most part the magico-mythic motifs and "archaic images" — they should really be called prototypes — collectively inherited by you and by me from past stages of development' (2000a: 256). So why, when Wilber knows this, does he employ allegedly transrational masculine and feminine 'types' which, located in polar mythic consciousness are actually 'archetypes' or even 'prototypes' when he knows that archetypes are far from transrational? And why, as we shall see next, does he go on to promote the connection of gender and archetypes within the thought of his Integral Institute disciples? The only answer is elevationism, of falling foul of the pre/trans fallacy.

This pre/trans confusion in regard to gender is perpetuated by other individuals aligned with Wilber. Willow Pearson, who is a founding member of Integral Institute and directs the Centre for Integral Sexuality and Gender Studies,[12] speaks of four archetypes and their shadow dimensions. Pearson claims the female archetypes of the Virgin, Whore, Amazon, and Hag each have a unique shadow manifestation as well as wisdom at their core.[13] This quadratic

12. http://it.integralinstitute.org/public/static/willowpearson.aspx
13. http://in.integralinstitute.org/talk.aspx?id=724

archetypal consideration could have been directly transposed from Moore and Gillette whose arguments were presented in chapter 2. But note there is a skewed set of values in operation. Moore and Gillette speak of the King, Warrior, Magician and Lover, all of which have their shadow side. Most archetypally-inclined men would be happy to identify with the 'wisdom' of these archetypes. The popular values assigned to the masculine archetypes are positive, even if their corrupt shadow can be readily acknowledged. This is not the case for Pearson's feminine archetypes: clearly it is much easier to read the Virgin and the Amazon as less shadowy than the Whore and the Hag. It suggests the feminine archetypes are in some way less integrated, with less internal complementarity than the masculine, a theme that will reassert itself in the next section dealing with Wilber's treatment of patriarchy and the evolutionary consciousness of men and women.

Further archetypal allusions can be identified when we find Wilber in conversation with John Gray, author of the best-selling *Men are from Mars, Women are from Venus* (1992). Gray's work treats gender in an archetypal manner, as having essential and deeply rooted differences which are shared by most/all men and women. Wilber and Gray's integral discussion, 'The Many Levels of Mars and Venus' repeats the notion of polarity, discussing the directional masculine mode of loving and the receptive feminine mode of loving.[14] Despite the title suggesting there are 'many levels' to Mars and Venus, which would go some way to an appropriate understanding of gender, we read simply of the directional masculine and the receptive feminine, even if these can be technically engaged by both men and women. It is puzzling how someone such as John Gray who, despite selling many books, is often considered to be a rather mediocre source of authority, can suddenly be considered integral, an exemplar of the next stage in human consciousness. It is as if simply agreeing and being associated with Wilber catapults one into the transrational realms, even if what is being discussed, before its integral association, was generally considered by any serious gender theorist as plain old irrational. A similar manifestation occurs in the next section with the integral adoption of men's rights advocate, Warren Farrell.

14. http://in.integralinstitute.org/talk.aspx?id=359

Ken Wilber and the Problem of Patriarchy

Wright (1996) argues that Wilber tries to pass patriarchy off as a biological necessity, and to a certain extent this is true. In short, Wilber claims that the introduction of the animal-drawn plough in place of the handheld hoe saw a massive reduction in female engagement from 'productive work' which was taken on by men with their physical strength advantage (2000a: 163). Following, he tells us, 'feminist researchers such as Janet Chafetz' (2000a: 164), Wilber argues it was in women's interests due to the likelihood of miscarriage from manual labour that society took on a patrifocal aspect. Wright refutes Wilber's claim and cites various examples of non-biologically determined reasons for the tightening grip of patriarchy including environmental stress (Fausto-Sterling 1985), the need to defend territory (Sanday 1981; Chafetz 1984) and also how patriarchy has been actively imposed upon previously egalitarian societies (Eisler 1987).

But Wright misses Wilber's ultimate aim in his discussion of patriarchy: yes, he seeks on one level to claim it is a biological necessity, but he also seeks to deny the actual existence of patriarchy or, at the very least, alter its meaning to his preferred term 'patrifocal'. Following his interpretation of Chafetz,[15] Wilber argues that the shift towards patrifocality 'cannot reasonably be ascribed to oppression or male domination, but to a *joint* decision on the part of men and women in the face of a set of natural givens' (2000a: 164, original italics). Wilber is keen to show that patriarchy manifested at the hands of both men and women as the best outcome for everyone at the time. Clearly, Wilber cannot deny that domination has occurred, thus we read the caveat that it is only when 'these natural differentiations...moved into *dissociations*' that the issue of dominance arises (2000a: 164, original italics). To think otherwise, for Wilber, is to falsely perpetuate the notion that

---

15. As evident by Wilber's distortion of Gilligan, Wright claims 'Wilber appears limited in his ability to accurately portray the views and the concerns of...feminist theorists' (1996: 35). More generally in regard to Wilber's overarching methodlogy of transcending and including, Leon Schlamm (2001) and George Adams (2002) argue that Wilber's focus on a particular type of highest-consciousness non-dualism requires the distortion of what other people (the transcended and included) mean when talking about their own traditions; in a sense, their meaning is denied.

patriarchy is a function of male dominance, and is to 'assume the complete pigification of men and the total sheepification of women' (2000a: 167), which is a bit like saying, 'how could there have been a holocaust? That would have meant the Jews were stupid, and we all know how clever they are!' To reiterate, Wilber does not simply say patriarchy was a biological necessity, but that patriarchy never even existed in terms of male dominance.

Wilber seeks to redefine and/or deny patriarchy in a similar way to Wilcox's (2004) notion of 'soft patriarchy' as outlined in chapter 3. Wilcox denied patriarchy by redefining what it is to be a patriarch, suggesting that within certain families it is merely symbolic. Wilber goes further by claiming the dominator dynamic of patriarchy was never real, and that the patrifocal reality was co-created by both men and women. It is not surprising that Wilber's take on patriarchy has found a colleague with at least one men's rights advocate, Warren Farrell, who is listed as one of the founding members of Integral Institute.[16] Farrell has contributed various talks to Integral Institute's explorations of 'Integral Sex and Gender Studies' including 'Integrating the Male Perspective'[17] and 'Going Beyond the Blame Game' in which Wilber and Farrell wax lyrical, suggesting that perpetuating the myth of patriarchy as male domination does no favours for women's empowerment.[18]

In a similar fashion to John Gray, Farrell has been elevated to the status of integral thinker by his association with Wilber, whereas before he was just a men's rights advocate fighting against the too-far-swung pendulum of feminism. Wilber goes on to lend his weight to Farrell's men's rights literature: his *Why Men Earn More* (2005) wields a glowing endorsement from Wilber, claiming it to be, 'nothing less than a guidebook for a woman to dramatically increase her salary by making smarter choices...Lying to women about why they are earning less is one of the most disempowering acts imaginable' (2005: ii) (all in the service of empowering women, of course).

Another blast from the manly past can also be discovered in connection with Wilber. Keith Thompson, another founding member

16. http://www.integralinstitute.org/public/static/abthistory.aspx
17. http://in.integralinstitute.org/talk.aspx?id=268
18. http://in.integralinstitute.org/talk.aspx?id=302.

of Integral Institute[19] and notable apologist for Wilber[20] is the mythopoetic agent responsible for the famous *What Men Really Want* interview (Bly and Thompson 1982) that set in motion the whole *Iron John* phenomenon. Thompson also edited the popular anthology *To Be a Man* (1991) that collected Bly, Farrell, and numerous other mythopoetic writers who have sought to reinterpret the relationship between men, women and patriarchy. At one point Wilber rented the house of Sam Keen (Wilber 1999: 66), author of mythopoetic classic *Fire in the Belly*. A further curious connection between Wilber and the mythopoetic men's movement is John Rowan, who wrote *The Horned God* (1987). Rowan, Like Bly, spoke of men in terms of neo-Jungian archetypes, but sought out those which also included feminine aspects. He also helped to produce the radical men's magazine *Achilles Heel*.[21] Rowan's main work is now psychotherapy, and he refers to Wilber on numerous occasions in his writings (1990, 1999 and 2000), including those focused specifically on men and therapy as initiation (1997).

Other writers who present a rather limited model of masculinity also find a friend in Wilber. In his book, *How to Manage Your Dick*, which shows men how to 'redirect sexual energy and discover your more spiritually enlightened, evolved self,' Sean O'Reilly lays out a plan of how to manage one's 'appetite survival system' of 'fighting, fucking, feeding, [and] fleeing' (2001: 9). O'Reilly cites Wilber as someone who has correctly identified this life force as 'Fuck It/Kill It' (2001: 10). Jeanne and Don Elium's *Raising a Son* (1996), which cites on numerous occasions Bly and Gilder in their modelling of masculinity, also refers to Wilber's Jungian/mythopoetic-inspired understanding of the Shadow in fathoming the behaviour of boys (1996: 123-25). While Wilber may not speak explicitly to masculinity, there is clearly something about his work that resonates with those who do.

If depoliticizing patriarchy was not enough, in a further act of revisionism Wilber also seems to want to do away with the word

19. http://www.integralinstitute.org/public/static/abthistory.aspx. Also suggested by, 'Keith and I go back a long way' (Wilber 1999: 251).

20. See Wilber, *Do Critics Misrepresent My Position? A Test Case from a Recent Academic Journal* [http://wilber.shambhala.com/html/misc/critics_01.cfm] and Christian De Quincey's *Deep Spirit: Critics Do. Critics Don't. A Response to Ken Wilber* [http://deepspirit.com/sys-tmpl/replytowilbercont1].

21. http://www.johnrowan.org.uk/background.html

'feminism', presumably finding it too suggestive of a struggle against the alleged patriarchy. In promotional material for the 2006 *Women's Integral Life Practice* seminar, Wilber reworks the phrase to 'three dimensional feminism'. In this material Wilber writes,

> the feminine aspect of you opens to infinity and lets it all come in with no regrets or resistance, and the masculine aspect then penetrates the world with this understanding in a very forceful firm directive way, to make it all happen. This is the gift.[22]

It doesn't sound particularly feminist, three dimensional or otherwise, rather a porno-spiritual fantasy: the feminine freely opens, infinity comes inside her, the masculine forcefully penetrates as a gift.[23] Wilber's vision of the feminine sounds here similar to Catholic mythopoets Rohr and Martos who described the feminine virtues as 'humility, obedience, openness, receptivity, [and] trust' which make the job of being king so much easier (1992: 132). Between the writing of the promotional material and the actual workshop, an Integral Salon was held in New York by the same facilitator (Willow Pearson who, above, promoted the archetypal aspects of the feminine), which by this time was reworked as 'integral femininity'[24] doing away altogether with the troublesome word 'feminism'.[25]

22. http://in.integralinstitute.org/i/emails/WomensILP.pdf

23. It is noteworthy, given Wilber's subtle and not-so-subtle habit of sexual innuendo that he does not include sexuality as part of higher levels of consciousness. He mocks a flatland world that elevates sexuality to 'a great Life Force that is, in and by itself, the ultimate spirit of the universe' (2000a: 500). Wilber gives the impression that sexuality has been painted as far more complex than it actually is, 'invested with a force, a power, a mystique, an aura, an authority, all out of proportion to anything that could actually be dug up from the libido itself' (2000a: 503). Certainly, Wilber sees sexuality as part of Spirit, 'but only one of the lower of several sheaths of Spirit: the sheath found in nature, in the biosphere' (2000a: 502).

24. http://kenwilber.com/blog/show/169

25. An example of how infectious Wilber's thoughts are in these matters can be seen in a trio of articles written by the feminist Elizabeth Debold (2005a, 2005b, 2006) called *Where Are the Women?* On first glance these articles look like an impassioned plea to include women's voices in the integral movement. But these articles soon turn into a Wilberian take on feminism, suggesting the reason women are absent is because they are too keen on holding on to the goodies they won during the rise of feminist consciousness: 'the new feminist freedom simply comes down to doing — and getting — what you want' (2005b: para. 8) and spinning Wilber's evolutionary wheel, 'why don't we abandon feminism as a postmodern ideology and instead embrace women's liberation as an evolutionary process?' (2005b: para. 11). Debold repeats Wilber's application of

Wilber's thoughts about biological determinism, the nature of patriarchy and the liberation of women reach some other peculiar conclusions. For Wilber, evolution unfolds in stages, each one transcending and including the previous. The biological destiny of gender is inherent in the biosphere stage, and while the biosphere dominated the evolution of human consciousness its demands were final. In this respect, to speak of women's liberation within the realm of the biosphere simply makes no sense. It is only in the birth of the noosphere[26] in around the sixteenth century (according to Wilber), which transcends and includes the biosphere, that women's liberation can usefully be discussed: 'And this inescapably means that the widespread emergence of the women's movement was not primarily the *undoing* of a nasty state of affairs that easily could have been different, but rather it marked the *emergence* of an altogether *new* state of affairs' (Wilber 2000a: 167, original italics). Again, Wilber attempts to erase male domination from history.

In this respect, ecofeminism particularly irks Wilber. Wright takes Wilber to task for claiming that ecofeminism is regressive and stuck in a magical mode of thinking which seeks unification with Gaia rather than turning to the integral realm in order to transcend but include it (Wright 1996: 31-33). Wilber demotes identification with Gaia and feminine principles to the pre-rational in much the same way as Christian mythopoets Arnold (1991: 214) and Dalbey (1988: 42) who argued that feminine earth-bound spirituality was primitive and idolatrous compared to the individuated nature of masculine spirituality. But even within the ecologically minded, Wilber sets up a further tension between the masculine and feminine. Ecofeminists, he tells us, prefer the horticultural days of the Great

Gilligan, referring to men and women's 'different voices', which is quite ironic as more than a decade previously Debold had co-authored a book called *Mother Daughter Revolution: From Good Girls to Great Women* (Debold, Wilson and Malavé 1993) that focused on Gilligan's argument of adolescent girls *losing* their voices, and what their mothers could do to help with this problem, rather than focusing on how that voice is *different* to men's.

26. The stage of higher consciousness popularized by Pierre Teilhard de Chardin (1959). Wilber cites Teilhard de Chardin several times in *SES* (2000: 115-19), although not specifically in reference to the noosphere. Wilber does not cite the noosphere's earlier advocate, Vladimir Ivanovich Vernadsky (1945), whose noospheric model was more of an evolutionary extension of the biosphere, than Teilhard de Chardin's separate spiritual manifestation. Wilber would probably find Vernadsky's interpretation equally compelling.

Mother, where women did more productive work; ecomasculinists[27] hark after an even earlier period before farming of pure and pristine nature (2000a: 474). Of course, Wilber assigns both ecofeminists and ecomasculinists to archaic consciousness, but nonetheless infers that even regarding concerns for Gaia, the masculine mode seems to penetrate deeper. Wilber finds it particularly ironic that ecofeminists present themselves as what Arnold would call 'gaialogians', as industrialization was the key factor in their liberation, lessening the need for physical strength in order to be productive: their 'existence as a movement depends upon industrialisation, the same industrialisation that they must aggressively condemn as leading to the despoliation of Gaia' (2000a: 676, n. 12).

It is, then, the emergence of the noosphere that allows for an appropriate integration of the male and female value spheres of agency and communion. But this is not as equal as it sounds, it does *not* mean that for the first time men and women could engage with both agency and communion. It is *women*, who can for the first time in the noosphere, act with agency as well as communion. Significantly, Wilber argues, 'in all previous history that role rather necessarily fell to the male as father' (2000a. 166). Wilber suggests that men have somehow attained a level of integration throughout history, ever since the notion of 'the father' and the domestication of the male was introduced, providing male agency a foothold in female communion. This suggests that evolution, with its directional impetus towards integration, has privileged men throughout the majority of the human era. It suggests that man has had little choice than act the way he has, as he is subject to that evolutionary force which allows him an honoured attainment of integration ('that role rather necessarily fell to the male as father') yet somehow takes away his freewill to improve the lot of women (who had to wait for evolution). And somewhat ironically, the birth of the noosphere gives women the ability to act with agency for the first time, yet it is not women's agency that brings about liberation, rather the evolutionary differentiation of the noosphere. Thus, for Wilber there was/is no male domination (patriarchy), 'women do not have to take their power back because they never gave it away; they

27. By which Wilber appears to mean a few men he has found who have written about ecology.

co-selected, with men, the best possible societal arrangements' (2000a: 598, n. 12). Biological reality has stacked the cards against women, and it is the release from that reality, not women's agency that offers liberation (an evolutionary/masculine 'gift'?). But even in the noosphere Wilber says women should not expect complete parity, 'given the unavoidable aspects of childbearing, a "parity" in the public/private domain would be around 60-40 male/female' (2000a: 676, n. 14).[28] Dashed are the hopes of many who thought that in the noosphere would be realized more flexible workplace policies.

In short, according to Wilber there was never a patriarchy, rather a biologically determined biospheric reality, which since the dawn of 'the father' privileged man with agency/communion integration that women have only in the modern period caught up with and who will not even in the noosphere find complete parity. For Wilber it is the masculine mode of agency that ultimately makes higher stages of consciousness more accessible to men who, 'being less personally attached to sociocentric relationships, find it easier to take a universal and postconventional "big picture" view, and thus more men make it into the universal, postconventional moral stages than do women' (Wilber 1996a: para. 158).[29] Wright (1996, following McIntyre 1995) notes that the first significant postconventional moral stage for Wilber is called vision-logic and is symbolized by the centaur, reflecting a union between biospheric nature (horse) with noospheric culture (human), but that 'the centaur is a profoundly male symbol; it does not represent an integration of male and female' (Wright 1996: 30). So it appears that it is masculine agency within Wilberian integralism that makes it to the higher spiritual and ethical realms. Wilber asks his readers and devotees to view his model of integral spirituality from a gender perspective as being based on an integration of masculine and feminine and, ultimately, to transcend (but include) such notions. Given Wilber's presentation of the way gender unfolds through the human era one can only deduce that there is no such masculine and feminine integration in

28. See Henrietta Moore (1988: 12-41) and Michelle Rosaldo (1974) for arguments against the naturalized allocation of women to the private and men to the public sphere as a result of 'women's activities' such as childbirth.

29. One wonders what bells hooks and Maya Angelou, who Wilber describes as sharing his vision of 'postconventional worldcentric awareness' (Wilber 1999: 344), would make of such comments alongside his wider treatment of feminism.

Wilber's spirituality, rather one which privileges the masculine in the past, present and future.

Wilber's Masculinist Style

William Irwin Thompson has described Wilber's 'compulsive mappings and textbook categorizations' as a way of seeking to 'control the universe through mapping, and the dominant masculinist purpose of his abstract system [is] to shift power from the described to the describer' (1996: 12).[30] Thompson goes on to describe Wilber's work as 'a mode of psychic inflation and self-magnification; it is a grand pyramid of systems of abstract thought, piled on other systems of abstract thought, with Wilber's kept for the top' (1996: 13). Thompson doesn't elaborate on Wilber's masculinist tendencies, but the following section highlights some of these, moving from a masculinist style to a distinctly *muscular spirituality*.

On a superficial level, Wilber creates what might be described as a 'masculinist style', assuming we understand masculinist as reflecting those aspects that are stereotypical and in favour of the masculine. Christian de Quincey suggests Wilber's work has a 'robotic quality' (2000: 208), referring to a lack of interiority in Wilber's work, despite the Upper- and Lower-Left quadrants. Certainly Wilber's *IS* (2006) focuses more than ever before on technological imagery, describing the integral map as an 'IOS' or 'Integral Operating System' (2006: 2) which readers are requested to 'download' (2006: 300). Continuing the computer analogy, Wilber writes of 'IOS Apps', when describing how the operating system has applications such as medicine or business (2006: 26). Reminding us how each AQAL stage has the potential for dysfunction, Wilber writes, 'there is a silent virus in the operating system that can and often does crash the entire system' (2006: 107). Readers are told they can use their existent spiritual practice and 'plug it in' (2006: 205) to integral practice. Integral products and services are certified by a logo that reads 'Powered by AQAL technology'.[31]

---

30. Aside from textual mappings and categorizations, in Wilber (2006) there are over 30 tables and figures.

31. http://www.integralinstitute.org/public/static/certpoweraqal.aspx

We have already seen how Wilber privileges masculine transcendence (as opposed to an alleged integration of masculine transcendence and feminine immanence) in his treatment of evolution's forward/upward momentum, of transcending and including. With *IS*, Wilber amplifies this theme by creating a new focus on describing stages of evolution, or degrees of development within culture or individual consciousness as 'altitude' (2006: 35).[32] This focus on altitude further privileges a typically masculine model of transcendence rather than feminine immanence, or an integration of the two. Wilber clearly seeks to transcend the earth in a very masculine fashion, suggesting the integral perspective is a 'view from 50,000 feet',[33] a view that is not only transcendent, but achievable only via the thrust of jet engines, again employing technology (masculine) dominating nature (feminine). There are clear dangers here that have been identified from even Jungian and mythopoetic perspectives let alone the integral. James Hillman writes of the puer archetype, a Peter Pan whose 'vertical flights of spirit' become 'a contemptuous soaring over a corrupt and shoddy world' (quoted in Tacey 1997: 79), which must be tempered in order to remain associated with reality.[34] Wilber allocates different altitudes to a 'tier': first tier for all those people stuck at stages below the integral, second tier for genuine integral thinkers, and third tier for particularly special people such as Wilber himself. Aside from continuing the theme of transcendence and elevation,

32. The level of altitude is distinguished by colour, a visually attractive representation of which can be found at *Holon News*, 'A Brief Explanation of Altitude' http://holons-news.com/altitudes.html

33. Wilber, *Forward to Integral Medicine: A Noetic Reader*, http://wilber.shambhala.com/html/misc/integral-med-1.cfm

34. Tacey notes that those suffering from a puer archetype complex tend to suffer a 'narcissistic borderline personality. A recurring problem is lethargy, exhaustion, tiredness' (80). Wilber likes to show off photos of his sculpted physique, and his website contains a selection of these under the title 'Narcissism Central' [http://www.kenwilber.com/personal/photos/index.html]. Various critics refer to Wilber's narcissistic tendencies, as highlighted by a chapter in Falk's (2006) critical take on Wilber entitled 'Bald Narcissism' (ch. 9, 81-102). Wilber (1999) is littered with comments about how people find him so inspiring and even reproduces numerous pages of adoring fan mail (1999: 45-53). More unfortunate in regard to the puer characteristics, Wilber also suffers from Rnase-L Enzyme Dysfunction Disease, a variant of ME (Myalgic Encephalomyelitis) and CFIDS (Chronic Fatigue and Immune Dysfunction Syndrome) [http://www.www.kenwilber.com/Writings/PDF/hi_folks.pdf and http://www.kenwilber.com/blog/show/214].

tier identification was also behind another masculine performance of Wilber's: the 'Wyatt Earp episode'.

On 8 June 2006, Wilber posted to his blog a lengthy entry[35] raging against his critics which caused a storm of commentary in the integral blogosphere.[36] In the entry Wilber dons the character of Wyatt Earp and peppers his post with masculinist gun-slinging and insults to his critics such as 'suck my dick' and 'get the fuck out of here!' In a follow-up post[37] Wilber reveals that the crudeness was all a cunning test to identify second- and third-tier individuals. Readers who found it rather lacking in taste and hostile are alleged to be responding from a first-tier perspective, their interpretation reflecting their own Shadow material; readers who identified the entry as such a test are second- and third-tier. Prophetically, Wilber writes that the gun-slinging rhetoric will no doubt be used as part of an allegedly studious examination of his psyche.[38] One is reminded of Ann Burlein's comments back in chapter 3 about the Christian white supremacist Pete Peters: 'by invoking biblical language of "spiritual warfare", he can deny violence as he invokes it' (2002: 70). By invoking third-tier language of 'sucking dick', Wilber can deny sexual violence as he invokes it.

This kind of heavyweight attitude is nothing new and flows through into Wilber's comments on the voluminous nature of his work. Wilber does indeed read and write a lot (although a good deal of it is repetitive), and he likes to remind us. In one discussion Wilber claims to have read to at least Ph.D. level in 23 disciplines[39] (although he has never actually completed a terminal degree). Of his critics, Wilber writes, 'misrepresentation of my work is quite common, simply because there is so damn much of it'.[40] Of his epic *SES*, Wilber writes, 'as those who have seen some of the research notes will attest, many of the paragraphs in *SES* are summaries of short books' (2000a: xiv). Indeed, the *SES* endnotes are 'a small book in themselves' (2000a: 7); volume 2 is 'more or less fully

35. http://www.kenwilber.com/blog/show/46
36. For example Frank Visser, *Not So Fast Cowboy* http://www.integralworld.net/index.html?visser13.html
37. http://www.kenwilber.com/blog/show/48
38. http://www.kenwilber.com/blog/show/46
39. http://www.kenwilber.com/blog/show/242
40. Wilber, Do Critics Misrepresent My Position? http://wilber.shambhala.com/html/misc/critics_01.cfm

written' (2000a: xxv). There is no doubt about it: Wilber has a bigger bibliography than most men, and the undeniable stamina to keep on going.

Wilber's Muscular Spirituality

Wilber does indeed pay special attention to muscularity, both physical and stylistic, which lends itself to Wilber's version of integral spirituality being described as 'muscular spirituality'. Wilber is well known for his enjoyment of weightlifting, and this spills over into his presentations of the spiritual. John Horgan, who interviewed Wilber for his chapter 'The Weightlifting Bodhisattva' in *Rational Mysticism* (2003) notes that he had 'decorated his living room in refined bachelor style: black leather furniture, a huge bank of stereo equipment, an elevated platform heaped high with weightlifting equipment' (2003: 59). Horgan goes on to write, 'Wilber described spiritual practice in athletic terms. "It's like lifting weights and exercising muscles. The more you do it, the bigger the muscles get"' (2003: 61).[41]

More than simply being analogous, Wilber recommends weightlifting as spiritual practice. If his own sincerely impressive physique was not inspiration enough, Wilber has reeled into Integral Institute Shawn Phillips, bodybuilder and author of *ABSolution: The Practical Solution for Building Your Best Abs* (2002). From early in his career Phillips experienced altered states of consciousness via the gym, 'what I was connecting with in the gym was a universal energy source. I would just feel it flowing. ...I called the gym my church' (quoted in Robertson 2005: para. 11).

Phillips was appointed lead facilitator and faculty member at Integral Institute to enable people to partake in weight training as spiritual practice. He developed *Focused Intensity Training* (FIT), which has been included in Wilber's *Integral Life Practice* program. Phillips' and Wilber's two-part Integral Institute podcasts, 'Getting FIT in All Three Bodies: Strength, Vitality, Transcendence' lays out the integral fitness model.[42] In their discussion, Wilber claims that after meditation, strength training has been the single most

41. Tony Schwartz's first impression of Wilber echoes Horgan's: 'he is tall, lean, and muscular from working out with free weights every day' (1995: 352).

42. Part 1: http://in.integralinstitute.org/talk.aspx?id=572; Part 2: http://in.integralinstitute.org/talk.aspx?id=597

transformative practice he has engaged, a genuinely transcendent experience. Elsewhere athletic spiritual analogies complement the technological, such as 'spiritual cross-training' (Wilber 2006: 197; 202) and the trademarked '3-Body Workout', part of the *Integral Life Practice* which continues the exercise-DVD marketing spiel with the promise of '1-minute modules: instant practices for people on the go'.[43]

Ladd and Mathisen (1999) highlight two waves of Muscular Christianity which are interesting to compare with Wilber's focus on muscularity. The first wave of the late 1800s and early 1900s focused on developing the body in order to produce a robust and healthy character, better placing the individual for a more manly relationship with God. The second wave, beginning after World War II and continuing to this day, focused on muscularity as an evangelical tool: on using sport as a way of engaging men's interest in God. Clearly, Wilber cannot be considered an extension of Muscular Christianity, as he does not represent a Christian worldview (rather he transcends and includes it), but he does share commonality with both waves of Muscular Christianity. Wilber does believe that sport has the ability to bring one closer to whatever passes for God: strength training as a genuinely transcendent experience. His appeal to sporting metaphors such as 'spiritual cross-training' and equally masculine technological metaphors such as 'integral operating system', fulfils a comparably evangelical function: they pique the curiosity of potential customers who might otherwise find spiritual concerns too feminine.

A Further Take on Wilberian Masculinism

This final section looks at how Wilber's muscular brand of spirituality plays out in the writings of another author, David Deida, who is a founding member of Integral Institute.[44] Deida is selected not because he develops Wilber's thoughts in any particular way, but because he communicates them in a more distilled fashion, free from the density and scholastic aspirations of Wilber's writing. In a sense, Deida is the 'real face' of integral thought. He does not employ any Wilberian theory as such in his books, but he does use notions of

43. http://www.myilp.com
44. http://www.integralinstitute.org/public/static/abthistory.aspx

masculine and feminine in much the same way. Just as Warren Farrell and John Gray have taken on the mantle of 'integral' by aligning themselves with Wilber, thus transforming their ideas which were previously considered by some to be rather pedestrian, so too does Deida. Should anyone be in doubt of his feelings, Deida writes in one essay that Wilber is the most beautiful philosopher of our time who authenticates genius and is glorious in almost every way.[45]

The title of his most popular book says a lot: *The Way of the Superior Man: A Spiritual Guide to Mastering the Challenges of Women, Work and Sexual Desire* (2004). Wilber's blurb on the back cover, returning the above compliment, says the book is 'a guide for the noncastrated male. ...Few are the books that discuss strong sexuality within strong spirituality, instead of tepid sexuality diluted by a mediocre spiritual stance'. The muscular motivational speaker, Tony Robbins, is also quoted on the cover praising the book for helping men 'fulfil their true purpose and to be authentically masculine'. Language such as the 'noncastrated male', 'strong' and the 'authentically masculine' immediately reminds one of mythopoetic literature, and Deida continues in this vein.

Deida sets up the masculine and feminine as polar in the same way as Wilber and the mythopoets: 'sexual attraction is based on sexual polarity, which is the force of passion that arcs between masculine and feminine' (Deida 2004: 3). Deida claims people with a masculine sexual essence are driven by mission and 'unless you discover this deep purpose and live it fully, your life will feel empty to the core' (2004: 5). People with a feminine sexual essence, however professionally successful, 'won't be fulfilled unless love is flowing fully in your family or intimate life' (2004: 6). Deida makes the appropriate noises about disconnecting sex and gender, noting that the masculine essence can belong to a woman, and vice versa, but he is clearly talking about men, or as Wilber says, 'the noncastrated male'. Similarly, Deida claims to be starting from a position of respect, where all genders and sexual orientations are treated as equals (2004: 10), moving into a new stage of sexual awareness, rather than reverting back to an old one. But, repeatedly Deida makes statements which make it difficult to interpret his thoughts on gender as being anything other than a step backwards, another

45. http://www.bluetruth.org/blog/_archives/2006/12/9/2561836.html

example of a supposedly integral presentation of gender falling foul of the pre/trans fallacy.

Throughout *The Way of the Superior Man* Deida repeatedly uses the phrase 'your woman' which immediately sends first-tier alarm bells ringing. A significant amount of his claims about the nature of gender would be laughable if they were not so serious, such as 'the feminine always seems chaotic and complicated from the perspective of the masculine' (2004: 15). But more than this, other passages take on a rather sinister and misogynistic flavour: 'for the feminine truth is a thin concept' (2004: 59). Elsewhere Deida holds little sympathy with 'no means no' campaigns: 'what she wants is not what she says' (2004: 108).

Deida also sets up a familiar distinction where women are connected with the earth (and, given his polar logic, presumably with men transcending it). Indeed, woman and the earth (world) seem to be synonymous for Deida: 'Neither woman nor world are predictable. ...Neither woman nor world can be second-guessed, or fooled' (2004: 33). Deida suggests there are only two ways to deal with woman and world: either renounce sexuality and 'the seemingly constant demands of woman and world' or '"fuck" both to smithereens, to ravish them with your love unsheathed' (2004: 33).[46]

Despite Deida's impassioned pleas for loving women in all their authentic femininity, the whiff of misogyny continues. Sounding particularly mythopoetic, Deida notes of a man's ability to take criticism, 'if he doesn't have a good relationship to masculine energy (e.g., his father), then he will act like a woman and be hurt or defensive' (2004: 35). Charging someone with 'acting like a woman' hardly honours authentic femininity. Continuing this path, Deida begins to take on the unhinged persona of Tom Cruise's character Frank T. J. Mackey in the movie *Magnolia* whose mantra is 'respect the cock and tame the cunt' with his seedy passage, 'You've had tit.

---

46. There may be a further level of violence in this statement: to 'ravish' with a 'love unsheathed' sounds suspiciously like potentially unwanted condom-free sexual intercourse, with all the added danger of this in the modern world. But then violence is an essential part of man for Deida: again exposing his mythopoetic roots, Deida says, 'although your woman doesn't want you to be a killer, she is turned on by your capacity to kill' (2004: 134). He continues, 'the dark masculine energy of the warrior, the one who could face death and kill when necessary, is an essential part of you' (2004: 135).

You've had pussy. …It wasn't even that good, as long as it did last. Your need is far deeper than any woman can provide' (2004: 157). It is simply unreasonable to claim, as Deida does, that he starts from a position of respect and gender equality, to then come out with such disrespectful and hostile statements, second-tier or otherwise.[47]

In some less frenzied passages Deida could be mistaken for a Promise Keeper. In chapter 3 we read of Tony Evans' suggesting to his evangelical brothers that they should turn to their wives and say, 'Honey, I've made a terrible mistake. I've given you my role. I gave up leading this family, and I forced you to take my place. Now I must reclaim that role' (1994: 79). The evangelical call to 'servant leadership' was built on the idea that many men have abdicated their role as leader in the family. Deida writes,

> If you want your woman to be able to relax into her feminine and shine her natural radiance, then you must relieve her of the necessity to be in charge. This doesn't mean you need to boss her around. It means you need to know where you are heading and how you are going to get there, in every way, including financially and spiritually (Deida 2004: 122).

This ability to make decisions (to be the servant leader) is what Deida describes as 'the masculine gift' (2004: 77). Deida asks us to accept that men making the decisions about money and God is a gift to 'your' woman, so she is 'able to relax'. This is yet another reworking of patriarchy, this time saying, 'don't you worry about a thing, let me make the decisions while you enjoy your natural radiance'. The 'superior man' is evidently an evangelical mythopoetic soft patriarch attempting to pass himself off as a sexual-spiritual radical by saying naughty words like 'fuck', 'tit' and 'pussy'.

47. Deida says, 'If you feel it is demeaning for a woman to be the "object" of your polar attraction, then you have probably disowned your masculine core. You have energetically emasculated yourself by condemning and suppressing your native desires' (2004: 83). This focus on 'native desires' which is so prevalent in Deida's work is another example of falling into the pre/trans fallacy. Assuming, for the sake of argument, that such 'native desires' did exist they would be of the order of Jungian archetypes (or what Wilber rightly defined as 'prototypes' (2000a: 256)) and of a pre-rational nature. Such native desires should therefore be 'transcended and included', but Deida simply 'includes' them.

Conclusion

Wilber's map of the integral is organized by the AQAL matrix, of which two aspects are masculine and feminine 'types'. Wilber interprets Carol Gilligan's research from *In a Different Voice* (1993) to allocate meaning to these masculine and feminine types: namely that the masculine (predominantly men) tend to operate via agency and transcendence, and the feminine (predominantly women) tend to operate via communion and immanence. Peggy Wright (1995 and 1996) argued that Wilber privileges the masculine mode in this equation. Furthermore, Wilber's gender types have an archetypal quality about them, arguably falling foul of his own theory, the 'pre/trans fallacy', which highlights the confusion between the pre-rational and the transrational (the integral). Wilber's special emphasis on the masculine and the archetypal treatment of both the masculine and feminine has some commonality with the mythopoetic, evangelical and Catholic men's movements.

Wilber argues that patriarchy existed as a biological necessity and was co-created by men and women rather than being a manifestation of masculine domination. Consequently, Wilber resists certain historical notions of feminism, suggesting that feminism makes no sense until the evolution of consciousness had reached a point where it was possible for feminism to exist. This stage of evolution is represented by the noosphere, which Wilber argues gave women for the first time a foot in both masculine agency and feminine communion, an integration enjoyed by men ever since the familialisation of the human male by the concept of 'the father'. Wilber claims that even in a full realization of the noosphere women can only expect a 60-40 parity in the public sphere. Again, this privileges the masculine mode, both historically and in the future. Wilber's reworking of patriarchy has some commonality with the evangelical men's movement concept of soft patriarchy, and has also been shared by Warren Farrell, who is popular within the mythopoetic movement and with men's rights activists. Wilber's relegation of the feminine and Gaia to the pre-rational also has clear echoes of Patrick Arnold and Gordon Dalbey, two rather misogynist exponents of Catholic and evangelical mythopoeticism.

Wilber perpetuates a certain 'masculinist style' which enables his flavour of integral spirituality to be interpreted as a form of 'muscular spirituality'. William Irwin Thompson (1996) writes of

Wilber's compulsive masculinist categorizations and mappings, and Wilber's work is peppered with technological and sporting metaphors, as well as gun-slinging responses to his critics. Wilber also consolidates this muscular style by advocating weightlifting as a path to transcendental experiences. His employment of such muscularity aligns Wilber with the methods employed by the two waves of Muscular Christianity as defined by Ladd and Mathisen (1999), suggesting a robust body is a way to become closer to God (or non-dual awareness) and also employing sporting (and technological) imagery as an evangelical tool for his brand of integral spirituality.

Beyond Wilber, another writer influenced by his thoughts continues a form of muscular spirituality. David Deida employs archetypal (polar/mythic) models of masculinity and femininity, which perpetuate women being connected with 'world' and man's transcendence. Despite claiming to celebrate the feminine, Deida also carries a distinct whiff of misogyny. Deida also shares some commonality with Promise Keepers in suggesting women should be absolved of making decisions, as this is the 'masculine gift'.

In his examination of the mythopoetic movement, Michael Schwalbe (1996) argued that what drew men to Jungian psychology were 'rational paths to the mysterious and ineffable part of us,' that is, in an amusing Jungian synchronicity, 'beyond the ken and control of the conscious ego' (1996: 67). Integral spirituality, while clearly not being 'beyond the Ken' offers a similar (trans)rational path to the mysterious which is appealing to men. This is achieved, as we have seen, by promoting spirituality that privileges masculine modes of consciousness, making men feel better by denying the historical realities of patriarchy, and advocating an integral life practice that is articulated in sporting, muscular and technological terminology.

Wilber's integralism is initially encouraging when it comes to gender, promising an opportunity for both the masculine and feminine to be honoured. Wilber sincerely believes his treatment of gender is revolutionary for those who can fly at an appropriately high altitude to see his concepts for what they allegedly are: in the introduction to the revised edition of *SES* Wilber, referring to readers of the first edition informs us that, 'women forgave me for my patriarchal obnoxiousness, men told me of weeping throughout the last chapter' (2000a: xxiv). However, those cruising at a more modest altitude must conclude that the net effect of Wilber's theories is the perpetuation of a severely problematic masculine spirituality purporting to be that which transcends and includes both genders. This is a disturbing model on which to base an increasingly popular alternative spirituality.

Wilber's brand of integral spirituality is yet another example of a masculine spirituality which perpetuates patriarchy by excluding the feminine and atypical masculinities. In the quest to find a masculine spirituality that does not perpetuate patriarchy it therefore seems reasonable to seek out those excluded atypical masculinities: the next chapter does this via an examination of gay spirituality.

Chapter Six

Gay Spirituality: A Way Out for Men

Having argued in the previous chapters for masculine spirituality and the men's movement to be treated with appropriate granularity, it seems rather at odds to offer a chapter on gay spirituality, which not only spans a number of ways of doing masculinity, but also political and ideological positions, and faith traditions.[1] However, gay spirituality does have some commonality beyond the fact that it is engaged by men who identify themselves as being gay: it offers the possibility for men to practice a spirituality which, for the most part, avoids the patriarchal traps which have littered the mythopoetic movement and the various Christian men's movements. Gay spirituality does not market itself as a masculine spirituality, as such, but the fact that it is a spirituality performed solely by men makes it one of the easiest types of spirituality to describe as masculine.[2] The aim here is not to argue for the necessity of a gay spirituality for the lives of gay men: that argument has been eloquently made in many other texts, a number of which are referred to below. The validity of gay spirituality is taken as a given and offered instead as simply another type of masculine spirituality that repeats some old mistakes but, more importantly, resists others and in doing so

1. Rollan McCleary (2004) provides a good survey of the broad spectrum of gay spirituality. This chapter deals chiefly with contemporary gay spirituality in America. McCleary argues that in the non-English speaking world gay spirituality looks quite different, 'as an idealizing preference for the masculine, individualistic, elitist, or even ascetical' (2004: 210); see Jack Malebranche (2006) for a strange example of this form of gay spirit in an American context.

2. Clearly, in this context, gay spirituality refers to the spirituality of gay men, not lesbian women. It would be particularly interesting to compare how female masculinities (Halberstam 1998; Noble 2004) interact with spirituality. However, useful literature on butch spirituality does not appear to be forthcoming, although a 2004 interview with Jade River, founder of the Re-formed Congregation of the Goddess International, suggests such conversations are certainly taking place within the lesbian community [http://www.lgbtran.org/Exhibits/OralHistory/JRiver/JRiver.pdf].

offers a useful alternative masculine spirituality which can provide some inspiration for any man.[3]

In order for such a wide spectrum of spiritualities to be accommodated in such a small space, this chapter uses a few necessarily broad categories. 'Popular gay spirituality' is explored first, meaning the kind of gay spirituality that resists categorization by faith tradition: it can appeal as easily to Christian mysticism as to Buddhism or Paganism. Popular gay spirituality opens a window on what is sometimes referred to as 'gay consciousness' or 'gay spirit' and it is this that provides the most obvious alternative to the patriarchal norm seen thus far. This section is followed by a brief look at what constitutes the nearest thing to a gay men's movement: the Radical Faeries. Popular gay spirituality provides an opportunity for alternative masculine performances informed by a sex-positive, earth-bound spirituality in stark contrast to the monolithic masculinity and sex-conquering transcendence of the previous chapters. Popular gay spirituality also highlights an interesting trend: while its 'gayness' may seem a radical departure from the heteronormative spiritualities of the previous chapters, there is also some clear commonality. In particular, popular gay spirituality draws noticeably on neo-Jungian archetypes[4] and neo-paganism in much the same way as the mythopoetic movement.

The second section turns to Christian gay spirituality, or gay theology. Despite the fact that the exploration of the Catholic men's movement concluded with the suggestion that it is characterized by a certain queerness, gay theology has almost no commonality with the Christian men's movements. Gay theology is underpinned by a critical awareness of how patriarchy operates within society and spirituality to shut down atypical masculinities in a way that is almost wholly absent in either the mythopoetic or Christian men's

---

3. This aim runs a small risk of glossing over the fact that the validity of gay spirituality in its various forms is *not* taken as a given by many of the leaders of the world's spiritual traditions, a fact attested by even a cursory glance at the news headlines. Putting gay and straight spirituality in dialogue like this also begins to address Björn Krondorfer's (2007) important question 'who's afraid of gay theology?' Krondorfer highlights the fact that there is a woeful lack of exchange between gay and straight men in theology and religious studies, and that only a few gay scholars receive any heterosexual attention.

4. The adoption of Jungian insight within gay spirituality was consolidated by Robert Hocke's (1989) *Jung, Jungians and Homosexuality*.

movements. While this political awareness is certainly present in popular gay spirituality, it is centralized in gay theology. These two sections approximately offer alternatives to the masculine spiritualities of the previous chapters: popular gay spirituality provides some continuation with mythopoetic and integral spirituality, and gay theology with the Christian men's movements. Popular gay spirituality and gay theology are not simply examples of masculine spiritualities which resist heteropatriarchal norms, although this is valuable enough; they are also exemplars for straight masculine spiritualities seeking to escape those norms, for there is much about them which need not be considered 'gay' at all.

The final section confirms this suggestion, examining queer theory and theology which, while being born out of queerness in terms of sexuality, is more profound when understood simply as a troubling device to subvert norms. Queer spirituality can therefore be seen as a way 'out' for all men, gay or straight. Gay liberation theologian Richard Cleaver argues that 'coming out' for gay men means 'moving out of a situation of bondage' (1995: 42). It is precisely the bondage of patriarchy from which all men need to 'come out'.

Of course, there is a danger here of idealizing gay spirituality. It must be pointed out that while this chapter argues that gay spirituality is a good thing, it does present some problems. It is rather lazy to identify gay men as excluded from heteropatriarchal society's norms and conclude that they do not conspire with such norms, and that there is some inherent value to the alternatives they provide. This myth was exposed by lesbian feminists in the early days of gay liberation, who noticed that gay men had a tendency to enjoy some of the benefits of patriarchal society. This process has continued over the years as some openly gay men have developed economically and professionally privileged positions in society with greater ease than lesbian women. Judith Halberstam writes of how 'white male gay hegemony' operates, ignoring women's issues and those of non-white gay men (2005: 220). Halberstam argues that gay men have countered the shame projected on to them by society by rebuilding the self via pride, 'rather than taking apart the social processes that project shame on to queer subjects in the first place' (2005: 224). Gay spirituality is exactly part of this 'rebuilding the self', and while no one wants to take away the hard-won pride of gay men, the fact that they on occasion ignored and even adopted some of the functions that operated to oppress them remains a stumbling block.[5] Gay theology, in particular gay liberation theology makes a more conscious effort to examine those oppressive social processes.

Highlighting the problems of gay spirituality serves a dual function. On one hand, critics are absolutely correct to point out its limitations which must be overcome. But on the other hand, paradoxically, these limitations may act as a bridge between heteronormative spirituality and the ideal of gay spirituality. Were there some abyss between the spiritualities of the previous chapters and this one, it would be hard to envisage how straight men could look to gay men for inspiration. But the limitations of gay spirituality provide a zone of familiarity for straight men, a kind of spiritual decompression chamber. So when the following sections highlight these limitations, two points are being made: that gay spirituality can be subject to some of the same criticisms as the previously discussed masculine spiritualities, but also that the limitations function as a sign post inscribed with the words 'This Way Out'.

Popular Gay Spirituality

While gay spirituality may seem at odds with the heteronormative spirituality of the mythopoetic and Christian men's movements, it certainly shares some commonality. Mythopoetic men, in particular, would find themselves in familiar territory were they ever to pick up some of the key texts outlining popular gay spirituality. The primary vehicles for exploring identity within the mythopoetic movement were myths and fairytales, and the primary characters within them are of an archetypal nature. McCleary argues that fairytales are a form of 'gay scripture' principally due to the employment of magical motifs and the adventures of an elitist *puer* character told in a tone which is often aristocratic or camp (2004: 144). Certainly myths and archetypes abound in popular gay spirituality, via both Jung and Joseph Campbell.[6] Among these key

5. See Richard Goldstein (2003) and Paul Robinson (2005) for further elaboration on a shift to the Right among same gay people, a process described by Lisa Duggan as homonormativity, 'a politics that does not contest dominant heteronormative assumptions and institutions, but upholds and sustains them' (Duggan 2003: 50).

6. Archetypes, the Shadow and general references to Jung take on an almost mantric quality in McCleary's survey of gay spirituality.

texts is Toby Johnson's (2000) *Gay Spirituality: The Role of Gay Identity in the Transformation of Human Consciousness*, which includes in gay identity a particular appreciation of myth as a way of understanding the human condition (2000: 83-85).[7] While gay experiences may differ from those of many mythopoetic men, the mythological methodology used to explore them is clearly the same. Similarly, another key text is Mark Thompson's collection of interviews with prominent gay men, *Gay Soul* (1994), which is littered with archetypal references.[8] Two of Thompson's interviewees (Robert H. Hopcke and Mitch Walker) are Jungian analysts who unsurprisingly appeal to the use of archetypes at some length in understanding gay spirit. Clearly, employing archetypes in a gay context is not so different from a straight mythopoetic context: both lead to conformity (Tacey 1997: 17), the only difference being the type of conformity.[9] Instead of celebrating the deep masculine or Wild Man within, gay neo-Jungians aspire to the Androgyne.[10]

The Androgyne is *the* gay archetype, combining both masculine and feminine qualities and providing the uniqueness of gay spirit: 'a potent blending of male strength and competence and of female sensitivity and feeling makes for a more interesting human being with a more complex and fascinating personality' (Johnson 2000: 123). In Thompson's *Gay Soul* (1994), most of the interviewees allude in some way to the combining of masculine and feminine in gay spirit and seven of the sixteen speak positively in terms of androgyny: James Broughton (1994: 14), Paul Monette (1994: 26), Andrew Harvey (1994: 56), James M. Saslow (1994: 138), Ram Dass (1994: 160), Ed Steinbrecher (1994: 202) and Robert M. Hopcke (1994: 216).

7. Johnson is particularly fond of Joseph Campbell, focusing an entire book on his work: *The Myth of the Great Secret: An Appreciation of Joseph Campbell* (1992).

8. Thompson makes particular use of Jungian archetypes and the Shadow in his later memoirs, *Gay Body: A Journey Through Shadow to Self* (1997).

9. Despite these differing types there is not as much resistance to the mythopoetic models of masculinity as one might imagine. Michael DeVoll and Christopher Blazina (2002) suggest gay men should follow the example of Bly's Wild Man and Moore and Gillette's King, Warrior, Magician, Lover in finding archetypes on which to base their gender performance in society. Clearly they assume Bly, Moore and Gillette were on to a good thing for straight men.

10. There are occasional explorations of more traditionally mythopoetic archetypes such as John R. Stowe's (1999) appeal to the Warrior.

In some ways the Androgyne should be celebrated, for unlike the Wild Man s/he at least does not establish an identity for men via the celebration of violence and killing (Zipes 1992: 16). But nevertheless the Androgyne's ostensible diversity is limited, repeating the old mistake of gender essentialism, suggesting there is one type of singular being at the heart of gay spirit, albeit one which echoes both the masculine and feminine. In Thompson (1994) only one person, Will Roscoe, picks up on the shortcomings of androgyny, noting that it is little more than a heterosexual model, contained within the male/female binary (1994: 104).[11] The centralising of the Androgyne within gay spirituality can be seen as one of the 'theologies at the margins' of which Marcella Althaus-Reid writes, whose end game is simply one of inclusion, 'reconciling themselves with androcentrism by getting reabsorbed into the system via heterosexual ideals of equality' (Althaus-Reid 2003: 51). In this way 'male strength and competence and female sensitivity' remain uncritically accepted as the price of gay inclusion, despite the claim that 'androgyny manifests the ability of consciousness to incorporate, and thereby overcome, opposites' (Johnson 2000: 124). This is the primary shortcoming of popular gay spirituality: inhabiting a marginal position in and agreeing with many of the assumptions of the heteropatriarchal economy rather than fully rejecting it.

In the mythopoetic movement the rediscovery of the Wild Man suggested the returning to the natural order of things, and for a renewed hope for the role of men in the future. The androgynous gifts of a rather essentialist gay spirit repeat this carving out of male privilege, but from a different perspective. Indeed, gay spiritual identity can become rather grand. Andrew Ramer writes, 'I think the future of the world, the hope of the world, depends upon us, that men who love men are the only people who can save the planet' (in Thompson 1994: 69). Andrew Harvey claims that 'homosexuals' should claim their positions as 'mystical and spiritual leaders' (in Thompson 1994: 57).[12] Johnson writes, 'there is an

11. This is why Roscoe (1991 and 1998) prefers to discuss the *berdache* of Native American Indian traditions who is not so much considered a merging of masculine and feminine, rather an altogether different, third gender.

12. In his novel *On the Edge* (1998), Edward St Aubyn offers a scathing (and hilarious) portrayal of gay spiritual grandiosity via a character based on Andrew Harvey.

enlightenment that goes with being gay, an understanding of the real meaning of religion' (2000: xi). There is a line between celebrating gay identity and elevating it to numinous significance that appears easy to cross. However, there is a notable parallel between 'gay enlightenment' and liberation theology's appeal to 'the epistemological privilege of the poor': the idea that the experience of being poor and suffering under oppression gives one a special insight into the world, and perhaps even the nature of God.

But popular gay spirituality is not defined solely by its limitations. Perhaps paradoxically, some of the notes of caution raised above are also where gay spirituality succeeds: their value relies on interpretation. The carving out of a 'gay identity', while prone to essentialism is also a much-needed alternative to heteronormative ways of doing masculinity. The Androgyn, while uncritically adopting the norms of feminine and masculine imposed upon us by a largely patriarchal order, does at least muddy the waters and offer a third, albeit limited way. That gay men should step up to be spiritual leaders is, of course, to project a whole range of assumptions on to gay men, but it would also be useful to have such gay spiritual leaders. The value of these themes is to interpret them not as solutions, but as paths to solutions and partial solutions. It is in this light of partial solutions that the following benefits of gay spirituality should be seen, as characteristics and flavours that can be added to a larger mix comprising different and less problematic ways of doing masculinity.

Johnson argues that gay spirituality is experienced from an outside perspective, non-dualistic, incarnational, evolutionary, insight-provoking, transformational and adaptively virtuous (2000: xvi). For Johnson, perspective works in a few ways. First, that gay people even exist necessitates an acknowledgment that there are different sexual perspectives from which to see the world. This can result in the challenging of social norms and the re-focusing of attention: without raising children, for example, an individual has more time to contribute to the wider community via art, service or spiritual guidance. Non-dualism relates not just to metaphysics but also to a different way of relating to another individual within a sexual (and social) relationship, liberated from the 'traditional' ways of men and women's interactive dynamics. Incarnation is about living a sex-positive spirituality, rather than one which seeks to deny or transcend bodily reality. Evolution is about whether or not religion is capable of keeping up with social change, exemplified by a more openly communicated gay consciousness: if it can do so, this means a different way of understanding religious authority, tradition and community. Insight refers to an ability to think metaphorically and understand the mythical nature of religion. Transformation is about understanding how negative actions come about and how to address this in ourselves and others: it is about facilitating a change in consciousness. Adaptive virtues include the theme of androgyny, as well as a host of positive characteristics including love, innocence, transparency, selflessness and generosity. All of Johnson's points, with the possible exception of mythical insight which speaks of his particular fondness of Joseph Campbell, while being rather woolly all go some way to counteracting the patriarchal masculinities presented in the previous chapters. Importantly, there is little about Johnson's points that is inherently 'gay' (inasmuch as men's sexual attraction to other men),[13] which suggests they could be beneficially adopted by any man, gay or straight.

The creedal statement about gay men by Harry Hay, the 'founder of the modern gay movement' (Timmons 1990), while rather idealistic nevertheless provides another useful schema for the benefits of gay spirituality:

- They are *not*, by nature, territorially aggressive and do not impose their political claims on others.
- They are *not*, by nature, competitive but are passionately interested in sharing with others.
- They are *not* interested in conquering nature but are interested in harmonious living with all of nature.
- They are *not* interested in denying bodiliness and carnality but are passionately involved in celebrating all aspects of human sexuality. (Quoted in Stemmeler 1996: 104)

Here we see a range of positions which again resist the patriarchal tendencies of other masculine spiritualities. Again, there is nothing specifically gay about these statements: any straight man could align himself with them while remaining unquestioned in his

---

13. It could, of course, be argued that the experience of marginalization as a result of being gay provides specific insights which are 'inherently' gay, insights which straight men must derive from different processes.

heterosexuality. Most notably, Hay identified the uniqueness of gay consciousness as being based on relational dynamics. Hay argued for the need to move beyond binary thinking, of subject and object, to a condition of 'subject-SUBJECT':

> The Hetero monogamous relationship is one in which the participants, through bio-cultural inheritance, traditionally perceive each other as OBJECT. To the Hetero male, woman is primarily perceived as sex-*object* and then, only with increasing sophistication, as person-*object*. The Gay monogamous relationship is one in which the participants, through non-competitive instinctual inclinations, *and contrary to cultural inheritances*, perceive each other as Equals and learn, usually through deeply painful trials-and-errors, to experience each other, to continuously grow, and to develop *with* each other, *empathically* — as SUBJECT (Hay 1996: 210; original emphases)

Subject-SUBJECT at once provides a model for same-sex attraction, and also a critique of patriarchy, which objectifies women as part of its project of domination (although Hay would see women's objectification of men as also being part of the heterosexual subject-OBJECT model). William Rodgers (1995) argues this subject-SUBJECT perception of the world has a distinct impact on spirituality. Within its various forms, gay spirituality sees the earth's creation not as something separate, but as an inherent part of the individual, lending itself to a greater respect for the earth and the increasing likelihood of its sustainability. Of course, these themes are common among ecofeminists, but less so for spiritualities connected with men and as such remains an important precedent.

Buddhism is a further aspect to popular gay spirituality that resists the types of masculinities promoted by the Wild Man. American Buddhism in general owes a good deal of its popularity to gay culture, having been promoted by gay writers such as Allen Ginsberg and John Giorno. Ginsberg was even instrumental in allocating Buddhism a certain institutional presence by developing Naropa University in Boulder, Colorado, one of the few universities in the United States that follows and promotes Buddhist ethics. Gay Buddhism is often referred to as 'Queer dharma': McCleary argues that, 'Queer' is the appropriate word, since 'gay' has essentialist implications Buddhist process cannot endorse' (2004: 77), questioning notions of the Self within a context of non-duality.[14] Similarly, in seeking a 'queer Dharmology' Roger Corless (2004) argues that Buddhist non-duality is more compatible with Hay's subject-SUBJECT consciousness than with regular subject-OBJECT consciousness.

Andrew Harvey, an interviewee in Thompson's *Gay Soul* has also done a great deal to strengthen the connection between gay spirituality and Buddhism (and 'Eastern' thought in general) in books such as *A Journey in Ladakh* (1983) and the hugely popular *The Tibetan Book of Living and Dying* (Sogyal, Gaffney and Harvey, 1992); his cross-traditional *The Essential Gay Mystics* (1997), has been summarized as being chiefly Tantric, Taoist or Zen-like (McCleary 2004: 208). Harvey is also in large part responsible for the popularity in the United States of the Sufi poet Jalal al-din Rumi in numerous books such as *The Way of Passion* (1994), many of which contain rather camp 'recreations' of the mystic's poems.[15] Johnson (2000: 216-25) also holds Buddhism in high regard. *White Crane*, a gay spirituality journal at one time published by Johnson, takes its name from 'the ancient traditions of China and Japan, [where] the white crane is a symbol of happiness and wholeness'[16] and follows a distinctly Eastern aesthetic and often contains articles about gay Buddhist spirituality. The Buddhist element of popular gay spirituality, while not necessarily inferring any proactive resistance to masculine domination (Campbell 1996; Gross 1993), does at least promote a mindfulness and compassion among its adherents which resists the typically combative models of masculinity within the mythopoetic and Christian men's movements. As Mark Muesse notes, '[Buddhist] meditation provides an effective treatment for the negative consequences of masculine conditioning' (2002: 9).

14. A similar point is made by Carol Queen and Lawrence Schimel whose phrase 'pomosexual' is a resistance to minority sexual identity politics and which alludes to the 'Zen notion of multiple subjectivities' (1997: 21). From a more social rather than literary influence, Queer dharma also draws on the life and work of Issan Dorsey (Schneider 1993: 216), a former drag performer who studied Buddhism with Shunryu Suzuki Roshi, founder of the San Francisco Zen Centre. Dorsey's work located gay Buddhism within general gay culture when in 1987 he founded Maitri, one of San Francisco's most respected care providers serving people debilitated by AIDS.

15. Over the years Bly has engaged in his own spirited translations of Rumi and other mystical poets such as Hafez, Ghalib and Kabir; see, for example, Bly (2004).

16. http://www.whitecranejournal.com/history.asp

Not So Radical Faeries

The nearest gay spirituality gets to being an actual movement is with the Radical Faeries, a loose coalition of gatherings and groups that began in 1979, drawing inspiration from the work of Harry Hay and Mitch Walker. The Radical Faeries are at once an interesting example of how men can do masculinity in different ways but nevertheless in a way that is not really so radically different from what we generally understand to be the men's movement.

The typical Faerie is 'firmly committed to counterhegemonic values' (Hennen 2004: 519) and in particular seeks to subvert a normative understanding of masculinity. Most notably s/he does this by wearing, 'fantastic outfits that include wings encrusted with glitter, tutu-like skirts, and wands like Glinda's in The Wizard of Oz' (Anable 2002: 18) and goes by names such as 'Dragonfly, Zinnia, Lavinia, Moongaze, PopTart, Aunt Tildy, Witchhazel, and Frank' (Hennen 2004: 501). Peter Hennen (2004) argues that Faerie drag operates in two distinct ways. The chief difference of Faerie drag compared to 'normal' drag is that Faeries tend not to seek the illusion of femininity: there is no denial of masculinity, simply a mixing of beards and hairy chests with high-camp dresses, a playful parody (2004: 521). A second, less prevalent form involves a deeper engagement of drag reflecting greater concern with sexual identity. Again, this does not seek the illusion of femininity, instead 'signalling something that at least *looked* like a third gender rather than simply juxtaposing masculine and feminine elements' (2004: 522).

What is interesting about these forms of Faerie drag is there is no denial of masculinity in favour of a feminized persona, the like of which straight men are often so fearful. Instead, masculinity is celebrated by putting those beards and hairy chests in dialogue with rhinestones and fake pearls. This is similar to the kind of drag 'straight' men engage in on those rare and often disturbing occasions when they wear dresses. Of course, there is a different set of power relations at play there, but nevertheless there is commonality with Faerie drag.[17] Even in the more subtle form of Faerie drag which

17. While he writes specifically of gay drag queens, Steven Schacht's suggestions about the nature of drag are useful here. Schacht argues that the gendered and sexual identities of both the performer and the audience are crucial in understanding the subtleties of drag as a phenomenon (2002: 164). Traditionally straight (perhaps even loutish) men in drag performing in front of a comparable audience are almost certainly

seeks to construct a third gender, masculinity is not denied, but extended: one of Hennen's subjects 'has long beautiful hair that cascades down his back...He also sports a neatly groomed van dyke beard and moustache, wears simple madras skirts, perhaps a smart vest' (2004: 522).

It is interesting to see photos of early Faerie gatherings when the cross-dressing campness was slightly less prevalent than it is today. The scene is highly reminiscent of mythopoetic gatherings: groups of largely naked bearded men would stand in ritualistic circles; staffs, totems and other 'pagan' items can be seen. Fifteen years later almost identical scenes were being performed at Iron John retreats throughout the United States. That mythopoetic gatherings resonated with a certain homoerotic energy was noted in chapter 2, and chapter 4 outlined claims by conservative Catholics that Richard Rohr's mythopoetic spirituality retreats are tainted by inappropriate amounts of male nudity and sexualization. Certainly the Faerie gatherings, beginning in 1979, pre-dated *Iron John*, however some key gay spirituality texts from the 1990s borrow from a neo-Jungian tradition of archetypes popularized by Bly, so there is arguably mutual influence between the two movements.[18] Both movements draw earlier still on a wider feminist rediscovery of the goddess and earth-focused spirituality, albeit reaching different conclusions. It is tempting to speculate that Bly and Hay had some dialogue in the 1970s around these themes, with each evolving on different trajectories, although there is no evidence to suggest this. Will Roscoe (Personal Communication, February 2007), Hay's friend and editor has no recollection of the two men communicating. This commonality between Faerie and mythopoetic spirituality is highlighted by Rodgers (1995). Aside from highlighting a Faerie pre-occupation with archetypes (the Androgyne), Rodgers notes that the most prevalent of Faerie

not attempting to articulate any subversive comments about the nature of gender, rather mocking the subject of their parody: chiefly women and perhaps gay men (either as effeminate men or, more subtly, gay men in drag). Schacht notes that even gay drag can be an exercise in masculine dominance and misogyny (2002: 165). See Leila J. Rupp and Verta Taylor (2003) and Steven Schacht & Lisa Underwood (2004) for further insights into drag performances.

18. Another similar tangent that would be interesting to explore is how Bly's Wild Man intersects with the bear community, a gay subculture that celebrates hirsute, stocky and particularly masculine gay men; see Hennen (2005) and Wright (1997 and 2001).

spiritual beliefs draw upon Wicca and neo-paganism, most notably an appreciation of the Goddess/Earth Mother. It is worth noting here that before his turn to *Iron John*, Bly had positioned himself on the spiritual spectrum by establishing in 1975 the annual Conference of the Great Mother, which continues to this day.

Another popular Faerie image is the Horned God, the subject of John Rowan's (1987) feminist mythopoetic book. Rodgers notes the presence of the Horned God at Faerie gatherings is perplexing as in Wiccan and neo-pagan traditions he is the consort of the Goddess, and thus heterosexual. Hennen highlights a similar heteronormative and masculinist call to the Faeries by James Broughton, focusing on phallic glory and fertility: 'The penis is a wand of the soul. ...Praise it. Give thanks for its awesome powers. ...in the holy balls in your scrotum the treasure of your semen is kept' (quoted in Hennen 2004: 526). Stuart Timmons' (1990: 267) account of the first Faerie Conference confirms this theme, noting how the participants spontaneously crafted a huge phallus in the earth.[19] Rodgers suggests this type of ostensible heternormativity is part of the Faeries engaging in an act of queer reclamation of ancient religious rites and homosexual acts established in the work of Arthur Evans (1978 and 1988). This is no doubt a valid argument, yet at the same time the Faeries are operating within an economy in which the mythopoetic movement would also feel comfortable.

Hennen concludes that while there is a real commitment to resisting gender norms among the Faeries, their success is only partial (2004: 529), and that the changes they do bring about operate on the individual level (2004: 530), falling into line with Halberstam's (2005: 224) criticism of white male gay hegemony failing to address the wider dynamics that oppress queer subjects. However, Faeries do also generate some wider influence: Rodgers (1995) notes that the traditional Wiccan ritual circles, comprising carefully balanced masculine and feminine polar energies, have been challenged and broken down by the inclusion of Faerie participants who do not recognize such polarity.

Given that Faerie drag does not seek the illusion of femininity, and that Faerie spirituality shares some commonality with mythopoetic spirituality, Faerie masculinity is more of an extension

19. See Eugene Monick (1987) and Aaron Kipnis (1992) for a mythopoetic handling of the phallus.

of normative masculinity than a radical departure from it. Ironically, by appreciating Faeries in this way, as following a recognizable trajectory from the norm, by expanding rather than denying, Faeries may have a greater potential to act as radical agents of change within the broader spectrum of masculinities. While Faeries might not achieve their ideal goal of producing a radical queer *sexual* alternative, they do succeed in producing a queering (i.e. subverting) of masculinity and spirituality that is tentatively graspable from a position of heteronormativity.

Clearly, the main function of the Faeries or a wider understanding of gay spirituality is to provide a spiritual tradition in which men can express their gay sexuality, however this is not its only function. Popular gay spirituality trades on various themes outlined above that promote different ways of doing masculinity, many of which have nothing specifically to do with being gay. Richard A. Isay, who in 1973 was responsible for the removal of homosexuality from the list of disorders recognized by the American Psychiatric Association, suggests that while gay men may not have a unique vision, they are certainly more interesting, having dealt with more issues in their lives, both from without and within (in Thompson 1994: 12). This may ultimately be the real meaning of Johnson's (2000) subtitle 'The Role of Gay Identify in the Transformation of Human Consciousness': not something specific about gayness, but rather something specific about a group of men who have looked longer and harder than usual at what it means to be a man. This is the lesson for all men, the transformation of human consciousness.

Some preliminary seeping of this 'gayness' into popular straight male culture has already happened with such barren terms as the 'Sensitive New Age Guy'. More recently the term 'metrosexual' has gained some popularity, although this clearly revolves more around an end game of marketing products than actually saying anything about gender, sexuality, emotions or ethics.[20] Toby Johnson suggests the term 'mesosexual': 'that is, in the middle of the continuum between heterosexual and homosexual'.[21] This sounds

20. Anyone who believes the metrosexual has anything 'sensitive' about him should consider his prototype: Alex from *A Clockwork Orange* (Burgess 1962), whose dandyish aesthetic is a thin veneer atop rape and pillage. Marian L. Salzman, Ira Matathia and Ann O'Reilly (2005) unwittingly expose the conversation around metrosexuality and the 'future of men' to be little more than a marketing opportunity.

21. http://www.tobyjohnson.com/mesosexual.html

initially appealing but like the Androgyne it appeals to a heteronormative binary, even if advocating a middle way. Some other term which avoids such binarity is needed, such as 'parasexual' or 'perisexual':[22] Ed Steinbrecher (in Thompson 1994: 199; 206-209) suggests 'metasexual'. The ultimate promise of these terms, albeit unrealized in any popular way, is to destabilize normative models of masculinity, and it is to this that the final section on queer spirituality turns.

Gay Theology

Elizabeth Stuart (2003) outlines four distinct phases which provide a useful taxonomy of gay and lesbian theology: gay liberal, gay liberation, erotic/lesbian theology, and queer. Gay liberal theology showed that gay experience was normal, healthy and worthy of interacting with the Divine. In order for gay people to realize this experience they had to cast off the oppressive authority imposed upon them and pursue their spiritual gifts, which may be better suited to fulfilling the gospel message than those of heterosexuals. Popular gay spirituality, as outlined above, employs a similar methodology to Gay liberal theology. Gay liberation theology differed by focusing on the cause of gay oppression and its theological and ethical implications for gay men and lesbians rather than simply celebrating gay virtues. Lesbian theology had stronger ties to feminist theology than gay male theology, whether liberal or liberation. It centralized an erotic bodily experience of the Divine, coupled with a deep appreciation of friendship. Queer theology, instead of asking gay and lesbians to come out, instead seeks to liberate all people from constructions of sexuality and gender.

John J. McNeill is a good example of gay liberal theology, and an immediate similarity can be seen with popular gay spirituality. McNeill's *The Church and the Homosexual* (1976) resulted in him being silenced by the Vatican on matters of homosexuality, a silence he broke with the publication of *Taking a Chance on God* (1988) and later *Freedom, Glorious Freedom* (1995). These texts follow the liberal goal of creating a proud theology inclusive of gay people. In particular McNeill (1995: 162-76) shares commonality with popular

22. Gregory M. Pflugfelder (1999: 97-145) develops this term, but gives it a different meaning about how homosexual practices were legally described in Edo-period Japan.

gay spirituality by making significant use of masculine and feminine archetypes, or Jung's *anima* and *animus*, this time projecting them less on to the person and more on to history. McNeill, quite reasonably, follows Richard Tarnas (1991) in suggesting the past three thousand years of history has been under the domineering influence of the masculine archetype (manifest in patriarchy) and that we are currently entering a phase where the feminine archetype is being realized. Instead of seeking a dominance of the feminine archetype, McNeill asks for a balance between the two. It is in achieving this balance that gay consciousness comes into its own: 'a positive gay identity on all levels—social, political, cultural, and spiritual—all over the world has a teleological purpose in the development of the *anima/animus mundi*' (McNeill 1995: 174). McNeill's use of archetypes within a historical context makes their use less problematic than within popular gay spirituality, suggesting less investment in an essentialist *personal* identity. This is an example of how gay theology, even when clearly intersecting with popular gay spirituality, tends to be more subtle. However, McNeill is still convinced of the notion of a rather singular gay identity and the role it can play within spirituality and theology, resulting in a familiar essentialism. This phase is nevertheless a crucial part of the evolutionary process which enabled gay liberation theology.

It is with gay liberation theology that we begin to see a powerful shift in the gay voice, with results that extend beyond its immediate concerns into the wider community. Stuart (2003) shows there are some problems with gay liberation theology, chiefly that it still relies rather uncritically on a gay identity and experience, making a sharp distinction between the oppressors and the oppressed, and in doing so chooses not to deal with those closeted gay people who partake in that oppression (2003: 47-48). However, gay liberation theology sets out an unprecedented challenge to the continuum of masculine spiritualities. Robert Goss aligns his gay and lesbian theological manifesto firmly within a context of liberation theology, a 'critical analysis of the social context that forms our experience, our struggles, and our emergent, innovative, and transgressive practice' (Goss 1993: xvii). His analysis involves an exploration of how homophobia functions within society, namely through a language of hatred, the medicalisation of homosexuality, Christian/ institutional oppression of gay people, the homophobic panic surroundings AIDS, and violence against gay people. In this way, 'a gay/lesbian liberation theology begins with resistance and moves to political insurrection' (Goss 1993: xvii). Similarly, Gary David Comstock (1993: 21) aligns his 'gay theology without apology' within the context of liberation theology and also examines how gay people have been subject to the machinations of patriarchy, the ebb and flow of public opinion and the financial and even military policies that have been imposed upon society in the United States (Comstock 1993: 67-76). Richard Cleaver also frames gay liberation in a similar way, paying special attention to the necessity for class awareness (1995: 84-111).

The fundamental importance behind gay liberation theology is that it began to ask the right questions about what was behind the oppression of gay (in our context) masculinity. If we are generous enough for a moment to assume a good number of the men in the mythopoetic and Christian men's movements were not actually consciously seeking to reaffirm patriarchy, but were responding to a genuine desire to address the problem of masculinity within society, then we can put their mistakes down to *not* asking the right questions. This failure is part of the 'strategic anti-intellectualism' identified by Michael Schwalbe (1996: 148) of the mythopoetic movement (and also applicable to the Christian men's movements). The vacuum left by a lack of critical questioning of the underlying causes of their anxiety was filled by the simple perpetuation of its causes: the often unconscious repetition of their patriarchal conditioning, a feminist backlash. In this hypothesis, when Bly identified the 'soft male', those men with whom the image resonated should have asked, 'what is it that seeks to deny the soft male?' Instead, those men responded with (and herein lies the answer to that question) their patriarchal conditioning, reverting back to a model of masculinity more closely aligned with the patriarchal model (the Wild Man). This is comparable to gay men who respond to their intuitive feelings of gayness with a self-denying and self-hating homophobia, shutting themselves firmly in the closet. Interestingly, Comstock (1996: 290) notes that within his on-campus pastoral work his advice was sought on issues of masculinity more from straight students than gay ones, not because they expected him to *share* their experiences, but because they knew he was willing, as a gay man, to talk about such experiences, to ask the right questions. This resonates with Isay's comments that gay men are more interesting than straight men, having dealt with more issues in their lives: the key variable is engaging with the right issues, either willingly or reluctantly as a result of social exclusion.

The right questions are inevitably political. Donald Boisvert (2002), taking his cue from Marx, defines gay spirituality as being a critical religious discourse that resists oppression which has a grounding in political analysis and engagement. Right from the start of the 'gay spiritual movement' Hay (1996: 186) sought to combine his Marxist analysis with a spiritual reality, seeing no conflict between the two. This is the gift that gay spirituality/theology has to offer to gay men: the opportunity to critically and spiritually engage with the patriarchal order that oppresses them and others. It is also an invitation for straight men to do likewise. Gay spirituality is the only men's spiritual environment where there is a sustained engagement with the political. It was suggested in chapter 2 that the profeminist critics of the men's movement lacked a subtle appreciation of the spiritual, and that profeminism might attract more numbers were it more open to the spiritual. That there is a certain resistance to the spiritual within the profeminist movement that attests to being 'gay affirmative' is particularly odd given that Hay and others show that the spiritual is a significant part of gay identities. The left-leaning straight man with a spiritual conscience now finds a third counterintuitive option: the 'spiritual' mythopoetic movement with no real sense of the political, the profeminist movement with no real sense of the spiritual, or the gay spiritual movement with no real sense of the straight. What is our man to do?

A Spiritual Queer-For-All

Stuart's final category of gay and lesbian theologies is queer theology which rather than asking gay and lesbians to come out, instead seeks to liberate all people from constructions of sexuality and gender (Stuart 2003: 89). Nikki Sullivan suggests that to queer something is 'to make strange, to frustrate, to counteract, to delegitimise, to camp up—heteronormative knowledges and institutions, and the subjectivities and socialities that are (in)formed by them and that (in)form them' (Sullivan 2003: vi). To queer something is to disrupt and problematize the norm, particularly (although not exclusively) in terms of gender, thus 'queer theologies are a refusal to normalisation, to the recycling of old borders and limits' (Althaus-Reid 2003: 50).

Lots of men in popular gay spirituality and gay theology describe themselves as queer, reclaiming the word from its pejorative use within a homophobic discourse. Queer was born of an examination of sexuality but, as Sullivan's definition suggests, there is much more to it. Yet, while queer has its origins in gay and lesbian studies there has also been some resistance to it within the gay and lesbian community, as it requires letting go of a hard-won 'gay identity', questioning as it does all notions of stable identities. It was suggested above that there were certain aspects of popular gay spirituality and gay theology that could be adopted by straight men as part of a resistance to the patriarchal spiritualities presented in the previous chapters. As we move into the queer realms, those aspects become less identifiably 'gay' and therefore are even easier to apply to straight men or, more specifically *any* man, as queer also troubles a 'straight' identity. A good deal of this section discusses the application of queer theory for straight men, which at first glance may appear like the co-option of the queer in a continued campaign of heteronormativity, and a glossing over of the spiritual experiences of queer people. However, the aim is not to focus on straight men *per se* but simply to offer them as the missing variable in the equation of queer potential for *all* men.

There has been some anxious wringing of hands amongst straight theorists about employing queer theory, under the shadow of Judith Butler's comment, 'normalizing the queer would be, after all, its sad finish' (1994: 21). The general concern is that if straight folks start meddling with and appropriating queer theory then those gay and lesbian voices moblized by it, often for the first time, will once again be silenced. However, straight voices have always been a part of the queer chorus, such as Eve Kosofsky Sedgwick, although there has been a tendency for these straight voices to be female, either because there is some existing minority-voice alliance between straight women and queer people or the slightly broader reasoning that straight men have been less inclined to question notions of normativity and sexual identity, enjoying as they do its privileges.

It is therefore of particular interest that the primary anthology about straight queerness (Thomas 2002b) was edited by a man (or perhaps, if the editor was a woman, the volume simply would not have stood out as unusual). In his contribution to that volume

Straight with a Twist: Queer Theory and the Subject of Heterosexuality
Calvin Thomas (2000a) charts those queer theorists who do and do
not allow for straight inclusion, as well as the tensions experienced
within his own straight relationship with queer theory. Thomas'
survey is cautiously extended by Annette Schlichter (2004) who
suggests straight adoption of queer theory is often about the desire
of intellectuals to appear transgressive. Schlichter questions the
value of straights employing queer theory when it has 'become a
form of cultural capital in the academy' (2004: 557), noting that when
Sedgwick was originally advocating the queer cause it was still a
distinctly risky business. This is certainly a reasonable concern,
especially when looking at the rare articulations of queer straight
masculinity.

Robert Heasley offers one such articulation with a provisional
typology of queer masculinities of straight men, which he bases on
those masculinities 'that disrupt, or have the potential to disrupt,
traditional images of the hegemonic heterosexual masculine' (2005:
310). Heasley includes: straight sissy boys, who generally lack the
skills to succeed in traditionally masculine performances; social-
justice straight-queers, who actively subvert heteronormativity;
elective straight-queers, who flirt with queerness as a means of
self-liberation; committed straight-queers, who more thoroughly
embrace the concept of queer to expand their notions of gender
and sexuality; males living in the shadow of masculinity, who resist
heteronormativity, but who do not wish to risk being identified
with being queer or gay.

Heasley's initial description, a disruption of the hegemonic
heterosexual masculine, is reasonable enough, but this is not
necessarily queer. Within his typology only the social-justice straight-
queers, the committed straight-queers and perhaps the elective
straight-queers can actually be considered queer. Sullivan's
definition suggests a proactive position: to camp up, to make strange.
Being queer takes more than not fitting with the norm. Heasley
might look approvingly upon the suggestion in chapter 4 that the
Catholic men's movement is in some way queer, as its members can
manifest a masculinity which appears not to fit the norm defined
by its evangelical counterpart. However, it was also argued that
queerness in the Catholic men's movement is more a happy accident
reflecting long-held traditions than a proactive campaign to challenge
heteronormativity. When the meaning of queer is stretched (or more

accurately, reduced) in this fashion there is indeed a danger that its articulations will 'run the risk of becoming deadening clichés through their repetition' (Butler 1999: xxi). As Butler says, normalizing the queer would indeed be its sad finish, but this tautological statement is true only because queer simply cannot be normal. Heasley stretches queer too far not by including straight masculinities,[23] but by bringing it too close to normal: for example it takes more than not liking sport to make a man queer.

Ultimately, queer theory, while being born out of a gay and lesbian discourse, has nothing specifically to do with being gay or lesbian. Critics of the expansion of queer need to focus not on the presence of those who elect heterosexuality, but the regulatory functions of the normal which, while connected are nevertheless separate. Focusing on the red herring of the straight runs the risk of missing the queer end game: the destabilization of sexual categories and the liberation of all people from the alleged norm. This is the appeal of the term 'Genderfucker' as it brings with it the subversive value of queer, but without the complete implication that one must 'be' queer in a gay/lesbian sense: 'Let us remember here that the Genderfucker may also be straight' (Althaus-Reid 2003: 68). There is nothing normal about the straight Genderfucker.

Turning attention to queer theology we can see again that queer is not just about the experiences of queer individuals. Stuart locates the queer right at the heart of the matter, claiming that 'Christianity is a queer thing' (2003: 105), noting the historical subversions of heteronormativity: the vowed celibate shows heterosexuality need not be standard, and that desire is ultimately directed to God; the celibate is single, yet bonded in the Church with Christ; celibates became 'mothers' and 'fathers' presiding over 'brothers' and 'sisters' where there was no kinship; religious women often took men's names. Graham Ward (1999) tightens the queer focus further still, arguing the body of Jesus and his gendered identity are continually displaced: from the beginning Jesus is conceived without a male progenitor; later, his flesh is transfigured through the performance of miracles, his physical body is transposed and consumed at the eucharistic supper, his body broken and sexually charged during the crucifixion, his identity confused by his disciples after

23. Elsewhere, Butler (1993: 230) acknowledges the value of queerness for straight people.

the resurrection, and finally his body wholly displaced by the ascension.

This kind of argument is fundamentally different to that of popular gay spirituality and gay theology along the lines of John Boswell (1980) or Ronald E. Long (2004) who want to highlight a gay presence in the history of religion. Instead, queer theology suggests the whole concept of the spiritual and of gender is built on fluid categorization, not just different categorization. Clearly this type of queer theology stretches to breaking point much of what has been shown so far to be a rather prescriptive 'masculine spirituality', and in doing so opens up a variety of religious experiences which would otherwise have been discouraged as overly feminine.

Stuart locates erotic theology as a separate category from queer theology, but there is certainly an overlap, as 'sexual storytelling' is an important part of queer theology: 'Queer liberation is a thoroughly erotic liberation' (Goss 1993: 172). For Boisvert, sexual storytelling is about 'the necessary and strategic importance of reappropriation, of naming and reclaiming without shame the homoerotic element in religious belief and practice' (2006: 166). Stuart argues that while erotic theologies seek to challenge notions of sexuality, they still run the danger of privileging the sexual experiences of the individual above all else and 'often end up virtually ceasing to be theologies at all' (2003: 62). Of course, most sexual storytelling is resisted not in order to preserve theology as a viable category, but to silence a particular type of theological voice: 'Queer bodies, specifically tumescent gay bodies, are simply too messy; they break too many assumed boundaries' (Boisvert 2006: 173). Such messiness is what Althaus-Reid describes as 'indecent theology' which 'brings back the sense of reality' (2000: 71). Certainly sexual storytelling is essential for queer people who feel the need to bear witness to their sexuality as part of their spiritual experience, however a sexual 'sense of reality' is something that should be applicable to all people.

Krondorfer suggests queer sexual storytelling is a problem for straight men, that erotic confessions of men penetrating one another cause an anxiety that is probably too high for most to overcome (2007: 268-69). This may well be the case, but it need not be. Straight men can learn a lot from sexual storytelling, and not just about the esoteric knowledges of gay sexual positions. Sexual storytelling is a lead for straight men to combine their own sexual experiences, from the mundane to the exotic, with their spiritual experiences. Despite a certain fascination with the psychoanalytic phallus (Monick 1987) and what has even been called a 'phallic spirituality' (Poling and Kirkley 2000), for the most part there is surprisingly little actual penis in masculine spirituality. Generally, sexual practice is suppressed in the mythopoetic and Christian men's movements, either by being ignored or treated as something which must be controlled: think of Arterburn's (2000) *Every Man's Battle: Winning the War on Sexual Temptation One Victory at a Time*. Within integral spirituality Ken Wilber relegated sexuality to a rather lowly rung on the consciousness ladder.

A good example of how gay and straight treatments of sexuality differ is masturbation, a practice engaged by the majority of straight men, but there is almost no discussion of it within straight spiritual literature[24] while it abounds in gay texts, in particular references to Joseph Kramer's *Body Electric* workshops (Thompson 1994: 170-80). Sharon Marcus' (2005) observations concerning Library of Congress classifications indicates that even in the quiet of the stacks masturbation has to do with anything other than straight men: 'Laqueur's *Solitary Sex* has been designated HQ447 – 'masturbation'. Like its call number, the book lies between homosexuality and feminism and forms a bridge between them' (2003: 213). Obviously there is nothing specifically gay about masturbation, rather gay men realize it more fully as part of a 'sense of reality', combining their sexual and spiritual practices.

Clearly the most fundamental challenge by queer theory to the masculine spiritualities of the previous chapters is to any notion of the authentically masculine. There can be no archetypes in queer theory, as archetypes are exemplars of stable identity. Without a stable masculine identity it is difficult for patriarchy to function as it operates by privileging a stable masculine identity and oppressing and even denying all identities which are other to it. Queer theology offers men all the benefits of gay spirituality but without the identity of 'gayness'. Queer theology allows for the fact that there are any

24. With the occasional exception such as Scott Haldeman (1996), although perhaps it should be noted that in a later article (Haldeman 2007) the author mentions the previous was written when he was 'at least purportedly "straight"' rather than his now open gayness (2007: 97-98).

number of ways of doing masculine spirituality, some of which might not even involve men (Halberstam 1998; Noble 2004). Unlike some expressions of gay spirituality, queer theology is not just about articulating the queer experiences of the individual; like liberation theology it is about actively critiquing and subverting oppressive regimes. Queer theology is *the* way out for any person who wants to articulate a non-patriarchal masculine spirituality.

Conclusion

Popular gay spirituality is primarily about gay liberation and the securing of a gay spiritual identity. While gay spirituality initially appears at odds with other forms of masculine spirituality, being on the wrong side of a heteronormative binary, there are nevertheless some commonalities with the mythopoetic movement via an appreciation of myth/fairytales, Jung, archetypes and a rather essentialist understanding of gender. In particular gay spirituality identifies the archetype of the Androgyne as emblematic of gay spirit, incorporating aspects of both the masculine and the feminine, and in doing so achieving some kind of unique vantage point from which to view the world. While critics note that the Androgyne operates within a heteronormative economy by adopting traditional notions of feminine and masculine (albeit blending them), the masculinity it encourages undermines the combative and domineering models of masculinity presented in the previous chapters, and in doing so has value.

Popular gay spirituality promotes various other themes which resist patriarchal tendencies. Toby Johnson suggested gay spirituality is insight-provoking and adaptively virtuous; Harry Hay introduced the subject-SUBJECT consciousness and claimed gay men are less competitive and interested in conquering nature. Both Johnson and Hay argued for a sex-positive spirituality. Popular gay spirituality also resonates with Buddhism, which suggests a more peaceful, contemplative masculine spirituality in contrast to the sword-wielding soldiers of the Christian men's movement. As well as actively encouraging transgressive masculine performances, the Radical Faeries also promote non-patriarchal themes, including a focus on earth-based spirituality that shares some commonality with ecofeminism. While gay spirituality is not so radically different from mythopoetic spirituality, it nevertheless is one of the few places where a masculine spirituality can avoid perpetuating the patriarchal status quo.

Gay theology, like popular gay spirituality, began with a celebration of gay identity, this time within the Church. Gay liberation theology moved beyond this identity to critically examine why gay men were being oppressed in the first place, and in doing so theologians such as Robert Goss and Gary David Comstock aligned their work with traditional liberation theology. Gay theology provides an alternative masculine spirituality to the Christian men's movement, challenging patriarchy as an oppressor rather than promoting its 'softer' version of servant leadership. McCleary's survey of the broad spectrum of gay spirituality concludes with the succinct comment that it is 'nothing less than an essentialist-grounded special illumination, the basis of a dynamic worldview. It is one that gays must be free to analyse and cultivate for themselves in a process from which any evolving society can benefit' (McCleary 2004: 338). Indeed, all masculine spiritualities can benefit.

Instead of focusing on the promotion of a gay identity, queer theology aims to destabilize notions of sexual identity within theology and at the same time the heteronormative institutions in which it functions. Growing out of gay and lesbian studies, queer can also be applied to straight people who seek to subvert categories of gender and in doing so challenge patriarchal oppression that relies on such stability. Queer theology loosens the ties between the non-patriarchal manifestations of gay spirituality and gay identity, thus making the gifts born from gayness more widely applicable.

While some clear commonality between the mythopoetic movement and popular gay spirituality can be identified via an appreciation of myth/fairytales, Jung, archetypes and a rather essentialist understanding of gender, it has been suggested that this commonality could make it possible for men familiar with mythopoetic spirituality to learn some lessons from gay spirituality. There is no such comparison between gay and queer theologies and the Christian men's movements. Those in the Christian men's movements who want to adopt less patriarchal models of masculinity must fundamentally depart from the movements' status quo. This does not require departing in any way from their faith tradition: Goss maintains as a central principle that 'Jesus used the symbol of God's reign (*basileia*) to speak of the liberating activity of

God among people' (Goss 1993: 72); Comstock argues, 'as ethical norms the Exodus and Jesus events function as a principle. ...central to each of these events is the unacceptability of pain and suffering inflicted upon one person or people by another' (Comstock 1993: 10). It requires departing from an understanding about what makes a Christian *man*, and in this regard both gay and queer theology provide some useful pointers.

It is noteworthy that while gay spirituality is included here as an example of 'masculine spirituality' it is done so because it happens to be a spirituality experienced and performed by men. Gay spirituality does not really describe itself in terms of masculine spirituality in the same way as the mythopoetic or Christian men's movements, nor is it masculine in an androcentric sense as with integral spirituality. So it is possible even after this whirlwind tour of gay spirituality to again ask the question: 'can we distinguish masculine spirituality from patriarchal spirituality' and still answer 'no'. We still have no useful (non-heteropatriarchal) application of the phrase 'masculine spirituality'. The next chapter reduces the likelihood of finding such as useful application even further by questioning whether we can really assign the phrase 'masculine spirituality' any accurate meaning at all.

Chapter Seven

SEXUAL DIFFERENCE, SPIRITUALITY AND SPACE

We have now seen various examples of how men have framed their definition of masculinity within spiritual contexts. For the most part, this definition has relied uncritically on heteronormative understandings of masculinity, whether based in archetypal realities, conservative biblical models of family dynamics, or the biologically determined trajectory of evolution. These understandings of masculinity are complemented by heteronormative expectations of femininity. When gender is understood in these ways the net effect tends to be a patriarchal spirituality. Gay spirituality is the one significant manifestation of masculinity and spirituality that resists patriarchy to a certain degree. The key difference between gay spirituality and other types of masculine spirituality is that it offers a more fluid understanding of what constitutes masculinity, which suggests a more critical examination of gender is crucial in resisting patriarchy. Indeed, secular and Christian mythopoeticism as well as integral spirituality, for all their allegedly masculine traits, rely on poorly developed understanding of sex and gender.

This chapter steps back from the more descriptive activities of previous chapters to consider some of the theoretical considerations which underpin masculine spirituality. In particular, different understandings of sexual difference are explored. Most of the literature regarding masculine spirituality understands sexual difference in biological terms via sex role theory, but this is of rather limited use and certainly does little to challenge the patriarchal nature of masculine spirituality: indeed, it is often used to perpetuate it. Another way of thinking about sex difference is explored via the work of Luce Irigaray, who speaks in these terms as a way of securing feminine (or women's) specificity on its own terms rather than being defined by men. The initial similarities between these two forms of sexual difference will be highlighted and unpacked. Further still, Judith Butler's understanding of sexual difference is suggested as particularly useful, one which moves beyond a rigid binary of masculine/man and feminine/woman.

Different ways of thinking sexual difference are then applied to masculine spirituality, noting how expectations that men should perceive the spiritual in ways appropriate to their biological sex leads to some confusion between understandings of sex and gender, of male spirituality and masculine spirituality. Indeed, such terminological confusions are shown to make discussions of 'masculine spirituality' problematic both in regard to the masculine and the spiritual; when Butler's more fluid understanding of the masculine is applied, the term becomes even more unstable.

The final section looks at the way sexual difference and masculine spirituality are expressed via spatiality: that the 'up' and 'out' are masculine and the 'down' and 'in' are feminine. This equation is shown to be another way for patriarchy to manifest, with the masculine up and out values often being allocated preferable status to the feminine down and in. Attempts at complementarity and holism to counter these skewed values are also critiqued as unavoidably reasserting those same values. Understanding sexual difference outside of a binary model suggests thinking space in equally diverse ways: Gilles Deleuze and Félix Guattari's rhizome is suggested as one such metaphor which allows space to be perceived outside of horizontal/vertical directionality and its consequent rigid gendering.

Sexual Difference

Perceptions of masculine spirituality rest largely on the particularity of the masculine experience, of sexual difference. Most popular proponents of masculine spirituality, while they do not articulate it as such, understand sexual difference via sex role theory, which argues that individuals should take on character attributes appropriate to their biological sex. For men, this generally involves asking the question highlighted by Joseph Pleck: 'what makes men less masculine than they should be, and what can be done about it?' (1987: 22). Masculine spirituality, as presented in the previous chapters, is riddled with statements about appropriate ways for men to understand their spiritually in accordance with their sex: archetypes, servant leaders and so forth. Two decades ago Pleck claimed that sex role theory was 'an event in psychology's history'

(1987: 38), yet it still seems to have a strong hold on masculine spirituality. We must look elsewhere for a more appropriate understanding of sexual difference, and for the tools for a critical examination of the theoretical basis of masculine spirituality.

One of the most influential advocates of sexual difference from a feminist position (philosophically, politically and spiritually) is Luce Irigaray, who argues 'sexual difference is probably the issue in our time which could be our "salvation" if we thought it through' (1993a: 5). There are very few people referred to in these pages who would disagree with this statement, but the conclusions drawn from it can vary immensely. The initial message that comes from Irigaray is that men and women's natures are different and particular: 'Man describes, narrates, states, collects, organizes. He doubles the world or creates it…Woman, for her part, chats, tattles, gossips, weaves inventions, fables, myths' (1993a: 138).

On one level, this appears to share some commonality with most treatments of masculine spirituality and its employment of sex role theory: men experience the spiritual in one way, women another. Indeed, Morny Joy, who provides an insightful examination of Irigaray from a religious perspective, identifies her habit of 'mythopoetic divinations' (2006: 27). Joy is troubled by Irgaray's 'uncritical claims to myth as a form of history that insist on promoting genuine "feminine" values' (2006: 29).[1] Irigaray exists in a zone of paradox in relation to the presentations of masculine spirituality as seen in the previous chapters. That she appeals to a mythical past to construct genuine gender values is clearly similar to the mythopoetic movement; that there are even such things as 'feminine values' appears closely aligned with Wilber's modelling of the 'feminine type'. It is therefore not surprising that there has been a long and inconclusive debate as to whether Irigaray's treatment of gender is essentialist and heteronormative (Butler 1999: 39-40; Butler and Cornell 1998; Fuss 1989: 70; Holmlund 1991; Schutte 1997; Stone 2006; Whitford 1991). Despite the fact that Irigaray seeks to resist phallocentrism in her discussion of sexual difference by

---

1. Joy also charts Irigaray's appeal to an ancient gynocracy in which mother/daughter relationships flourished. This period was supplanted by patriarchy and 'the resultant spiritual barrenness in the mother/daughter relationship is still evident today' (2006: 92). There is a striking similarity here with Bly who charged patriarchy (at least the form perverted by the industrial revolution) with driving a wedge between fathers and sons.

creating (possibly for the first time) a space in which to accurately think the feminine, critics such as Annamarie Jagose see Irigaray as 'not so much a departure from the phallic order as its reproduction in reverse' (Jagose 1994: 29).

However, these similarities do not mean that Irigaray would be welcomed by proponents of masculine spirituality, and certainly she would not be too keen on them. Her emphasis on feminine values would be considered by many in the mythopoetic movement as part of the contemporary denial of the deep masculine, resulting in the 'soft male'. In the Christian men's movements Gordon Dalbey and Patrick Arnold saw such appeals to a matriarchal past as spiritually primitive: if Arnold ever got around to reading Irigaray he would have placed her high on his list of 'gaialogians'. Wilber, too, would see such an appeal as a retreat to a period of less evolved consciousness, of being bound to the magical-archaic earth rather than transcending and including it. Irigaray would rightly see such resistance to her work as part of a phallocentric economy which denies the feminine. Her appeal to spiritual feminine values, whether or not one considers them essentialist at heart, is a resistance to such a denial: that is the double-edged sword of her work, 'the pharmakon, the remedy and the poison both' (Jagose 1994: 41). This does not mean that Irigaray's presentation of sexual difference is free of problems — far from it — but that to address them requires first having genuinely accommodated her critique of patriarchy rather than glossing over or denying it. To reiterate, the difference between the initially similar sexual differences articulated by masculine spirituality and Irigaray, is the former is interested in what is appropriate for biological sex defined within a masculine economy, whereas the latter is interested in sexual difference as a way of articulating the experiences of women (and, as argued below, atypical men) outside of that masculine economy.

The psychoanalytical feminist theorist, Bracha Ettinger, offers an alternative formulation of sexual difference which seeks to open up a 'feminine' possibility, but which avoids some of the essentialist and heternormative charges laid against Irigaray. Ettinger argues that sexual difference does not work on the personal level: 'Sex difference is a thinking apparatus...It holds and unfolds archetypes and ideals for the soul' (2004: 78). While Ettinger, like Irigaray, is keen on making rather absolutist remarks about the nature of man and woman, her feminine matrixial model is complicated by in-between space, '*a web of movements of borderlinking, between subject and object, among subjects and partial-subjects, between me and the stranger, and between some partial-subjects and partial objects*' (2004: 76), a less black and white difference, 'not the difference of that which is *opposite* versus that which is the *same*' (2004: 78) [original emphases]. Ettinger's sexual difference seems less about the nature of man and woman, and more about how to think about sexual difference in new ways: 'Feminist protest, militancy, political campaigns of equality, cultural battles of difference…are not rejected or out of place, but infiltrated and transformed from within by a different dimension' (Pollock 2004: 23).

Just as the sexual difference articulated by masculine spirituality and the feminist positions exemplified by Irigaray appear initially similar, so too the response to their critics. Mythopoets of all flavours would argue that a questioning of sexual difference results in less manly, soft men. Some feminists, understandably protective of women's desire to articulate experience on their own terms, also see a questioning of sexual difference as resulting in an 'insistence on sameness' (Grosz 1994: 208), or 'the androgyn' (Gatens 1991: 140). However, a questioning of sexual difference can also open up possibilities rather than simply closing them down: a more subtle appreciation of sexual difference charts the difference not between man and woman (or man and man or woman and woman), but *person* and *person*.

This argument is elegantly articulated by Judith Butler in *Gender Trouble* (1999: xxvi), as she highlights 'the tenuousness of gender "reality"'. Butler questions the presumption of a binary gender system in which there is some obvious connection between sex and gender, arguing instead for an appreciation of gender in which '*man* and *masculine* might just as easily signify a female body as a male one, and *woman* and *feminine* a male body as easily as a female one' (1999: 10). Butler's understanding of gender questions Irigaray's alleged essentialism by problematizing the relation between, and our definition of, *feminine* and *woman*. Gender is 'a shifting and contextual phenomenon…a relative point of convergence among culturally and historically specific sets of relations' (Butler 1999: 15). Irigaray's model of sexual difference, based upon the particularity of a rather singular feminine experience, is therefore based on an unstable term.

But where does this actually take us? At an absolute level it becomes problematic to use the words masculine and feminine at all, even the words man and woman, in both their gender-implied meaning and also physically, given a non-pathological (and therefore non-*corrected*) accommodation of intersex. While this space is graspable, and quite valid, it is not an easy one in which to live. A more sensible route is to maintain notions of masculine and feminine, of man and woman, of sexual difference, but to assign them a much looser, more fluid status. We certainly should not and cannot use these categories as primary criteria of difference. We can enjoy the creative character of gender and difference, 'tenuously constituted in time, instituted in an exterior space through a *stylized repetition of acts*' (Butler 1999: 179): performance art at its most fundamental. It is the borderland, the mestiza consciousness presented by Gloria Anzaldúa (1987): a space of in-between, but with the understanding that there really is nothing in which to be between; *in-between is the norm*, if it is possible to speak of the norm. Instead of sex difference being cast in terms of man and woman, masculine and feminine, either through a patriarchal economy or one which inverts it, we can think of 'a thousand tiny sexes' (Deleuze and Guattari 1987: 213), so that 'sexual difference itself move[s] beyond binarity into multiplicity' (Butler 2004b: 197).

Sexual Difference and Spirituality

As mentioned above, most articulations of masculine spirituality pursue an understanding of sexual difference based in sex role theory. Archetypal models of masculinity, hardwired in the brain, speak of a male sex role: king, warrior, magician, lover. That a man should lead his family according to biblical values speaks of a male sex role, even if of a secondary nature to biblical authority. Wilber's understanding of masculine and feminine types, even though potentially belonging to both men and women, speak of a male sex role: men focus on agency and ranking, whereas women focus on communion and linking.

Given that sex role theory is a rather outdated way of thinking about sex difference, it should come as little surprise that there is a good deal of confusion throughout much of the popular masculine spirituality literature about the nature of sex and gender: of one being biologically innate and the other socially constructed. The biologically derived nature of sex role theory underpins the literature, but there is also some awareness of how gender functions: the two strands are used interchangeably, and not because of some subtle appreciation of the interplay between the two, but because the terms are never addressed from the start in a satisfactory manner. A brief look at the titles of some of the main books referred to in previous chapters indicates this confusion: Arnold's subtitle refers to 'masculine spirituality' whereas Rohr and Martos' refers to 'male spirituality', when they are writing about the same thing. Wilber's magnum opus *Sex, Ecology, Spirituality*, refers to sex with its biological nature, yet his masculine and feminine types refer more to gender, while ultimately defaulting in meaning back to sex. Male spirituality, when applied accurately, should refer to a spirituality based in the biological reality of being male, whereas masculine spirituality should refer to one based in social constructions of gender. Even academic writing on the subject seems to gloss over these distinctions: on just one page J. D. Castellini *et al* (2005: 42) refer to 'male spirituality', 'men's spirituality' and masculinity without any inclination to unpack the differences in these terms; the title of their paper refers to male spirituality, but their conclusion argues that relationships with God are 'strongly affected by gender' (2005: 54). Similarly, Ian M. Harris (1997), whose paper title refers to male spirituality, writes interchangeably of both sex and gender in his discussion. Castellini and Harris' papers provide a useful opportunity to see how definition of terms, or lack of, both in regard to masculinity and spirituality, has made its study a sometimes confusing business.

Castellini, who uses the phrase 'male spirituality' identified the following motivations for men's involvement with spirituality: relationship with God; faith/prayer community; self-awareness, or relationship with self; isolation or existential emptiness; fear or grief; father-son relationships; coping strategies; male bonding, or relationships with other men. Castellini's findings beg some interesting questions about how 'masculine' and 'spiritual' masculine spirituality actually is. Of the motivations Castellini identified, only two (relationship with God and faith/prayer community) can accurately be described as spiritual (keeping in mind the Pauline distinction of *pneumatikos* and *psychikos anthropôs*). All the other motivations could equally be discussed in exclusively non-spiritual contexts. Of the motivations Castellini identified, only two (father-son relationships and male bonding) are uniquely 'masculine' (in terms of pertaining only to men), and neither of these count among the two motivations that are uniquely spiritual. In Castellini's findings there is no single variable that is at once uniquely masculine *and* spiritual. In chapter two it was argued that it was a mistake to describe the mythopoetic movement as the 'spiritual men's movement' because nearly everything it articulates is not spiritual, but psychic. While the psychic *can be* spiritual, it is not necessarily so, as its main site of exploration is within the individual, rather than the spiritual whose ultimate concern should be transpersonal. Castellini's findings suggest male/masculine spirituality, like mythopoetic spirituality, is actually more psychic than spiritual.

Similar conclusions can be drawn from Ian M. Harris (1997) who undertook several surveys among predominantly Christian men, the results of which he collated into the 'Ten Tenets of Male Spirituality'. These are: finding inner wisdom; searching for truth; speaking from the heart; confronting the dark side; loving; working for a better world; passing a test; belonging to something great; following scripture; believing in destiny. Harris locates these tenets within a spiritual context, but even the hardest atheist would happily sign up for all but the last two (following scripture and believing in destiny); as it is the participants of Harris' study ranked those two tenets as the least important. The highest ranked tenet was 'belonging to something great', which resonates with the mythopoetic fascination with wilderness: conflating something larger than the individual with the spiritual, when it is not necessarily the case. Furthermore, not one of those tenets is 'masculine' or 'male': they are simply factors that influenced the study participants who happen to be men.[2] Rather than 'Ten Tenets of Male Spirituality' Harris has actually defined 'Ten Tenets of Spirituality Perceived By Some Men', a perfectly worthy exercise, but of a very different nature (a similar point can be made about most of the motivations behind the Castellini study).

It is this reluctance to engage much of the fundamental theory regarding sex and gender, as well as the more obvious ideological differences, that has resulted in such a disconnect between most

---

2. To his credit, Harris does acknowledge this in his conclusion, but this does not alter the fact that the general impression of his study is to bring some definition to 'male spirituality'.

popular literature about masculine spirituality and other dialogues between gender and religion, such as feminist theology. In short, masculine spirituality is rather backward in its understanding of gender, as much of the previous chapters attest. The above discussion of sexual difference offers a persuasive refutation of most forms of masculine spirituality. Despite the fact that Irigaray should secure to some extent the function of masculine spirituality, arguing as she does for stable notions of gender identity, she would nonetheless reject it for being a perpetuation of an economy of maleness which allows little or no reality for women. If, with Butler, we conclude that the categories of masculine and feminine are too problematic to be used in anything but the loosest sense, we must also conclude that the term 'masculine spirituality' has little, or at least rather loose value.

To discard masculine spirituality in this manner also means, to a certain extent, discarding feminine spirituality. Clearly, for Irigaray and other feminist proponents of feminine/women's spirituality, the first charge of perpetuating an economy of maleness does not hold. However, Butler's understanding of gender certainly problematizes what we understand as feminine spirituality. To discard feminine spirituality feels more counterintuitive than masculine spirituality, familiar as we are with the well-articulated and attractive themes of the goddess, nurturing, weaving and so forth. But of course, these themes are not discarded, rather the assumed connection with the feminine and consequently the category of woman: either these themes are no longer considered feminine at all, or they remain feminine and equally applicable to men as women. All we can really talk about in any productive fashion is 'men *and* spirituality' and 'women *and* spirituality'.

This reframing of terms avoids some of the problems highlighted by the Castellini and Harris studies: it is much easier to talk with some accuracy about men's experiences of the spiritual, rather than the immensely complex implications of 'male spirituality', 'masculine spirituality' or even 'men's spirituality'. To speak in these terms in any useful way is to require at the very least a sound understanding of the following: the biological nature of the religious experience and how this differs between male and female subjects; the constructed and performative nature of gender and how masculine spirituality is about female masculinities as well as male; the dynamics of power and regulation behind a possessive spirituality 'belonging' to men. All these questions are being fruitfully explored elsewhere, but unfortunately not in the material under discussion. Until that moment, *all we can speak of are different people's experiences of the spiritual.* The resultant spiritualities take us back to the queer realms of the previous chapter, spiritualities which resist all static sexual categories, at once politically subversive and playful.

There are some articulations of sexual difference and spirituality which can be usefully employed, but they are not those based in sex role theory. For example, within the allegedly essentialist articulations of Irigaray's sexual specificity there is room for multiple readings: her project of *écriture feminine* can be considered to offer some promise for men and spirituality, at least for its potential, if not current reality. Consider the following statement:

> Are women's ways of breathing, women's breath different from those of men? The feminine breath seems at once more linked with the life of the universe and more interior. It seems to unite the subtlest real of the cosmos with the deepest spiritual real of the soul (Irigaray 2004: 166).

Initially, we are left to wonder if indeed Irigaray believes there is actually some particularity to women's breath. If so, we are then left to wonder if indeed Irigaray believes that particularity is intrinsically more spiritual than the breath of men. There is a good chance this is actually what Irigaray means, but her intentions can be appropriated for the cause of an accommodation of men and spirituality. How we get there is made clear through Butler's reading of Ettinger: again it is Ettinger who offers what might be called an *écriture liminale.*

Butler (2004a: 98) suggests that Ettinger's matrix predates notions of identity, questioning the ability to use the word *feminine*, which further muddies the waters of sexual difference. Indeed, Ettinger's notion of sexual difference, of female sexual specificity, 'is not the same thing as anatomy or morphology' (Pollock 2004: 8), offering more of a theoretical feminine alternative to a Freudian-Lacanian phallocentric economy than something explicitly connected with women in any 'actual' sense: 'the Matrix is not about women, but about a feminine dimension of plurality and difference of the several in joint subjectivity' (Ettinger 1996: 152). In the end, Ettinger's sexual difference is focused on the feminine, but as Butler suggests, its pre-ontological nature produces a feminine space for *all*; thus, importantly, 'the feminine under the Matrix marks not the phallus-negated other, but a different site of sexual difference that is not about binary logic' (Pollock 2004: 11).

What, then, if we re-read Irigaray in this light? Irigaray's ethics of sexual difference may well intend to create a space for women and the feminine, but its 'difference' can also be seen as more fundamental. Irigaray's *Divine Women* can then be interpreted as *Divine People Outside of a Phallocentric Economy of Sameness*.[3] Now re-read 'the feminine breath seems at once more linked with the life of the universe and more interior. It seems to unite the subtlest real of the cosmos with the deepest spiritual real of the soul'. If this statement must be read literally, then certainly it must be rejected as nonsense, but if feminine breath is simply that which resists patriarchy then it is certainly reasonable, and is also inclusive of some men: 'the only task, the only obligation laid upon us is: to become divine men and women, to become perfectly, to refuse to allow parts of ourselves to shrivel and die that have the potential for growth and fulfilment' (Irigaray 1993b: 68-69). This is the kind of spirituality with which men need to be engaged, and which the concluding chapter will build upon.

Masculine Spirituality and Space

One of the most fundamental, yet little questioned ways that sexual difference is articulated within spirituality, is that the spiritual has a spatial nature and that this in turn is gendered. Much of the conversation about masculine and feminine spirituality is based on the assumption that the 'up' and 'out' are masculine and the 'down' and 'in' are feminine. Despite the fact that mythopoetic archetypes are interior beings (Bly 1990: 227; Moore and Gillette 1992a: 51) we find examples of an outward masculine nature in the Christian mythopoets. Remember Dalbey's comments about the idolatrous nature of feminine 'earth-bound theologies' which must be transcended (1988: 42). Similarly, Arnold writes, 'in contrast to feminine spirituality, which is inward and interior and rooted in Mother Earth, male spirituality is outwardly orientated and spatial' (1991: 39). Wilber's vision of the integral continues this path, relegating Gaia-focused spiritualities to archaic consciousness

3. See also Grosz (1995: 121).

(down/in) in favour of a masculinized altitude or transcendence (up/out).

Spiritually, this theme has been going on for a very long time to the point where it has become highly naturalized. The equation of earth as Mother has clearly been ingrained in much of human culture since ancient times; even more theologically 'advanced' suggestions such as the feminine nature of the soul, with all its interiority, initially appear quite plausible. However, this distinction has significant repercussions throughout most of our understandings of both masculine and feminine spirituality, guiding our language, aesthetics and how we imagine ourselves to be connected to the spiritual realities beyond our mundane experiences. And, despite the adoption of the formula by some feminine spiritualities, the gendered nature of spiritual space provides another venue in which patriarchy proliferates.

The spatialization of the spiritual is only to be expected. George Lakoff and Mark Johnson have shown that metaphorical spatialization or 'orientation' is part of the method by which we understand and articulate the world around us: 'most of our fundamental concepts are organised in terms of one or more spatialisation metaphors' (2003: 17); just think of the subtitle of the previous chapter, 'a way out for men'. We therefore understand spirituality in part by metaphorically orientating ourselves within it. Another reason spirituality is spatialized can be deduced from Doreen Massey's theorizing of space. Massey highlights a common but faulty dichotomous logic which seeks to allocate things to either time or space. In this logic, that which is lacking a temporal dimension is considered in stasis, and is therefore spatial (1994: 271). Spirituality has a certain elusive character of timelessness, so is also, in that dichotomous logic, spatial. Furthermore, Massey critiques Fredric Jameson's equation that space is that which is unrepresentable (1991: 266). Again, spirituality has a certain elusive character of being unrepresentable, and can thus be perceived as spatial.

Nor should it come as any surprise that space (and spiritual space) is gendered. Henri Lefebvre (1991) argues that space is produced through social interaction. Gender is a fundamental aspect of social interaction and as such space is 'gendered through and through' (Massey 1994: 186). Much of the research about gender and space rightly shows how it is carved up into men's and women's spaces, largely in favour of men. Daphne Spain argues, 'gendered spaces provide the concrete, everyday-life grounding for the production, reproduction, and transformation of status differences' (1992: 233). But it is also interesting to consider how directionality in space is gendered, and thus the values assigned to the 'up' and 'out' of masculine spirituality and the 'down' and 'in' of feminine spirituality.

Lakoff and Johnson's exploration of orientational metaphors highlight some of the values given to up and down metaphors: happy is up, sad is down; conscious is up, unconscious is down; health and life are up, sickness and death are down; having control or force is up, being subject to control or force is down; more is up, less is down; high status is up, low status is down; good is up, bad is down; virtue is up, depravity is down; rational is up, emotional is down (2003: 15-17). They argue such spatialization is grounded in our bodies and physical and cultural experience, 'they are not randomly assigned' (2003: 18): happy is up because our posture is erect when happy; conscious is up because we stand up when awaking from sleep. Lefebvre, too, claims 'the whole of (social) space proceeds from the body' (1991: 405). But of course, there are factors at play which shape our physical and cultural experience. If we consider how gender functions in these spatial metaphors we see that most, if not all, of the up metaphors are equated with 'masculine values' and the down with 'feminine values'.[4] Certainly these equations 'are not randomly assigned' within a patriarchal economy, as they underscore its dynamics of power, but they are randomly assigned inasmuch as they bear little relation to the actuality of men and women's physical bodies *outside* of that patriarchal economy. Lakoff and Johnson argue that in the equation of, say, MORE IS UP, 'the IS should be viewed as a shorthand for some set of experiences on which the metaphor is based and in terms of which we understand it' (2003: 29). In the context of gender,

4. Lefebvre makes the same point in relation to what he describes as 'absolute space' which is of a religio-political nature: 'Altitude and verticality are often invested with a special significance, and sometimes even with an absolute one (knowledge, authority, duty)...horizontal space symbolises submission, vertical space power' (1991: 236). Irigaray (1993b) makes a similar point, referring to the two fishes of Pisces, the fish going upward is thought of exclusively as male, whereas the fish going down is female. In terms of gendered and directional value, the descent is considered first fabled, then diabolical (1993b: 60, n. 2).

the IS is the regulatory and power dynamics of patriarchy. These up/down in/out values have also been mirrored by the age-long and naturalized dichotomy that men belong to the public realm and women to the private.[5] The public is up and out, the private is down and in. In this respect, the values allocated to directionality appear as just another patriarchal tool.

Further spatial issues surrounding patriarchy can be 'mapped' onto the spiritual. Grosz's commentary on Irigaray notes that men have a tendency to erase the contribution of women/mothers to their lives and 'hollow their own interiors and project them outward, and then require women as supports for this hollowed space' (1995: 121). A projection outwards can also be seen as an act of colonization, itself a masculine endeavour (Mills 2005: 55; Phillips 1997), one which both abandons the feminine domestic sphere and also perceives the territory it conquers as feminine (Kolodny 1975). In this light, the typically transcendent nature of masculine spirituality can be seen as part of this projection outward from Mother Earth, which seeks to both flee and conquer the feminine in the spiritual domain.

Of course, historically, given that history itself has largely been a masculine project, these masculine values have been considered superior to feminine values, and their default status within society has made it unnecessary to bring special attention to them. However, second-wave feminism has seen more prominence given to those feminine values. The refocus on the up and out of masculine spirituality clearly comes as a responsive act of panic, a public relations offensive in the face of feminine spirituality's obvious good health and sustainability. Just as men's ministries are not really a response to the fading of men within the Church, but rather an anxiety about having to share power, so too a reassertion of the up and out: it is not masculine values that are in danger, rather the pre-eminence of masculine values.

The good health and sustainability of what we perceive to be feminine spirituality cannot help but cast masculine spirituality in a

---

5. We have already seen in chapter 5 that Ken Wilber bases much of his understanding of gender on a biologically determined split between public/private and masculine/feminine, one which would continue even in the noosphere. The same reasoning is implicit in most of the discussion about servant leadership in chapters 3 and 4, and to a certain extent also in the discussion of boys being initiated into 'public' manhood in chapter 2.

rather toxic light. Masculine spirituality is analogous to the oil and tobacco industries: everyone knows them to be bad, but such is the mass investment in them that it seems almost unimaginable to reject them out of hand. The alternative is to complement these historical anomalies with mitigating measures: carbon credits and health warnings. In recent years the tension between up/out and down/in has been unwittingly compounded by similar and well-intentioned attempts at holism and complementarity.[6] These voices understandably question certain skewed trends in spirituality which are largely perceived as pathologically masculine, and suggest they be tempered with the feminine (it is noticeable that only rarely is the feminine asked to complement itself with the masculine). For example, Matthew Fox, a straight theologian whose gender insights have given him a curiously privileged position within gay spiritual circles (Mcleary 2004: 300-301) claims, 'males are meant to mirror a "Father Sky" Divinity while also honouring the "Mother Earth" side in them' (quoted in Gelfer 2006b: 187). Fox's intention is for men to get in touch with their feminine side, which at first glance is a perfectly reasonable suggestion. But the problem is his equation compounds the connection between the masculine sky/up and the feminine earth/down, it secures the categories while trying to escape them: as Butler notes, 'to be not quite masculine or not quite feminine is still to be understood exclusively in terms of one's relationship to the "quite masculine" and the "quite feminine"'(Butler 2004: 42).

6. There is a comparable discussion to be had about the dimensional partner to space: time. Grosz argues that 'time, even more than space, needs to be thought in terms which liberate it from the constraints of the present' (2005: 178). Grosz's treatment of time, or rather futurity, is initially very appealing as it notes the patriarchal nature of the present and the past and looks to a future populated by women's becomings: 'the only time of sexual difference is that of the future' (2005: 176). If we can overlook the fact that (at least theoretical) sexual difference does exist in the present, we find that Grosz's rather dissociative focus on futurity is in part to do with a faulty project of complementarity. Grosz (building on Irigaray) follows Kant's formulation that time is masculine and space feminine, and believes the feminine must embrace time because they have historically been associated with space (which is here understood as limiting) rather than time/becoming (2005: 177). The most sensible response to Kant's equation is to reject out of hand the restrictive gendering of space and time. But Grosz and Irigaray's response is to accept that space and time are gendered and to complement Kant's skewing of the equation by 'feminising' time. This may work in terms of articulating women's potential becomings, but the danger is perpetuating Kant's mis-gendering and becoming, once again, 'not so much a departure from the phallic order as its reproduction in reverse' (Jagose 1994: 29).

A similar process occurs with Irigaray who suggests 'the link uniting or reuniting masculine and feminine must be horizontal and vertical, terrestrial and heavenly' (1993a: 17). Irigaray gives the impression she is seeking a whole, but it is a whole made of binary opposites, the traditional assumption of masculinity lending itself to the vertical and heavenly and femininity to the horizontal and terrestrial. Irigaray clearly has some awareness that there is a problem with the typical way sexual difference engages space, and its delimiting nature, suggesting, 'perhaps we are passing through an era when *time must redeploy space?*' (1993a: 17, original emphasis). Irigaray alludes to this awareness again in her discussion of place in Aristotle, saying, 'astonishingly there is no suggestion here of a spherical place where no clear-cut distinction between up and down would obtain' (1993a: 44-45), which implies a desire to escape the regulatory function of directionality.

Irigaray's appeal to holism is also evident with her further employment of the sphere image: she refers to sexual intercourse where, 'bodies also face the issue of fitting one inside the other, without thereby altering the other dimensions. Can this be understood as the constitution, together, of a spherical or almost spherical form?' (1993a: 45) But again Irigaray's sphere is a false totality, as it is made up of binary opposites, rather than one or two people (three, four or more?) who are total (spherical) in and among themselves. Irigaray's sphere is a yin-yang made flesh, one body forever light, the other dark, genitalia tessellating in some mythic symmetry. A true sphere would move beyond the two into the many, a twilight (or rainbow) experience.

Ultimately, we should not speak of spiritual spatiality in gendered terms, or at least not in such a rigid fashion. To rephrase Butler's earlier comments about the fluid nature of gender, '*up* and *out* might just as easily signify feminine spirituality as masculine, and *down* and *in* masculine spirituality as easily as feminine'. And complementarity, while seeking a solution to a masculine spirituality that is clearly problematic, does nothing but perpetuate the definitions it seeks to escape. Even holism, exemplified by Irigaray's sphere, seems rather weak as an answer to the complexity of the spiritual-spatial-sexual terrain. Indeed the sphere itself, despite its seemingly feminine curves, as opposed to the masculine straight line and right angle, also has a certain masculinist nature: of totality, of geometric perfection, a Wilberian integration. The sphere has none of Ettinger's accommodating topography: the web, borderlands, partial objects and subjects, no 'sense of reality'. To think spatially about spirituality and — if one must — gender, requires a different kind of orientating metaphor.

A good place to start in this reorientation process is Deleuze and Guattari's concept of the rhizome, which can be applied to both thought and space. Regular space is 'tree logic' or arborescent: Deleuze and Guattari seek a rhizomatic space, 'stranger to any idea of genetic axis or deep structure' (1987: 12). Immediately, rhizomatic or 'smooth' space sounds like an appropriate alternative to the inward/outward space sketched by Arnold or even Irigaray, having 'no beginning or end; it is always in the middle, between things, interbeing, *intermezzo*' (1987: 25).[7] Nor is arborescent or striated space just an incorrect set of assumptions. Gendered (*which we can arguably equate with striated*) space is actively imposed upon us in a regulatory manner: 'One of the fundamental tasks of the State is to striate the space over which it reigns, or to utilize smooth spaces as a means of communication in the service of striated space' (1987: 385). In our main context, the State can be considered patriarchy, which imposes gendered striation such as the private/public dichotomy on to spirituality. One example of the utilization of smooth (gender troubled) space in the service of striated space would be the neo-liberal mobilization of gay subjects, of homonormativity.

This leads to what one might call a Deleuzian spirituality.[8] Deleuze and Guattari have little patience for God, 'the centre or the signifier; the faciality of the god or despot' (1987: 135), often being compelled in the same sentence to employ 'the judgment of'. They do, however, have a soft spot for shamanism, 'the most beautiful and most spiritual' (1987: 176), including several positive references to Carlos Castaneda, or at least the lessons of his Don Juan. This is not because they romanticize shamanism as a pre-Capitalist space, but because there is something essentially schizoid about the shaman, dwelling

7. Here in the Pacific, instead of the rhizome/tree couplet we could offer the alternative *archipelago/continental*, with the latter's dual meaning of both continental-mass unity and also the historical lineage of continental philosophy.

8. Rhizomatics within a spiritual context appears to share some commonality with what is currently being described as 'participatory' or 'peer to peer' spirituality, as defined by Ferrer (2002) and Heron (2006). Theologically, Althaus-Reid (2003) has made deft use of Deleuze.

in between worlds, simultaneously *in different* worlds. For the same reason they embrace the role of sorcerers who have, 'always held the anomalous position, at the edge of the fields or woods. They haunt the fringes. They are at the borderline of the village, or *between* villages' (1987: 246). The shamanistic space Deleuze and Guattari refer to is clearly spiritual, and rhizomatic/nomad space is also spiritual (although by no means exclusively so). Consider their quite beautiful image of sand and ice deserts:

> There is no line separating earth and sky; there is no intermediate distance, no perspective or contour; visibility is limited; and yet there is an extraordinarily fine topology that relies not on points or objects but rather on haecceities, on sets of relations (winds, undulations of snow or sand, the song of the sand or the creaking of the ice, the tactile qualities of both). It is a tactile space, or rather "haptic," a sonorous much more than a visual space. The variability, the polyvocality of directions, is an essential feature of smooth spaces of the rhizome type, and it alters their cartography. The nomad, nomad space, is localized and not delimited. (Deleuze and Guattari 1987: 382)

This is a good description of the kind of spiritual space free of gendered spatial restrictions, free from assumptions about the individual, not delimited.[9] It suggests a mood of non-duality or mystical union ('no line separating earth and sky') as well as an attunement to the desert, and the localized nomad within it, that resembles an eco-spirituality that might appeal to the mythopoetic imagination.

In much the same way that Deleuze and Guattari's rhizomatic/nomad space can be read as spiritual and free of gendered nature, so too Ettinger's matrixial space. It has already been mentioned that the matrix is pre-ontological, and thus pre-gender. In terms of the matrix as spiritual space, consider its dangers as sketched by Griselda Pollock (2004), 'of madness, of psychosis, with no signifiers to relieve phantasms and hallucinations that bleakly register both the trauma and the solace of what we now come to recognise as the matrixial dimension' (2004: 21). Is this not another, darker weaving

---

9. It is interesting to note that the largest living thing on the planet, the 'humongous fungus' discovered in 2001 in Oregon's Blue Mountains and covering an area of 9.65 square kilometres is of a rhizomatic nature, and has challenged science's understanding of what constitutes an individual entity: 'Extensive *A. ostoyae* genets develop because of host continuity and lack of spatial restrictions imposed by conspecific genets' (Ferguson, Dreisbach, Parks, Filip, and Schmitt 2003: 621).

of a place we have heard of before? Of sacramental mystery? Âtman? Non-dual awareness? The 'thresholds of *I* and *non-I* emerging in co-existence' (Ettinger 1992: 176)?[10]

Ettinger's matrix, 'a web of movements of borderlinking' also makes sense as spiritual space when read in light of Veikko Anttonen's understanding of spiritual territory. Anttonen, extending Victor Turner's understanding of liminality, argues that anomalous aspects of terrain such as rocks, springs or cracks in the ground take on a sacred nature due to acting as a border, being the gate between the sacred and the profane (Anttonen 1996: 49-50). Bodily openings also function as border zones, taking on a sacred nature (1996: 52). Lefebvre makes a similar point regarding the special nature of boundaries in his theorizing of how space is produced (1996: 193). The whole idea of border territory, of the space between the masculine up and out and the feminine down and in — a queer space — then becomes charged with spiritual significance.[11]

While it may not be possible to avoid thinking of spirituality in spatial terms, as Lakoff and Johnson seem to suggest, it *is* possible to resist gendering spatiality in such a rigid fashion, especially a less earth-bound spatiality as the spiritual. As the above discussion of up and down shows, various values attributed to directionality reflect long-held patriarchal assumptions, and these should be resisted. Certainly there is ample opportunity to orientate within the spiritual along border zones and between spaces rather than at the polar ends of a deep vertical axis, and these spaces almost inevitably resist gendering which tends to be framed by binary opposites. Ultimately, it may be best to do away altogether with the gendering of spiritual space, to abandon perceptions of the masculine as outward and transcendent. This is hardly a controversial statement given the generally pathological nature of masculine spirituality, but again, what of the feminine? An

10. There is a mind-bending tangent for the psychoanalytically gifted to unpack here about how pre-individuated spaces such as Ettinger's matrix and the Lacanian Real function spiritually, about how one might truly grapple with their spiritual-spatial-(pre)gendered nature.

11. Anzaldúa's borderland and mestiza consciousness is again ripe for appropriation in this sacred context. Anzaldúa always knew these ideas would be stretched beyond their initial sexual and ethnically specific context. In one interview (Reuman 2000) Anzaldúa expressed the only real annoyance she had with this was not being cited frequently enough as the metaphor's originator (2000: 5-6).

abandonment of the masculine as outward and transcendent necessitates an abandonment of the feminine as inward and immanent. Who is prepared to let go of 'feminine spirituality', the ransom, at a theoretical level, for abandoning masculine spirituality?

The removal of feminine along with masculine space looks suspiciously like another project of erasure on behalf of the malestream author, but can be understood as a liberation of feminine space from its current enclosure into the full territory of spiritual space. Feminine space itself has been produced within and by a masculinist economy: for Lefebvre, the whole development of space has happened under the 'dominance of the male principle…Whence the use and overuse of straight lines, right angles, and strict (rectilinear) perspective' (1991: 410-11).[12] Lefebvre thinks an alternative, feminine inversion of this condition would be 'a pity' (1991: 410), not because he is resistant to a feminist project, but because he sees the danger of the 'reproduction in reverse' charged against Irigaray.[13] In this liberated space the value of down and in remains intact, as does, for what it is worth, the up and out. The only difference is that any person can pick and choose any part of spiritual space, rather than that which their gender has assigned to them. In all probability, this will make little difference to the choices of most women, who will opt to remain associated with the values of down and in. But more men may choose to turn their backs on the wild frontier of transcendent space and begin the long journey back to earth: 'The first man is of the earth' (1 Cor. 15:47). There is value here for both the men who seek to change and the women and atypical men who are less likely to be oppressed in the process.

12. When discussing Roman representational space, Lefebvre could easily be referring to Wilber's spirituality and how it defines feminine space. Representational space was of a masculine nature: 'the masculine principle, military, authoritarian, juridical — and dominant; and the feminine, which, though not denied, is integrated, thrust down into the "abyss" of the earth, as the place where seeds are sown and the dead are laid, as "world"' (1991: 245). In Wilber's integral spirituality, the feminine is similarly 'integrated', the abyss of the earth being archaic consciousness. Remember also that David Deida equates women as 'world', both of which should be fucked to smithereens.

13. It is interesting to speculate how Lefebvre would have revised his theorizing of space in light of queer theory.

Conclusion

Masculine spirituality is based on an assumption that we can talk about 'the masculine'. This assumption is framed by a debate regarding sexual difference via sex role theory: that men and women should act in ways appropriate to their biological sex. Within patriarchy, the purpose of this distinction is largely to define women in a certain way, as other to men, and then to oppress them. But sexual difference can also function in alternate ways. Luce Irigaray argues for women's sexual specificity as part of a project that resists patriarchy. On a superficial level these two articulations of sexual difference look similar: that men do *this* and women do *that*. But Irigaray intends to offer the feminine as an alternative to patriarchy: women defined by and written in their own terms, not as the Other. Bracha Ettinger's take on sexual difference shows it to be, ultimately, a thinking apparatus outside of the phallocentric economy. Judith Butler provides a further, arguably more persuasive treatment of sex difference and gender which allocates a far more fluid meaning to the terms: where feminine can be applied to man as easily as masculine to woman. With Butler, sexual difference is liberated from binary opposition into the multiple: we no longer have to be one thing or another, but can exist between things.

   It soon becomes clear that insufficient attention has been allocated to sexual difference in the world of masculine spirituality. There is confusion between basic terms such as sex and gender that spans not only popular literature on the subject, but also the scholarly. A similar confusion takes place with the use of the term 'spirituality', exemplified by a conflation of anything larger than the individual with the spiritual. In the end it becomes difficult to say with any certainty what 'masculine spirituality' actually means, even on its own terms, let alone applying any external critical tools. When a more sophisticated understanding of sexual difference is applied to masculine spirituality it is again found wanting. Irigaray's understanding of sexual difference resists masculine spirituality as part of a patriarchal order. Butler problematizes it further by creating a zone of flexibility around the meaning and application of the term, 'masculine'. If the terms masculine and feminine are understood as less solid categories then so must the terms masculine spirituality and feminine spirituality.

One important way sex and gender difference is articulated is via a spatial understanding of the spiritual: that the masculine is up and out and the feminine down and in. Doreen Massey and Daphne Spain argue that space is gendered, usually to the detriment of women, and many of the values George Lakoff and Mark Johnson assign to the up and out and down and in confirm this, with the more positive up values more typically assigned to the masculine. In recent years one method used to counter a skew in directional values (usually towards the up and out) is to promote the idea of complementarity or holism: that men should get in touch with their feminine side. At first glance this is an admirable intention, but ultimately it does little more than compound the problem of the existence of gendered directionality and values rather than resisting them. The alternative is to stop thinking about spiritually in spatial terms focused solely around vertical and horizontal axes. Gilles Deleuze and Félix Guattari's rhizome offers one such example of a more dispersed and smooth space, which resists the regulatory function of striation that partly operates by gendering space. Ettinger's matrix is another option which shows that the 'feminine' does not necessarily have anything to do with women, rather a way of thinking outside gender binary logic in terms of borderlines and partiality. These queer spaces, always in the middle, between things, interbeing, intermezzo, take on a particularly spiritual nature due to their anomalous and liminal nature.

Ultimately, the understanding of sexual difference employed by masculine spirituality promotes a very limited way of being a man and doing masculinity. It should, then, come as no surprise that masculine spirituality manifests in the largely unsavoury ways outlined in the previous chapters. On the whole, reverting to biologically determined roles for men and women essentializes gender in a way that enables patriarchy to continue, and masculine spirituality plays its part in this process. When different understandings of sexual difference are applied to masculine spirituality the possibilities begin to proliferate, although in that process the term 'masculine spirituality' becomes increasingly less stable. In previous chapters it was suggested that participants of masculine spirituality can be unaware that it manifests in such explicitly patriarchal ways: they are often blind to the implications of their own project by good intentions coupled with poor critical awareness of their actions. The same can be said, in part, for the treatment of sex and gender. Certainly there are some men who actively seek to oppress women and atypical men by appealing to biological sex roles, but others simply drift by without ever giving the matter any serious thought and rarely face any impetus to change as the status quo ensures their continued privilege. How the relationship between men and spirituality might begin to change will be suggested in the next, concluding chapter.

Chapter Eight

Conclusion

I began by introducing masculine spirituality on its own terms, about how it is concerned with articulations of masculinity and spirituality that are appropriate for and resonate with men. On its own terms, and in an ideal world, masculine spirituality should complement feminine spirituality and provide a framework in which the different experiences of men and women — of different people — can be expressed and honoured within a spiritual context. This, I am convinced, is the underlying intention of most advocates of masculine spirituality. But unfortunately, good intentions do not necessarily result in comparably good effects. My argument has been that instead of innocently bearing witness to the experiences of men in what might otherwise be perceived as an overly feminine spiritual economy, masculine spirituality actually promotes an all-too-familiar patriarchal spirituality. This patriarchal spirituality encourages a certain type of hegemonic masculinity that dominates women and subordinate masculinities; it does this chiefly by defining masculinity by archetypes, revising the definition of and depoliticising patriarchy, and encouraging what it perceives to be an authentic masculinity via the adoption of sex role theory.

Archetypes

One of the common strands of the various forms of masculine spirituality addressed was the employment of archetypes to define, explain and promote a certain type of masculinity. The origins of archetypes in masculine spirituality, echoing Jung's idea of the collective unconscious, are internal to all men. For Robert Bly, archetypes were located deep in the psychic depths of the individual, for Robert Moore and Douglas Gillette the reptilian core of the human brain, for Patrick Arnold holy characters from the Bible. Whatever their source, archetypes have a habit of reflecting the society from which they are drawn, of being 'calcifications of a patriarchal world view' (Culbertson 1993: 222). We are told that because archetypes are located in some archaic or magical part of human consciousness we are bound by them, and to try and deny or escape their influence is a futile task and potentially damaging for society. This is unfortunate because the masculinity promoted by archetypes is of a patriarchal nature and results in a patriarchal spirituality.

Bly's Wild Man, the archetype of archetypes, sets this ball in motion. Like *Brut* cologne, the Wild Man is the essence of man, whose characteristics are offered as the antidote to today's 'soft male' who has too often succumbed to both the feminization of society and feminism. For a man to access the Wild Man he must retreat into his psychic depths, into the forest, into a pre-Christian pagan space of hirsute manliness. Bly intends the Wild Man, with his relationship with the young boy of the *Iron John* story, to be an example of how men can be initiated into adulthood and the deep masculine. This would be a worthy exercise if it enabled boys to flourish for both their own sakes and the good of the community, but instead *Iron John* 'celebrate[s] violence and killing as the means to establish male identity' (Zipes 1992: 16). This is the archetypal path established by Bly.

This path is then followed and extended by various other mythopoetic writers, chief among whom are Moore and Gillette who developed at length the archetypes of King, Warrior, Magician and Lover. In this quartet it is the explicitly patriarchal archetypes — the King and Warrior — which have received most attention. Moore and Gillette provide numerous examples in which kingly energy operates, supposedly for the good of the individual and society at large, by creating order out of chaos and meting out justice. Regular men are encouraged to 'access the king in the male psyche' and reproduce this cosmic equilibrium in their own lives and the people with whom they interact. But at best the King is a benevolent dictator, at worst a despot: hardly an appropriate model on which to base the spirituality of men. This disturbing precedent is continued with Moore and Gillette encouraging men to access the warrior in the male psyche, whose natural presence is indicated by the fact that chimpanzees resort to battle, and men's fascination with war movies such as *Apocalypse Now*, *Platoon*, and *Full Metal Jacket*. Moore and Gillette would have their readers believe it is natural for mythopoetically inclined men to imagine themselves operating within the presumably dark and oppressive jungle, senses alert for other hostile primates, or perhaps the Viet Cong.

The influence of Bly's Wild Man, and archetypes in general, reached beyond the mythopoetic movement to the Christian men's movement. In an evangelical context Gordon Dalbey relied heavily on Bly in his construction of a more manly Christianity revolving around the masculine roles of the father, warrior, lover of a woman, and provider. Fellow evangelical, Stu Weber, promoted the warrior archetype, of which Jesus was exemplar, 'on a white horse, in a bloodspattered robe, with a sword in His mouth and a rod of iron in His hand' (1993: 41). John Eldredge also made much of the theme of wildness and how Christian men have to take on warrior attributes. In a Catholic context, Patrick Arnold aligned masculine spirituality with the archetypes of Wild Man, Warrior and King, along with a host of largely Old Testament archetypal figures. Richard Rohr and Joseph Martos performed a similar Catholic archetypal turn, defining masculine spirituality as 'the wild man's journey'.

Again, these appeals to archetypal models promote largely oppressive and violent masculinities and consequently a patriarchal spirituality. Even when these themes are consciously removed and resisted, archetypal gender models remain problematic. Consider gay spirituality, which also makes significant use of archetypes. Certainly violence and domination is avoided by the focus on the Androgyne, yet it still raises two issues: first, that there is some singular archetypal model to which to appeal, resulting in the rather essentialized 'gay spirit'; second, that the Androgyne remains bound within a binary model of an equally essentialized notion of masculine and feminine, albeit combining the two. Consider also those women's archetypes referred to within integral spirituality: the Virgin, Whore, Amazon, and Hag. These archetypes do not speak explicitly of masculine domination (although there is an implicit element of misogyny about them), but they do lend themselves to a one-dimensional understanding of gender performance rather than the multidimensionality one can expect with something as complex as the spiritual. The whole notion of masculine and feminine 'types' on which Wilber's understanding of gender is based, are also of an archetypal nature and are equally one-dimensional. In short, treatments of gender that appeal to archetypes are either domineering, simplistic, or domineering *and* simplistic.

More generally, an appeal to myth, the context in which archetypes operate, produces further problems. All the versions of masculine spirituality outlined in the previous chapters look to myths for inspiration when suggesting how masculinity should function both socially and spiritually. In the Christian men's movements this appeal to some timeless natural order is extended with the uncritical adoption of certain biblical pronouncements. But myths, like archetypes, do not represent anything other than the social order from which they are drawn. To appeal to myths is to enter a cycle of perpetuation: myths are derived from patriarchal societies and then used as sources of inspiration, thus continuing patriarchal societies. Within various masculine spiritualities this problem is compounded by charging myth with numinosity, by elevating myth to spirituality. The lessons we are asked to learn from myths then take on a divinely ordained nature.[1] Again, there is a difference between intention and effect. The storytellers of masculine spirituality may well intend for myths to reveal and honour the beauty of sexual difference, but instead they act as shills for the patriarchal order. The function of myth is not, as claimed, to represent reality from which we have become dissociated, rather as Roland Barthes said, 'the function of myth is to empty reality; it is, literally, a ceaseless flowing out, a haemorrhage, or perhaps an evaporation, in short a perceptible absence. ...*myth is depoliticised speech*' (quoted in Zipes 1992: 19).

Revisioning Patriarchy

A further common theme in the various forms of masculine spirituality is the revisioning of patriarchy away from being seen as 'a system of social structures and practices in which men dominate, oppress and exploit women' (Walby 1990: 20). Bly's understanding of patriarchy is curious. On the one hand, it is possible to read his laments about the soft male, the feminization of society and the denial of the deep masculine as a backlash against feminism and therefore a reassertion of patriarchy. But Bly does not really believe we live in a patriarchy, or at least not a genuine

---

1. The spiritualization of myth also compromises the status of the spiritual, confusing the 'spiritual person' (*pneumatikos*) with the 'natural person' (*psychikos anthropôs*).

one. For Bly, genuine patriarchy (along with matriarchy) is a kind of benevolent historical anomaly since eclipsed by the Industrial Revolution: Bly at once denies the contemporary reality of patriarchy, while seeking to reassert its mytho-historical origins. Bly has always been vocal in denying he is in any way anti-feminist or patriarchal, and he does this by alluding to a scenario in which both the masculine and feminine are honoured, and by staying largely silent on the issue of actual women.[2] We are asked to believe that his mythopoetic themes of violent archetypes, the power dynamics of initiation and so forth do not result in patriarchy as it is commonly understood—as an oppressive structure—even if the evidence suggests otherwise.

While Bly's understanding of patriarchy can be seen as ambiguous, its revisioning is less so in the Christian men's movement. Leaving to one side both evangelical and Catholic mythopoeticism, we are immediately faced with the largely evangelical spin of biblical manhood, or as Ed Cole might refer to it, maximized manhood. In the Christian men's movement, men are encouraged to be the leaders of their families: patriarchs in a very literal sense. Promise Four of the Promise Keepers refocused on this theme by stating men should build strong marriages and families in accordance with biblical values, and those values are for the man to show leadership in his marriage and family.[3] Most men within the Christian men's movement consider men's role as leader to have been eroded by modern society and therefore it needs to be strongly *re*asserted, as demonstrated by Tony Evans' infamous words, 'I'm not suggesting that you *ask* for your role back, I'm urging you to *take it back*' (1994: 79, original emphasis).

But there is some awareness among even the most determined of Christian patriarchs that it is impossible to completely turn back the clock: women cannot, in the twenty-first century, really be expected to accept patriarchy in its rawest sense. It is at this point that the meaning and language surrounding patriarchy is repackaged

2. At least in *Iron John*: in other books such as *The Maiden King: The Reunion of Masculine and Feminine* (1998), co-authored with Marion Woodman, Bly speaks equally to women.

3. Rosemary Radford Ruether argues that the whole claim of the Christian Right to be promoting biblically ordained 'family values', the like of which resonate with many Christian men's ministries, is false and 'has its origins in the ideology of Victorian white middle-class America, not in the Bible' (2000: 225).

for the contemporary evangelical woman such as the Promise Reapers.[4] In order to distance themselves from actual patriarchy, these biblically inspired men claim instead to be 'servant leaders', at once assuming the traditional role of leading the family, yet also in service to it. In an academic analysis of the phenomenon, W. Bradford Wilcox promotes the concept of 'soft patriarchs' through which we are asked to understand men's leadership in the home as merely 'a salve for men's threatened manhood [rather] than a license for them to exercise authority over their wives or demand they stay at home' (2004: 143). The unsavoury reality of patriarchy is depoliticized and concealed within the Christian men's movement by the shift in language towards servant leadership and soft patriarchy and the shift in meaning towards patriarchy being more of a symbolic rather than actual order. There is also a good deal of commonality between the servant leader and various mythopoetic archetypes: we are asked to accept the soft patriarch in the same way as the King, as a fountain of well-intentioned benevolence for the greater good rather than tyrannical exploiter of power.

A similar revisioning of patriarchy takes place in Wilber's integral spirituality which denies that patriarchy is about dominating women, rather a biological necessity given men's natural propensity to 'productive work' ever since the introduction of the animal-drawn plough. In a further act of depoliticization and concealment, Wilber opts for the term 'patrifocal' instead of patriarchy, making it clear that to speak of patriarchy in terms of male domination is to 'assume the complete pigification of men and the total sheepification of women' (2000a: 167). Furthermore, not only is society's patrifocal nature enshrined in humanity's history, it is also secured in the present and future noosphere: 'given the unavoidable aspects of childbearing, a "parity" in the public/private domain would be around 60-40 male/female' (Wilber 2000a: 676, n. 14).

The phraseological turn from 'patriarchy' to 'patrifocal' is then complemented by demoting 'feminism' to 'three dimensional feminism' and 'integral femininity'. The hard-won liberation of women is presented not as freedom from male domination, but freedom from the restraints of living in the biosphere, an evolutionary gift. All these elements contribute to the erasure of

4. Promise Reapers, along with various other groups like Suitable Helpers and Heritage Keepers comprise women who support men's leadership roles promoted by ministries such as Promise Keepers; see Tanya Erzen (2000).

political and critical language to the benefit of the masculine. Continuing his understanding of parity within integral spirituality, Wilber follows the traditional spiritual formula which equates the masculine with transcendence and the feminine with immanence, and then bases his whole developmental schema on transcending and including, relegating feminine immanence to archaic consciousness, thus privileging and securing the dominance of the masculine principle.

These revisionings of patriarchy result in a stealth-like normalization of what might otherwise be considered extreme positions, especially when, as noted by Linda Kintz (1996), the sources are ostensibly respectable clean-cut individuals. Before long, proponents of masculine spiritualities, who may well consider themselves perfectly reasonable men, are advocating a reassertion of patriarchy via a very particular interpretation of myth, biblical values and evolution. A similar normalization process takes place in regards to violence. Consider the archetypes referred to above. Consider also the paramilitary culture constructed around men's ministries which move beyond the rhetoric of spiritual warfare to parading leaders' military pedigree, packaging ministry products with a military aesthetic, equipping members with swords, and appealing to extreme and combative sports. Even integral spirituality with its clear trajectory towards non-dual awareness appeals to a certain menace: Wilber's muscularity and gun-slinging rhetoric, David Deida's suggestion of fucking woman and world to smithereens.

In masculine spirituality, the combination of archetypes, myths and a revisioning of patriarchy make for a powerful force. Archetypes and myths are drawn from a patriarchal consciousness and function as a mirror in which patriarchy gazes, mistaking its own reflection for some kind of supernatural reality. Patriarchy thus perpetuates itself throughout history. But more disturbing, patriarchy then engages in an act of concealment by revisioning itself into something other than patriarchy. It muddies the waters of history, claiming it was never really his-story in the first place, rather his and her story, always reflecting the best outcomes for everyone at a particular moment in time, whether it be increased productivity with the dawning of the agricultural era, or increased involvement with the family by contemporary servant leaders. In the movie *The Usual Suspects*, the villain, Keyser Söze, secures the potency of his evil persona by creating an aura of both myth and doubt about his existence. As he sits before his clueless interrogator, Söze transparently shares his methodlology with the memorable line, 'the greatest trick the devil ever pulled was convincing the world he didn't exist'.[5] This is exactly what happens with masculine spirituality as it first secures and then denies the reality of patriarchy.[6]

Challenging Authentic Masculinity

The problematic themes that underpin masculine spirituality rely on some agreement via sex role theory about what are appropriate expressions of masculinity, about what constitutes 'authentic masculinity'. The whole mythopoetic movement is based upon the assumption that there are authentic aspects of masculinity expressed via archetypes, and that these can be accessed by all men. In itself, this might not be so problematic if those archetypes did not define masculinity primarily by identifying with the Wild Man, the King or the Warrior. The Christian men's movement builds upon this use of archetypal masculinity and adds to it the notion of biblical masculinity. In itself, this might not be so problematic if biblical masculinity did not result in a literal patriarch aspiring to spiritual and worldly warfare. Integral spirituality finds authentic masculinity in masculine and feminine types. In itself, this might not be so problematic if the masculine type did not result in agency, ranking and transcendence at the expense of communion, linking and immanence.

5. Readers who prefer more literary references may opt for Charles Baudelaire's original version, 'the Devil's cleverest wile is to convince us that he does not exist' (quoted and discussed in Denis de Rougement 1956: 17). C. S. Lewis made a similar point in the preface to *The Screwtape Letters*:

> There are two equal and opposite errors into which our race can fall about the devils. One is to disbelieve in their existence. The other is to believe, and to feel an excessive and unhealthy interest in them. They themselves are equally pleased by both errors and hail a materialist or a magician with the same delight (Lewis 1942: 9).

6. More generally this manifests with increasingly frequent references to 'post-patriarchy' or 'post-feminism', as if the feminist critique of patriarchy was in some way complete and successful. While a post-patriarchal and post-feminist future has very real potential, we are certainly not there yet.

The transcendence/immanence binary presented by integral spirituality highlights a further way sex role theory functions within most spiritualities: their spatial-gendered nature. In chapter 7 I showed how masculine spirituality is equated with 'up' and 'out' and feminine spirituality with 'down' and 'in'. Many of the values allocated to such directionality favour the masculine and also reiterate the private/public domain, thus consolidating patriarchal power. That the masculine is assumed to be up and out is yet another assumed aspect of authentic masculinity which (with the notable exception of the interior Wild Man) is rarely signified by immanence. All these forms of spirituality believe it is possible to identify with some certainty appropriate expressions of authentic masculinity. Unfortunately the understanding of masculinity these spiritualities settle upon tends towards the patriarchal: they promote a hegemonic masculinity which oppresses those it sees as the Other in women and subordinate masculinities.

It is only with gay spirituality that any significant challenges to these assumptions take place within the various forms of masculine spirituality. While gay spirituality does allocate some significance to archetypes, it does not appeal to those of a violent or oppressive nature, opting instead for the Androgyne. It does not appeal to biblical masculinity or indeed any type of authentic masculinity. If gay spirituality appeals to anything it is to a range of potential masculinities which actively subvert the gender expectations of other masculine spiritualities, thus the popularity of faeries, sparkling wands and tutus. Gay spirituality also resists to a certain degree the gendered nature of spiritual space, offering gay men with its ecological and neo-pagan inclinations an element of immanence. It is also about taking seriously what it defines as 'gay spirit' which allocates men a range of characteristics that are almost diametrically opposed to those set out by other forms of masculine spirituality.

I have already agreed with the criticism that gay spirit or consciousness is an essentialist idea, but it is certainly preferable to the essentialist understanding of gender exemplified by sex role theory. Toby Johnson claimed that gay consciousness is experienced from an outside perspective, non-dualistic, incarnational, evolutionary, insight-provoking, transformational and adaptively virtuous. Harry Hay argued that gay spirit was defined by not being aggressive or imposing, being interested in sharing and living harmoniously with others, and celebrating all aspects of human sexuality. Hay also promoted a subject-SUBJECT perception of the world, which avoids the heteronormative model of subject-OBJECT and its habit of othering. While these attributes of gay spirit are certainly romantic and rather simplistic, they are a refreshing change in comparison with the masculine consciousness presented elsewhere.

Another theme which gay spirituality addressed, and which is generally absent in other masculine spiritualities, is serious political analysis. Right from the start, Hay sought to combine his Marxist worldview with gay spirit. While popular gay spirituality had a tendency to focus more on the promotion of gay identity, the arrival of gay liberation theology offered a greater political analysis about how that identity was oppressed within the Church and society as a whole. Just as gay spirituality is an invitation to all men — gay or straight — to embrace a more fluid definition of masculinity, so gay liberation theology is an invitation to all men to (re)introduce an element of political awareness into their spirituality, to challenge the default conservatism prevalent elsewhere in masculine spirituality.

The conservatism in masculine spirituality is of two primary types. First, there are those of a consciously conservative nature, anti-feminist and clearly out to re-establish masculine privilege: Patrick Arnold would be a good example of this type. But a significant amount of the conservatism in masculine spirituality is not necessarily about actively pursuing a conservative agenda, but rather having seemingly no political awareness that their project is conservative to begin with, even conservative to the extreme. It is this lack of awareness which results in the often genuine puzzlement in the face of criticism: why are King and Warrior archetypes or servant leaders patriarchal, they seem to ask, we're just decent guys who want to do right by our family and friends? It is this lack of awareness that enables men to engage with scenes of paramilitary fantasy without asking any questions about what it actually suggests beyond being some natural signifier of masculinity.

Political awareness operates differently within Wilber's integral vision. In the document *Integral Politics: A Summary of Its Essential Ingredients*,[7] Wilber applies his AQAL model and principle of transcending and including onto politics. Wilber argues for a third—

7. http://www.kenwilber.com/writings/read_pdf/73

integral — way beyond the partial truth claims of Left and Right. It is beyond the scope of the present study to answer this question, but given that I have argued that Wilber's integration of masculine and feminine privileges the masculine, it would be interesting to examine whether his integration of Left and Right privileges one or the other.[8] Certainly one potential danger of integral politics which echoes the lack of general political awareness in masculine spirituality is to fall again into the trap of Wilber's own elegant model: the pre/trans fallacy. Remember, the pre/trans fallacy highlights two common mistakes made in considerations of spiritual matters: the pre-rational can be elevated to the transrational, and the transrational can be reduced to the pre-rational. For Wilber, integral politics should be transrational and based on a firm understanding, and then integrating of Left and Right. However, there is the danger with 'beyond Left versus Right' rhetoric that integral consumers never fully understand the implications of Left and Right, assuming instead they must simply move beyond them. Such a situation results not in the transrational, but the pre-rational: Left and Right are not integrated, rather never adequately addressed in the first place. There is then a danger that pre-rational, or pre-critical, political awareness can simply be populated by whatever skew to the Left or Right (if indeed there is a skew) integral politics happens to take.

Putting to one side the potential promises or failings of integral politics, what can be said with some certainty is that gay spirituality, particularly gay liberation theology, injects into the spectrum of masculine spiritualities a political consciousness that is otherwise either absent or noticeably conservative. In chapter 6, I suggested that a straight left-leaning (clearly pre-integral) man who seeks to bear witness to his spirituality is going to have a hard time combining these concerns in the various strands of men's movement. This is because the 'spiritual' mythopoetic and Christian men's movements have no real sense of the political, the profeminist movement has no real sense of the spiritual, and the gay spiritual

8. Harry Hay's Marxist alarm bells would probably start ringing on seeing the recent interest in Wilber's work in literature pertaining to corporate business, change management and leadership (Barrett 2006; Cacioppe 2000a and 2000b; Cacioppe and Edwards 2005a and 2005b; Edwards 2005; Küpers 2005; Landrum and Gardner 2005; Locander *et al* 2002; Lund 2004; Paulson 2002; Pielstick 2005; Steingard 2005; Van Marrewijk 2003; Van Marrewijk and Hardjono 2003; Volckmann 2005).

movement has no real sense of the straight. This is a significant problem for straight men. Short of conjuring a men's movement that both these men and women in general could trust,[9] one of the most useful ways forward is to trouble the categories of gay and straight, thus making the gifts of 'gay spirit' more freely available to *all* men.

Beyond the Gay Divide

In chapter 7, I discussed different ways of looking at sexual difference. Most advocates of masculine spirituality look at sexual difference in terms of there being appropriate ways of being masculine and feminine, of appropriate sex roles. An initially similar, yet more sophisticated understanding of sex difference was then presented by Luce Irigaray, who promoted sexual difference between men and women not to prescribe how men and women should behave, rather to secure a space for women's identity shaped outside the phallocentric economy. There are clear similarities between Bly and Irigaray as both appeal to a reasonably fixed idea of sexual difference founded in some benevolent patriarchal and matriarchal past. However, the differences are many. Bly makes a rather naïve pre-political appeal to some kind of natural order. Irigaray makes a highly political statement about patriarchal power grounded in a complex and shifting sea of psychoanalysis, linguistics, philosophy and *écriture feminine* which, whether one agrees with it or not, is of a totally different order. Further still, Judith Butler proposed another vision of sexual difference outside of a static understanding of male and female, allowing for masculine women and feminine men, where sexual difference is marked by multiplicity rather than binarity.

Back in the epigraph to my introduction to this book (see page 1) is the oft-cited passage from the Gospel of Thomas, 'When you

---

9. Starhawk famously described such a thing as being comprised of:

> men who could be passionate lovers, grounded in their own bodies, capable of profound loves and deep sorrows, strong allies of women, sensitive nurturers, fearless defenders of people's liberation, unbound by stifling conventions yet respectful of their own and others' boundaries, serious without being humourless, stable without being dull, disciplined without being rigid, sweet without being spineless, proud without being insufferably egotistical, fierce without being violent, wild without being, well, assholes (Starhawk 1992: 27-28).

make the male and the female one and the same, so that the male not be male nor the female female...then will you enter the kingdom' (22).[10] One way of reading it would be to claim that it calls for a theological erasing of sexual difference, or that it seeks something akin to the androgynous archetype of gay spirituality. This is the initial conclusion most people draw in conversations when I question the categories of masculine and feminine spirituality. Another reading of the passage would understand it quite differently. To make the male and the female one and the same is not to collapse them into one homogenized (presumably phallocentric) category, rather to recognize that all men and women possess one individual sexuality, *distinct to themselves*. To make the male not be male and the female not be female is not to deny maleness and femaleness, rather to acknowledge that there is no single way of being male or female. Thus, the author of Thomas is in agreement with Deleuze, suggesting that humanity must be understood as a thousand tiny sexes before it can enter the kingdom. The male and the female are the same, and at once neither male nor female, precisely because they are both characterized by multiplicity, dwelling and becoming on a Deleuzian plateau.[11]

This understanding of sexual difference as multiplicity is exemplified by queer theory.[12] While it was born out of gay and lesbian studies, queer theory ultimately moves into territory that

10. Even Jane Fonda has publicly pondered this passage, although unfortunately not as Barbarella, rather on the Charlie Rose Show (PBS, first aired 23 October 2006).

11. A similar Deleuzian understanding can be reached from the earlier part of this Thomas passage: 'when you make the inside like the outside and the outside like the inside, and the above like the below...then will you enter the kingdom'. The inside and outside, the above and below, share distinct commonality with Deleuzian striated space, which regulates spiritual territory in the service of the State. Troubling this equation, by making the inside like the outside and the above like the below, moves us into smooth space which I have argued resists rigid gender categorizations. Clearly also, making the above like the below resonates strongly with my argument in the previous chapter against the equation of masculine with up and out and feminine with down and in within a spatial representation of spirituality.

12. It is tempting to think that since the terminological discovery of the 'homosexual' and before queer theory everyone accepted the categories of gay and straight, but this is not true. While largely describing the spectrum of male-male desire, Chris Brickell's survey of nineteenth and twentieth century sexological texts shows there to be a substantial history of categorizing masculinities with much more nuance and fluidity than suggested by the homo/hetero binary: 'a complex and contradictory set of sexual ontologies that encoded liminality' (Brickell 2006: 427).

troubles the categories of gay and lesbian, as well as straight. In chapter 6, I argued for queer theory to accommodate straight men. This accommodation should be ingrained in queer theory as to resist a group of people categorized as straight is not a particularly queer thing to do, given its more fundamental resistance to categorization. However, there are some queer theorists who worry that 'straight' inclusion might have a deadening effect on the queer theme by its repetition and use by people wanting to appear transgressive where transgression possesses a certain cultural capital (Butler 1999: xxi; Schlichter 2004: 557). But there is a practical need for this accommodation, namely the heteronormative definitions of masculinity outlined in the previous chapters tend towards the patriarchal, which suggests resisting patriarchy is also about resisting those definitions. Opening up the queer realms to predominantly heterosexual men who want to resist oppressive forms of masculinity immediately provides a theoretical framework and also a community of like-minded individuals to those men, which should in turn enable further resistance.

Of course it would be wrong to suggest that the lack of engagement by predominantly heterosexual men with queer theory is to do mostly with a resistance to them by queer theorists. More likely is a prevailing homophobia among even those men who seek to challenge oppressive forms of masculinity. Björn Krondorfer (2007) asks the important question, 'Who's afraid of gay theology?' noting the general silence regarding gay theology among straight theologians. That such a dialogue between gay and straight scholars (even friends and allies) is delicate is well demonstrated by the flurry of responses to his question (Haldeman 2007; Livingston 2007; Longwood 2007; Musskopf 2007). David Livingston suggests discussing men's studies and/or gay theology can be a risky business for one's career. André Musskopf notes there is also some hesitance from gay theologians to engage with straight masculinities, as there is an assumption they are not working in the same field, and also that straight men appear rather slow and naïve in their self awareness compared to gay men. Scott Haldeman questions Krondorfer's categories of gay scholarship and both he and W. Merle Longwood question his assumed gay/straight binary. All these men nevertheless reiterate the value of Krondorfer's original question.

Certainly, most of these concerns have been echoed elsewhere in these pages. Clearly also it is difficult for some men to engage gay scholarship and even gay men without some vague sense of panic at the possibility of being considered gay by association. I do not believe that homophobia is hardwired in men, rather instilled by cultural values. However, this makes the occasional anxieties about being considered gay no less real. This was brought home to me not long ago when parking my car in town after visiting the library. I had two piles of books on the front seat: atop one sat Phil Downer's *Effective Men's Ministry*, on the other Bob Goss' *Jesus Acted Up: A Gay and Lesbian Manifesto*. I am not proud to say I moved Bob's book down the pile as it suddenly occurred to me some passer-by might think *I* was gay and choose to scratch my car in protest. A trivial example, perhaps, but for a moment it triggered in me an anxiety about gayness I had not previously felt in my social relationships with gay men. Assuming such anxieties do not prove insurmountable, engaging gay spirituality and theology is particularly important for straight men. Such engagement, as already suggested, shows there to be a variety of different ways of doing masculinity which do not have to shore up the patriarchal regime; it also begins the slow journey of undoing the homophobic tendencies in most men.

The gay divide is just one of many divides, or as Stephen Boyd describes them in his particular worldview, the 'sins' that prove problematic for a healthy masculine spirituality: classism, anti-Semitism, racism, homophobia, sexism, and femiphobia (1995: 147). Such divides or stumbling blocks for men within Christianity are unpacked further by Philip Culbertson (1992): the identification of God as Father; fear of the feminine; domination of the tradition by men; men's suppression of emotions; a focus on self-sufficiency, making it hard to pray for or seek help; misunderstanding the value of reciprocal relationships; the insistence that to *do* something is categorically more manly than to *be* something; the problem men have in knowing who they are when they are not in charge; the heritage of body-soul dualism and the dismissal of sexuality; the need to control structurelessness by putting everything in a hierarchical order; the assumption that incompleteness is a sign of failure; the preference for linearity over circularity (Culbertson 1992: 111). These divides and stumbling blocks highlight the alliances that must be made and the work to be done between men and other men and women if a healthy masculine spirituality is ever to be realized. These divides highlight what James Nelson (1988) described as the 'intimate connection' that must be re-established in masculine spirituality between aspects of the self, other men and women, and the Divine.

However, the way masculine spirituality is articulated by individuals such as Boyd, Culbertson and Nelson is unfortunately not the same as its more identifiable advocates. Ultimately, assuming a position which seeks to overcome such divides and stumbling blocks or, in short, patriarchy, I would argue for dispensing altogether with the phrase 'masculine spirituality'. The previous chapters have outlined in some detail the fact that masculine spirituality tends to be little more than a thin veil for patriarchal spirituality. Furthermore, the unstable and fluid nature of gender and therefore of 'masculine' as a category make it difficult to know with any certainty what 'masculine spirituality' actually means or to whom it refers. At the very least, it demands at a theoretical level a looseness of interpretation that the majority of masculine spirituality proponents would find highly unacceptable. Until there is some notable and non-marginalized movement of men that promotes a 'masculine spirituality' which actively resists patriarchy and allows for masculinities which encompass jewel-spangled and bearded faeries and probably also masculine women, it is better to focus instead simply on the category of 'men and spirituality'. To speak of men and spirituality offers a horizon of potential that sadly has been closed down by most existent masculine spiritualities.

Constructing a New Relationship Between Men and Spirituality

I want to conclude in more speculative territory. In the preface I told of how this project was originally about a rediscovery, or even a discovery for the first time of a positive masculine spirituality. I wanted to find a non-patriarchal spirituality that was not just lived by men, but also had something to do with being masculine. Unfortunately, before I could embark on that particular project it became evident there was first much unpacking to be done of patriarchal masculine spirituality. Now that I have modestly furthered this process it is possible once again to address my original intentions.

I have already argued for the importance of moving beyond the gay/straight binary and the adoption of queer theory as an important step towards undoing some of the problems facing men and spirituality. I have also argued for an abandonment of the term 'masculine spirituality' in favour of 'men and spirituality'. These are both sound moves, but they do not necessarily communicate well with men. I have spoken on my journey with a number of good men, some academically trained and some not, who find the call to queer theory too counterintuitive, or the distinction between masculine spirituality and men and spirituality too subtle to bother thinking about. Some men (and women), especially those who work on the ground in men's groups of both a voluntary and court-ordered/therapeutic nature, have experiences of men who are so dissociated from a sense of self that they simply could not comprehend such suggestions, let alone agree or disagree with them.

It is to these 'regular' men that the forms of masculine spirituality outlined in these pages appear so credible. Many men have an intuitive sense that there is something wrong with the way masculinity functions in society, but they have few, if any, tools for its development. Phenomena like Iron John or Promise Keepers can resonate with these men because they start a conversation about masculinity in accessible terms, a conversation that is otherwise largely absent. I have shown how these conversations have unfortunate consequences for men's perception of the spiritual, but this is exacerbated by there being no comparably accessible conversation about masculinity that can provide a useful alternative. Following are a few of the issues that would need to be addressed in order for such an alternative conversation to gain momentum.

An initial important task is to stop building a proprietary fence around men and spirituality, of assuming it is men's work. One theme discussed was the interchangeable use and lack of real interrogation of the terms 'male spirituality', 'masculine spirituality' and 'men's spirituality'. Male spirituality should refer to something biologically determined, masculine spirituality to something socially constructed, and men's spirituality to something 'belonging' to men. The different meanings of these terms are never fully explored in the popular or even academic literature. One descriptive phrase which does have some immediate usage is 'masculin*ist* spirituality', if masculinist is understood as a reassertion of heteronormative masculinity functioning within something akin to a 'men's rights' context. This book refers more accurately to masculinist spirituality than any other permutation. Whichever way, there is too often the assumption identified by Jeff Hearn and Keith Pringle that the work is 'by men, on men, for men' (2006: 5). There is therefore a need to break this assumption from the beginning with the terminology used to describe the work to reflect something more in line with 'on men, by everyone, for everyone'.

Certainly the defining and naming of a field of exploration is important and complex, and the discussion of men and spirituality must refer in some way to men. In the introduction I located my work within the subject of 'men's studies in religion'. Livingston (2007), commenting on Krondorfer's (2007) suggestion that men's studies in religion suffers a 'taxonomic envy...of the benevolent outsider' (260), argues there is a problem with the term as it has none of the 'political and ethical charge as that of gay theology, queer theory, or feminist theology' (83). Livingston suggests that there is no obvious place for men who step outside the 'masculine green zone' (hegemonic masculinity), as they may be looked upon suspiciously by both those who resist it and those who perpetuate it, and that having a suitable category for such men would be useful (85). He offers for discussion the terms Critical Male Theology, Kenotic Male Theology or Critical Masculinist Theology (85-86). Livingston's suggestion that men need to look critically upon their role within religion is certainly the correct place to start, but by now it should be evident that referring to a theology as male or masculine is problematic, and a masculinist theology, even within an intended critical framework, is likely to ring further alarm bells in various quarters.

Even taking into account the caveat of 'critical' the problem with these suggestions is that they still imply an assumption of men's work. We know a male or masculinist theology is *about* men (although little more) and *by* men. That male theologies are more about *who* than *what* is demonstrated by there appearing to be little apparent room for a woman to engage them, except perhaps in a deconstructive capacity. Certainly the intention may be worthy, such as a desire for a 'political and ethical charge', but describing them as male or masculinist may be counterproductive, especially for those people who, with some justification follow Hearn's advice that 'all new identities of men, including those that are anti-sexist, gay, bisexual, even pro-feminist, should be treated with wariness' (Hearn 1992: 231). Hearn's definition of 'critical studies on men' serves a useful function in that it clearly states both who and what the studies are about, but makes no comment on who should be engaged with them. Due to its openness and clear aims this field has blossomed in recent years resulting not just in a proliferation of books but large research projects undertaken by both men and women, the like of which have never been seen in a religious context.[13]

It may even be that the whole naming exercise is something of a diversion. It is not always necessary to coin new phrases to describe 'new' realities when it may be that the meaning of old phrases have simply been forgotten and can be rediscovered and reapplied. Between feminist and queer theories, an understanding of hegemonic masculinity and an old-fashioned dose of class awareness there seems little within the brief of critical male theologies that is unique. My feeling is that it is not the lack of a suitable category that is the problem for men who wish to engage critically with masculinities and religion, rather a lack of real commitment to that critical process on the part of most men. From personal experience, at least, there is not as much resistance as one might imagine from women and gay people to straight men who wish to step outside the green zone. And, quite frankly, leaving the corrupt nature of the green zone behind should relieve any man of his anxieties about how he is viewed within it. In short, our conversation begins with men making a genuine commitment to change via a process that involves both men and women.

Having suggested that it is not always necessary to create new categories to solve old problems, my next suggestion may appear rather contradictory: men need to let go of the assumption that they can 'rediscover' useful ways of doing masculinity. Much of masculine spirituality is about rediscovery, whether of archetypal or biblical aspects within men. I suspect there has never been a time in humanity's history where men and masculinities have functioned free from the problems we face today. And even if there was some Arcadian moment when matriarchy and patriarchy co-existed in mutuality, it would be naïvety to expect it could be recreated in the modern world. More often than not, attempting to reclaim the past because things were better there is simply an escapist retreat from

13. Via the CROME (Critical Research on Men in Europe) Network, Hearn and a significant number of other researchers have produced a voluminous body of work on men and masculinities for the European Commission (see, for example, Hearn *et al* (2004) for a general report and see Hearn *et al* (2006) for an example of their methodological framework).

the reality of the now. Men need to look forward to new ways of doing masculinity, which is an automatic rejection of 'authentic masculinity' that has been the basis for so many of our problems in these pages.

There are existing tools that can be used in this process of looking forward, the seeds of which already lie within the movements so far critiqued. One method for this genuine commitment in place in the mythopoetic movement and integral spirituality is the Jungian shadow. Dealing with patriarchy and privilege is in a very real sense dealing with the shadow, that often ignored and murky aspect of the self responsible for destructive behavioural patterns. But, unfortunately, identifying that the shadow exists is not the same thing as its engagement. Michael Schwalbe makes the insightful point that in the mythopoetic movement a Jungian understanding of gender reduced difference to simply being about complementary ways of thinking and being rather than the more tangible difference of power between men and women: 'Jungian psychology, ironically, kept the men from seeing and facing the shadow of patriarchy' (Schwalbe 1996: 223). But more than this the shadow is in some ways naturalized in the mythopoetic movement. Moore and Gillette for example, argue archetypes contain 'an active-passive bipolar shadow structure' (1991: 63): it is as if, like violence, shadow material is inevitable rather than something that can be dealt with and rejected.[14] Another tool for the call to genuine commitment available in the Christian men's movements needs little explanation: the Gospel demand for compassion, love and justice. Despite the fact that these existing tools have had little useful effect in the various masculine spiritualities, they still have a very real potential.

Turning away from the old and the authentic and looking forward is clearly also a refutation of archetypes. However, the repeated references to archetypes in masculine spiritualities suggest they have an almost unshakable hold on the popular psyche. Indeed, neo-Jungian thought in general appears to show no sign of loosening its grip on the spiritual imagination of many people. Perhaps, for those who find it impossible to be free of them, archetypes must be revisioned: let us turn them into calcifications of a liberatory rather

14. Similarly, in the discussion of integral spirituality Willow Pearson claimed the Virgin, Whore, Amazon, and Hag archetypes each possess 'a unique shadow manifestation' [http://in.integralinstitute.org/talk.aspx?id=724].

than patriarchal worldview. Some of the more enlightened members of the mythopoetic movement began this path by rejecting the explicitly oppressive archetypes such as King and Warrior: John Rowan (1987) sought out archetypes of a more profeminist nature; Glen Mazis (1993) focused on those archetypes referred to but undeveloped by Bly, namely the Trickster, Magician and Grieving Man; Aaron Kipnis (1992) wanted to promote the blessings of the Green Man. And of course, gay spirituality made this task central with the employment of the Androgyne.

But just as we have seen a revisioning of the meaning of patriarchy, so too we could see a revisioning of the meaning of archetypes. I suggest that rather than psychic realities hardwired in the reptilian brain, archetypes should be perceived simply as fictional characters that can be drawn upon for inspiration. Without even moving beyond the boundaries of normative masculinity there are various characters that might prove useful objects of meditation for a politics of liberation: the Saboteur and Agitator spring to mind; the more technologically inclined might find inspiration in the Hacker who stealthily exploits weaknesses in the computer systems of the status quo, redistributing harvested data for the greater good, or simply leaving a calling card as a joke. These kinds of revisioned archetypes also suggest a political consciousness that would need to be present in our conversation, and which has been discussed via gay liberation theology.

Of course some might say, with some justification, that there is already a men's movement having such conversations: the profeminist movement. The reasons why profeminism 'has almost no life outside the university' (Clatterbaugh 2000: 887) are complex, including a failure on behalf of its members to successfully communicate to 'regular' men and, more importantly, a failure of most men to move out of their comfort zone and commit to profeminist values. However, one aspect I have already mentioned, and which I believe could be easily rectified, is a profeminist reluctance to embrace spirituality, despite its intention to be gay-affirmative with the significant spiritual element that implies. This Leftist issue is neatly phrased in the subtitle of Jim Wallis' *God's Politics: Why the Right Gets It Wrong and the Left Doesn't Get It* (2005). I strongly believe the immediate way forward in our conversation is for profeminist men aligned with critical studies on men to develop a more subtle appreciation of the spiritual, and for spiritual men aligned with men's studies to commit more fully to profeminist politics. Such an alliance has the potential to be greater than the sum of its parts and could well capture the imagination of men who neither group have before managed to reach.

I have argued for the rejection of masculine spirituality due to its patriarchal nature and restrictive treatment of gender. But this does not close down in any way men discussing religion and spirituality in terms which resonate with being a man. It opens up a conversation which resonates with any number of ways of being a man (or masculine) that rejects patriarchy. It is a pro-man conversation because it is pro-person, which by necessity must involve the liberation of all people. Feminist and queer theories and theologies have done most of the work in making way for such a conversation. What is needed now is for predominantly straight men to step up and play their part in a process which will benefit the vast majority of people. This is hardly a new or radical suggestion, but its realization remains elusive. Such is the insidious nature of patriarchy. But as the saying goes, the bigger they are, the harder they fall.

BIBLIOGRAPHY

Abramowicz, Danny, *Spiritual Workout of a Former Saint* (Huntington, IN: Our Sunday Visitor Publications, 2004).

Adams, George, 'A Theistic Perspective on Ken Wilber's Transpersonal Psychology', *Journal of Contemporary Religion* 17. 2 (2002): 165–79.

Allen, L. Dean, 'Promise Keepers and Racism: Frame Resonance as an Indicator of Organizational Vitality' in Rhys H. Williams (ed.), *Promise Keepers and the New Masculinity: Private Lives and Public Morality* (Lanham, MD: Lexington Books, 2001), pp. 55–72.

_____ *Rise up, O Men of God: The Men and Religion Forward Movement and the Promise Keepers* (Macon, GA: Mercer University Press, 2002).

Allister, Mark, *Eco-Man: New Perspectives on Masculinity and Nature* (Charlottesville, VA: University of Virginia Press, 2004).

Althaus-Reid, Marcella, *Indecent Theology* (London: Routledge, 2000).

_____ *The Queer God* (London: Routledge, 2003).

American Academy of Pediatrics Committee on Adolescence 'Homosexuality and Adolescence', *Pediatrics* 92. 4 (1993): 631–34.

Anable, Steve, 'Folding My Wings', *The Gay & Lesbian Review Worldwide* 9. 2 (2002): 18–20.

Anderson, William, *Green Man: The Archetype of Our Oneness with the Earth* (San Francisco, CA: HarperCollins, 1990).

Andrescik, Rob, 'Edwin Louis Cole: The Legacy — 1922–2002.' *New Man* (November/ December 2002). Retrieved from http://www.newmanmag.com/display.php?id =6757.

Anttonen, Veikko, 'Rethinking the Sacred: The Notions of "Human Body" and "Territory" in Conceptualizing Religion' in Thomas A. Idinopulos and Edward Yonan (eds.), *The Sacred and Its Scholars: Comparative Methodologies for the Study of Primary Religious Data* (Leiden: E. J. Brill, 1996) pp. 36–64.

Anzaldúa, Gloria, *Borderlands: The New Mestiza = La Frontera* (San Francisco, CA: Spinsters/Aunt Lute, 1987).

Aquilina, Mike, 'Making New Catholic Men', *Our Sunday Visitor* (20 July 1997, pp. 10–11.

Arnold, Patrick, 'In Search of the Hero: Masculine Spirituality and Liberal Christianity', *America* 161, no. 9 (1989): 206.

_____ *Wildmen, Warriors and Kings: Masculine Spirituality and the Bible* (New York: Crossroad, 1991).

Arterburn, Stephen, Fred Stoeker, and Mike Yorkey, *Every Man's Battle: Winning the War on Sexual Temptation One Victory at a Time* (Colorado Springs, CO: WaterBrook Press, 2000).

Baker-Fletcher, Garth Kasimu (ed.), *Black Religion after the Million Man March: Voices on the Future* (Maryknoll, NY: Orbis Books, 1998).

Barrett, Richard, *Building a Values-Driven Organization: A Whole System Approach to Cultural Transformation* (Boston, MA: Butterworth-Heinemann, 2006).

Bartkowski, John P., 'Breaking Walls, Raising Fences: Masculinity, Intimacy, and Accountability among the Promise Keepers,' in Rhys H. Williams (ed.), *Promise Keepers and the New Masculinity: Private Lives and Public Morality* (Lanham, MD: Lexington Books, 2001), pp. 33–53.

Bawden, Bill, and Tom Sullivan, *Signposts: How to Be a Catholic Man in the World Today* (Ijamsville, MD: Word Among Us Press, 1999).

Beck, Don Edward, and Christopher C. Cowan, *Spiral Dynamics: Mastering Values, Leadership, and Change: Exploring the New Science of Memetics* (Cambridge, MA: Blackwell Business Press, 1996).

Bederman, Gail, 'The Women Have Had Charge of the Church Work Long Enough': The Men and Religion Forward Movement of 1911–1912 and the Masculinization of Middle-Class Protestantism', *American Quarterly* 41. 3 (1989): 432–65.

Benjamin, Walter, *Illuminations* (Fulham: Fontana Press, 1992).

Bennett, LaRon D., *The Million Man March: The Untold Story* (Brunswick, GA: BHouse Publishing, 1996).

Bethmont, Rémy, 'Some Spiritually Significant Reasons for Gay Attraction to (Anglo-) Catholicism', *Theology and Sexuality* 12. 3 (2006): 233–49.

Blake, Mariah, 'Manly, Yes: An Aventura Minister Pumps Testosterone into the Faith', *Miami New Times* (2006). Retrieved from http://www.miaminewtimes.com/2006-03-09/news/manly-yes.

Bliss, Shepherd, 'Revisioning Masculinity: A Report on the Growing Men's Movement' *in Context* 16 (1987, Spring). Retrieved from http://www.context.org/ICLIB/IC16/Bliss.htm.

Bloch, Jon P., 'The New and Improved Clint Eastwood: Change and Persistence in Promise Keepers Self-Help Literature' in Rhys H. Williams (ed.), *Promise Keepers and the New Masculinity: Private Lives and Public Morality* (Lanham, MD: Lexington Books, 2001), pp. 11–30.

Block, Stephanie, 'Coloring Outside the Lines', *The Wanderer* (1997, May). Retrieved from http://www.catholicculture.org/library/view.cfm?recnum=649.

Bly, Robert, *Iron John: A Book About Men* (Reading, MA: Addison-Wesley, 1990).

_____ *The Sibling Society* (Reading, MA: Addison-Wesley, 1996).

_____ *The Winged Energy of Delight: Selected Translations* (New York: HarperCollins, 2004).

Bly, Robert, and Keith Thompson, 'What Men Really Want', *New Age* (1982, May): 30–37; 50–51.

Bly, Robert, and Marion Woodman, *The Maiden King: The Reunion of Masculine and Feminine* (New York: Henry Holt & Company, 1998).

Boisvert, Donald, 'Talking Dirty About the Saints: Storytelling and the Politics of Desire', *Theology & Sexuality* 12.2 (2006): 165–80.

_____ 'Wherefore Gay Spirituality, or How Queer Can the Sacred Be?', *White Crane Journal* 54 (2002). Retrieved from http://www.whitecranejournal.com/54/art5405.asp.

Bonnett, Alastair, 'The New Primitives: Identity, Landscape and Cultural Appropriation in the Mythopoetic Men's Movement', *Antipode* 28. 3 (1996): 273–91.

Boswell, John, *Christianity, Social Tolerance, and Homosexuality: Gay People in Western Europe from the Beginning of the Christian Era to the Fourteenth Century* (Chicago, IL: University of Chicago Press, 1980).

Boyd, Stephen B., *The Men We Long to Be: Beyond Domination to a New Christian Understanding of Manhood* (San Francisco, CA: HarperSanFrancisco, 1995).

_____ 'Trajectories in Men's Studies in Religion: Theories, Methodologies, and Issues', *Journal of Men's Studies* 7. 2 (1999): 265–69.

Boyd, Stephen B., W. Merle Longwood, and Mark W. Meusse (eds.), *Redeeming Men: Religion and Masculinities* (Louisville, KY: Westminster John Knox Press, 1996).

Brewster, Chuck, 'Training Men of Significance' in Phil Downer (ed.), *Effective Men's Ministry: The Indispensable Toolkit for Your Church* (Grand Rapids, MI: Zondervan, 2001), pp. 209–14.

Brickell, Chris, 'Sexology, the Homo/Hetero Binary and the Complexities of Male Sexual History', *Sexualities* 9. 4 (2006): 423–47.

Brod, Harry, 'Introduction: Themes and Theses of Men's Studies' in Harry Brod (ed.), *The Making of Masculinities: The New Men's Studies*, (Boston, MA: Allen & Unwin, 1987a), pp. 1–20.

_____ (ed.), *The Making of Masculinities: The New Men's Studies* (Boston, MA: Allen & Unwin, 1987b).

_____ (ed.), *A Mensch among Men: Explorations in Jewish Masculinity* (Freedom, CA: Crossing Press, 1988).

_____ 'The Mythopoetic Men's Movement: A Political Critique', in Christopher Harding (ed.), *Wingspan: Inside the Men's Movement* (New York: St Martin's Press, 1992), pp. 232–36.

Brod, Harry, and Michael Kaufman (eds.), *Theorizing Masculinities* (Thousand Oaks, CA: Sage Publications, 1994).

Burgess, Anthony, *A Clockwork Orange* (London: William Heinemann, 1962).

Burgess, Adrienne, *Fatherhood Reclaimed: The Making of the Modern Father* (London: Vermilion, 1997).

Burlein, Ann, *Lift High the Cross: Where White Supremacy and the Christian Right Converge* (Durham, NC: Duke University Press, 2002).

Butler, Judith, 'Against Proper Objects', *differences* 6, no. 2–3 (1994): 1–26.

_____ *Bodies That Matter: On the Discursive Limits of 'Sex'* (London: Routledge, 1993).

_____ 'Bracha's Eurydice', *Theory, Culture & Society* 21. 1 (2004a): 95–100.

_____ *Gender Trouble: Feminism and the Subversion of Identity* (London: Routledge, 1999, 2nd edn.).

_____ *Undoing Gender* (London: Routledge, 2004b).

Butler, Judith, and Drucilla Cornell, 'The Future of Sexual Difference: An Interview with Judith Butler and Drucilla Cornell', *Diacritics* 28.1 (1998): 19–42.

Cacioppe, Ron, 'Creating Spirit at Work: Re-visioning Organization Development and Leadership – Part I', *Leadership & Organization Development Journal* 21.1 (2000a): 48–54.

_____ 'Creating Spirit at Work: Re-visioning Organization Development and Leadership – Part II', *Leadership & Organization Development Journal* 21. 2 (2000b): 110–19.

Cacioppe, Ron, and Mark G. Edwards, 'Adjusting Blurred Visions: A Typology of Integral Approaches to Organisations', *Journal of Organizational Change Management* 18. 3 (2005a): 230–46.

_____ 'Seeking the Holy Grail of Organisational Development: A Synthesis of Integral Theory, Spiral Dynamics, Corporate Transformation and Action Inquiry', *Leadership & Organization Development Journal* 26. 2 (2005b): 86–105.

Campbell, June, *Traveller in Space: In Search of Female Identity in Tibetan Buddhism* (New York: George Braziller, 1996).

Carbado, Devon W. (ed.), *Black Men on Race, Gender, and Sexuality: A Critical Reader* (New York: New York University Press, 1999).

Carrigan, Tim, R. W. Connell, and John Lee, 'Toward a New Sociology of Masculinity' in Harry Brod (ed.), *The Making of Masculinities: The New Men's Studies*, (Boston, MA: Allen & Unwin, 1987), 63–100.

Carter, David, *Stonewall: The Riots that Sparked the Gay Revolution* (New York: St. Martin's Press, 2004).

Castellini, J. D., W. M. Nelson, J. J. Barrett, Mark S. Nagy, and G. L. Quatman, 'Male Spirituality and the Men's Movement: A Factorial Examination of Motivations', *Psychology and Theology* 33. 1 (2005): 41–55.

Chafetz, Janet S., *Sex and Advantage: A Comparative Macro-Structural Theory of Sex Stratification* (Totowa: NJ: Rowman & Allanheld, 1984).

Chaudhuri, Haridas, *The Philosophy of Integralism. The Metaphysical Synthesis in Sri Aurobindo's Teaching* (Calcutta: Sri Aurobindo Pathamandir, 1954).

Clare, Anthony W., *On Men: Masculinity in Crisis* (London: Chatto & Windus, 2000).

Clatterbaugh, Kenneth, *Contemporary Perspectives on Masculinity: Men, Women, and Politics in Modern Society* (Boulder, CO: Westview Press, 1997, 2nd edn.).

_____ 'Literature of the U.S. Men's Movements', *Signs* 25. 3 (2000): 883–94.

_____ 'Mythopoetic Foundations and New Age Patriarchy' in Michael S. Kimmel (ed.), *The Politics of Manhood: Profeminist Men Respond to the Mythopoetic Men's Movement (and the Mythopoetic Leaders Answer)*, (Philadelphia, PA: Temple University Press, 1995), pp. 44–63.

Claussen, Dane S., (ed.), *The Promise Keepers: Essays on Masculinity and Christianity* (Jefferson, NC: McFarland, 2000).

_____ (ed.), *Standing on the Promises: The Promise Keepers and the Revival of Manhood* (Cleveland, OH: The Pilgrim Press, 1999).

Cleaver, Frances, *Masculinities Matter! Men, Gender, and Development* (London: Zed Books, 2002).

Cleaver, Richard, *Know My Name: A Gay Liberation Theology* (Louisville, KY: Westminster John Knox Press, 1995).

Cole, Edwin Louis, *Maximized Manhood* (New Kensington, PA: Whitaker House, 1982).

_____ *Real Man* (Southlake, TX: Watercolor Books, 2003).

Cole, Edwin Louis, and Patrick Morley, 'Majoring in Men', *Enrichment Journal* (2003, Spring). Retrieved from http://enrichmentjournal.ag.org/200302/200302_016_morley_cole.cfm.

Comiskey, Joel, *Groups of Twelve: A New Way to Mobilize Leaders and Multiply Groups in Your Church* (Houston, TX: Touch Publications, 1999).

Comstock, Gary David, 'Gay Men and Straight Men: Getting Unstuck and Crossing Over', *Journal of Men's Studies* 4. 3 (1996): 281–90.

_____ *Gay Theology without Apology* (Cleveland, OH: The Pilgrim Press, 1993).

Connell, R. W., 'Masculinities and Globalization', *Men and Masculinities* 1.1 (1998): 3–23.

_____ 'Men at Bay: The "Men's Movement" and its Newest Bestsellers' in Michael S. Kimmel (ed.), *The Politics of Manhood: Profeminist Men Respond to the Mythopoetic Men's Movement (and the Mythopoetic Leaders Answer)*, (Philadelphia: Temple University Press, 1995), pp. 75–88.

Connell, R. W., and James W. Messerschmidt, 'Hegemonic Masculinity: Rethinking the Concept', *Gender & Society* 19. 6 (2005): 829–59.

Connolly, William, 'The Evangelical-Capitalist Resonance Machine', *Political Theory* 33. 6 (2005): 869–86.

Corless, Roger, 'Towards a Queer Dharmology of Sex', *Culture and Religion* 5. 2 (2004): 229–43.

Cottman, Michael H., *Million Man March* (New York: Crown Trade Paperbacks, 1995).

Coughlin, Paul, *No More Christian Nice Guy: When Being Nice – Instead of Good – Hurts Men, Women and Children* (Minneapolis, MN: Bethany House Publishers, 2005).

Cross, Haman, and Thomas Fritz, 'Men of All Colors: Unity in Diversity' in Phil Downer (ed.), *Effective Men's Ministry: The Indispensable Toolkit for Your Church* (Grand Rapids, MI: Zondervan, 2001), pp. 190–98.

Culbertson, Philip, 'Christian Men's Movements' in Michael Flood, Judith Kegan Gardiner, Bob Pease and Keith Pringle (eds.), *International Encyclopedia of Men and Masculinities* (London: Routledge, 2007), pp. 65–67.

_____ 'Men Dreaming of Men: Using Mitch Walker's "Double Animus" In Pastoral Care', *The Harvard Theological Review* 86. 2 (1993): 219–32.

_____ *New Adam: The Future of Male Spirituality* (Minneapolis, MN: Fortress Press, 1992).

Culbertson, Philip, and Björn Krondorfer, 'Men's Studies in Religion' in Lindsay Jones (ed.), *Encyclopedia of Religion*, (Detroit, MI: Macmillan Reference USA, 2005), pp. 5861–66.

D'Acchioli, Vince, 'Vision that Drives Ministry' in Phil Downer (ed.), *Effective Men's Ministry: The Indispensable Toolkit for Your Church* (Grand Rapids, MI: Zondervan, 2001), pp. 36–45.

Dalbey, Gordon, *Healing the Masculine Soul: An Affirming Message for Men and the Women Who Love Them* (Waco, TX: Word Books, 1988).

_____ *Fight Like a Man: Redeeming Manhood for Kingdom Warfare* (Wheaton, IL: Tyndale House, 1996).

de Quincey, Christian, 'The Promise of Integralism. A Critical Appreciation of Ken Wilber's Integral Psychology', *Journal of Consciousness Studies* 7, no. 11-12 (2000): 177–208.

de Rougement, Denis, *The Devil's Share: An Essay on the Diabolic in Modern Society* (Haakon Chevalier trans; New York: Meridian Books, 1956).

de Young, Maury, *Hunting Season: Insights for Living from a Seasoned Hunter* (Kearney, NE: Morris Publishing, 2002).

Debold, Elizabeth, 'Where Are the Women?' *What Is Enlightenment?* (2005a, June–August). Retrieved from http://www.wie.org/j29/women.asp.

_____ 'Where Are the Women? Toward a New Women's Liberation', *What Is Enlightenment?* (2005b, September–November). Retrieved from http://www.wie.org/j30/debold.asp.

_____ 'Where Are the Women? Beyond the Divine Feminine', *What Is Enlightenment?* (2006, March–May). Retrieved from http://www.wie.org/j30/debold.asp.

Debold, Elizabeth, Marie Wilson, and Idelisse Malavé, *Mother Daughter Revolution: From Betrayal to Power* (Reading, MA: Addison-Wesley, 1993).

Deida, David, *The Way of the Superior Man: A Spiritual Guide to Mastering the Challenges of Women, Work and Sexual Desire* (Boulder, CO: Sounds True, 2004, 2nd edn.).

Deleuze, Gilles, and Félix Guattari, *A Thousand Plateaus: Capitalism and Schizophrenia* (Brian Massumi trans; Minneapolis, MN: University of Minnesota Press, 1987).

DeVoll, Michael G., and Christopher Blazina, 'Jungian Templates for Contemporary Gay Men; Or "What Does Mary Want with That Bear and What's the Diva Dishing?"', *Journal of Men's Studies* 11.1 (2002): 29–36.

Diamond, Jed, 'Twenty-Five Years in the Men's Movement' in Michael Kimmel (ed.), *The Politics of Manhood: Profeminist Men Respond to the Mythopoetic Men's Movement (and the Mythopoetic Leaders Answer)* (Philadelphia, PA: Temple University Press, 1995), pp. 313–20.

Dittes, James E., 'A Men's Movement for the Church?', *The Christian Century* 108, no. 18 (1991): 588–90.

Dobson, James, C., *Bringing up Boys* (Wheaton, IL: Tyndale House Publishers, 2001).

_____ *Straight Talk to Men: Timeless Principles for Leading Your Family* (Sisters, OR: Multnomah, 2003).

_____ *A Father, a Hero: Inspiration and Insights for Every Dad* (Sisters, OR: Multnomah Gifts, 2005).

_____ 'Two Mommies Is One Too Many', *Time* (2006). Retrieved from http://www.time.com/time/magazine/printout/0,8816,1568485,00.html.

_____ *What Wives Wish Their Husbands Knew About Women* (Wheaton, IL: Tyndale House, 1975).

Downer, Phil, 'Becoming a Spiritual Parent' in Phil Downer (ed.), *Effective Men's Ministry: The Indispensable Toolkit for Your Church* (Grand Rapids, MI: Zondervan, 2001a), pp. 175–81.

_____ (ed.), *Effective Men's Ministry: The Indispensable Toolkit for Your Church* (Grand Rapids, MI: Zondervan, 2001b).

Duberman, Martin B., *Stonewall* (New York: Dutton, 1993).

Duggan, Lisa, *The Twilight of Equality? Neoliberalism, Cultural Politics, and the Attack on Democracy* (Boston: Beacon Press, 2003).

Edwards, Mark G., 'The Integral Holon: A Holonomic Approach to Organisational Change and Transformation', *Journal of Organizational Change Management* 18.3 (2005): 269–88.

Eilberg-Schwartz, Howard, *God's Phallus and Other Problems for Men and Monotheism* (Boston: Beacon Press, 1994).

Eisler, Raine, *The Chalice and the Blade: Our History, Our Future* (San Francisco: Harper & Row, 1987).

_____ 'What Do Men Really Want? The Men's Movement, Partnership, and Domination' in Kay Leigh Hagan (ed.), *Women Respond to the Men's Movement: A Feminist Collection* (San Francisco: HarperCollins, 1992), pp. 43–54.

Eldredge, John, *Wild at Heart: Discovering the Secret of a Man's Soul* (Nashville, TN: Nelson Books, 2001).

Elium, Jeanne, and Don Elium, *Raising a Son: Parents and the Making of a Healthy Man* (Berkeley, CA: Celestial Arts, 1996).

Erickson, Dan, and Dan Schaffer, 'Modern Man in Contemporary Culture' in Phil
    Downer (ed.), *Effective Men's Ministry: The Indispensable Toolkit for Your Church* (Grand
    Rapids, MI: Zondervan, 2001), pp. 15–24.
Ernster, Barb, 'Moving Men into Catholic Men's Movements', *National Catholic Register*
    (2005). Retrieved from http://www.thecall.org/coverage_movements.htm#moving.
Erzen, Tanya, 'Liberated through Submission? The Gender Politics of Evangelical
    Women's Groups Modeled on the Promise Keepers' in Dane S. Claussen (ed.), *The
    Promise Keepers: Essays on Masculinity and Christianity* (Jefferson, NC: McFarland,
    2000), pp. 238–54.
Ettinger, Bracha, 'Matrix and Metamorphosis', *differences* 4.3 (1992): 170–208.
_____ 'Metramorphic Borderlinks and Matrixial Borderspace' in John Welchman (ed.),
    Rethinking Borders (Basingstoke: Macmillan, 1996), pp. 125–59.
_____ 'Weaving a Woman Artist With-in the Matrixial Encounter-Event', *Theory, Culture
    & Society* 21. 1 (2004): 69–94.
Evans, Arthur, *The God of Ecstasy: Sex-Roles and the Madness of Dionysos* (New York:
    St. Martin's Press, 1988).
_____ *Witchcraft and the Gay Counterculture: A Radical View of Western Civilization and
    Some of the People It Has Tried to Destroy* (Boston, MA: Fag Rag Books, 1978).
Evans, Tony, 'Sexual Purity' in A.I. Janssen and Larry K. Weeden (eds.), *The Seven
    Promises of a Promise Keeper* (Colorado Springs, CO: Focus on the Family, 1994), pp.
    73–81.
Evola, Julius, *Eros and the Mysteries of Love: The Metaphysics of Sex* (Rochester, VT: Inner
    Traditions, 1991).
Falk, Geoffrey D., *'Norman Einstein': The Dis-Integration of Ken Wilber* (Toronto: Million
    Monkeys Press, 2006).
Faludi, Susan, *Stiffed. The Betrayal of the American Man* (New York: W. Morrow and Co.,
    1999).
Farrar, Steve, *Point Man: How a Man Can Lead His Family* (Sisters, OR: Multnomah,
    2003, rev. edn.).
Farrell, Warren, *Why Men Are the Way They Are: The Male-Female Dynamic* (New York:
    McGraw-Hill, 1986).
_____ *Why Men Earn More: The Startling Truth Behind the Pay Gap – and What Women
    Can Do About It* (New York: AMACOM, 2005).
Fausto-Sterling, A., *Myths of Gender* (New York: Basics, 1985).
Ferguson, B.A., T.A. Dreisbach, C.G. Parks, G. M. Filip and C.L. Schmitt, 'Coarse-Scale
    Population Structure of Pathogenic Armillaria Species in a Mixed-Conifer Forest in
    the Blue Mountains of Northeast Oregon', *Canadian Journal of Forest Research* 33. 4
    (2003): 612–23.
Ferrer, Jorge, *Revisioning Transpersonal Theory: A Participatory Vision of Human Spirituality*
    (Albany, NY: SUNY Press, 2002).
Flanagan, Russ, 'Prison for Myspace Perv', *The Express-Times* (2007). Retrieved
    7 February 2007 from http://www.nj.com/news/expresstimes/pa/index.ssf?/
    base/news-9/117073856948440.xml&coll=2.
Forman, Robert, *Grassroots Spirituality: What It Is, Why It Is Here, Where It Is Going*
    (Charlottesville, VA: Imprint Academic, 2004).
Francis, L.J., and T.H. Thomas, 'Are Anglo Catholic Priests More Feminine? A Study
    among Male Anglican Clergy', *Pastoral Sciences* 15 (1996): 15–22.

Fuss, Dianna, *Essentially Speaking: Feminism, Nature, and Difference* (London: Routledge, 1989).

Gallagher, Sally K., and Sabrina L. Wood, 'Godly Manhood Going Wild? Transformations in Conservative Protestant Masculinity', *Sociology of Religion* 66. 2 (2005): 135–60.

Galli, Mark, *Jesus Mean and Wild: The Unexpected Love of an Untamable God* (Grand Rapids, MI: Baker Books, 2006).

Gatens, Moira, 'A Critique of the Sex/Gender Distinction' in Sneja Gunew (ed.), *A Reader in Feminist Knowledge* (London: Routledge, 1991), pp. 139–57.

Gebser, Jean, *The Ever-Present Origin* (Athens, OH: Ohio University Press, 1985).

Gelfer, Joseph, 'A Conversation with Matthew Fox', *Ashé! Journal of Experimental Spirituality* 5. 2 (2006b): 182–90.

_____ 'Review of 'No More Christian Nice Guy' By Paul Coughlin', *Journal of Men's Studies* 14. 2 (2006a): 259–60.

Getz, Gene A., *The Measure of a Man* (Ventura, CA: Regal Books, 2004, rev. edn.).

Ghose, Aurobindo, *The Life Divine* (Calcutta: Arya Publishing House, 1939–40).

_____ *The Synthesis of Yoga* (Madras: Sri Aurobindo Library, 1948).

Gibson, James William, *Warrior Dreams: Paramilitary Culture in Post-Vietnam America* (New York: Hill and Wang, 1994).

Gilder, George F., *Men and Marriage* (Gretna: Pelican Publications Co., 1986).

Giles, Doug, 'Dirty Harry Goes to Church', *Townhall* (2004). Retrieved from http://www.townhall.com/columnists/DougGiles/2004/11/27/dirty_harry_goes_to_church.

Gilligan, Carol, *In a Different Voice: Psychological Theory and Women's Development* (Cambridge, MA: Harvard University Press, 1993, 2nd edn.).

Gingold, Alfred, *Fire in the John* (New York: St Martin's Press, 1991).

Goldstein, Richard, *Homocons: The Rise of the Gay Right* (New York: Verso, 2003).

Goodrick-Clarke, Nicholas, *Black Sun: Aryan Cults, Esoteric Nazism, and the Politics of Identity* (New York: New York University Press, 2002).

Gorsuch, Geoff, *Brothers! Calling Men into Vital Relationships: A Small Group Discussion Guide* (Colorado Springs, CO: NavPress, 1994).

Goss, Robert, *Jesus Acted Up: A Gay and Lesbian Manifesto* (San Francisco: HarperSanFrancisco, 1993).

Gray, John, *Men Are from Mars, Women Are from Venus: A Practical Guide for Improving Communication and Getting What You Want in Your Relationships* (New York: HarperCollins, 1992).

Gross, Rita M., *Buddhism after Patriarchy: A Feminist History, Analysis, and Reconstruction of Buddhism* (Albany, NY: State University of New York Press, 1993).

Grosz, Elizabeth, *Volatile Bodies: Toward a Corporeal Feminism* (St. Leonards, NSW: Allen & Unwin, 1994).

_____ *Space, Time and Perversion* (St Leonards, NSW: Allen & Unwin, 1995).

_____ *Time Travels: Feminism, Nature, Power* (Durham, NC: Duke University Press, 2005).

Hagan, Kay Leigh (ed.), *Women Respond to the Men's Movement: A Feminist Collection* (San Francisco: HarperCollins, 1992).

Halberstam, Judith, *Female Masculinity* (Durham, NC: Duke University Press, 1998).

_____ 'Shame and White Gay Masculinity', *Social Text* 23, no. 3–4 (2005): 219–33.

Haldeman, Scott, 'Bringing Good News to the Body: Masturbation and Male Identity' in Björn Krondorfer (ed.), *Men's Bodies, Men's Gods: Male Identities in a (Post-) Christian Culture* (New York: New York University Press, 1996), pp. 111–24.

_____ 'On Writing Religion, "Gay" and "Straight": An Open Letter to Björn Krondorfer', *Theology & Sexuality* 14. 1 (2007): 95–99.

Hall, Donald (ed.), *Muscular Christianity: Embodying the Victorian Age* (New York: Cambridge University Press, 1994).

Hamer, Dean, *The God Gene: How Faith Is Hardwired into Our Genes* (New York: Doubleday, 2004).

Hanson, Ellis, *Decadence and Catholicism* (Cambridge, MA: Harvard University Press, 1997).

Harding, Christopher (ed.), *Wingspan: Inside the Men's Movement* (New York: St Martin's Press, 1992).

Harris, Ian M., 'Ten Tenets of Male Spirituality', *Journal of Men's Studies* 6. 1 (1997): 29–53.

Harvey, Andrew (ed.), *The Essential Gay Mystics* (San Francisco, CA: HarperSanFrancisco, 1997).

_____ *A Journey in Ladakh* (Boston: Houghton Mifflin, 1983).

_____ *The Way of Passion: A Celebration of Rumi* (Berkeley, CA: Frog Ltd, 1994).

Hay, Harry, *Radically Gay: Gay Liberation in the Words of its Founder* (ed. Will Roscoe; Boston: Beacon Press, 1996).

Hayford, Jack, 'The Pastor's Role' in Phil Downer (ed.), *Effective Men's Ministry: The Indispensable Toolkit for Your Church* (Grand Rapids, MI: Zondervan, 2001), pp. 56–65.

Healy, James, 'Man to Man: A Renewed Focus for Ministry', *The Catholic World* 235. 1407 (1992). 137–41.

Hearn, Jeff, *Men in the Public Eye: The Construction and Deconstruction of Public Men and Public Patriarchies* (London: Routledge, 1992).

_____ 'The Implications of Critical Studies on Men', *NORA. Nordic Journal of Women's Studies* 3. 1 (1997): 48–60.

_____ 'From Hegemonic Masculinity to the Hegemony of Men', *Feminist Theory* 5.1 (2004): 49–72.

Hearn, Jeff, Ursula Müller, Elżbieta H. Oleksy, Keith Pringle, Janna Cherenova, Harry Ferguson, Østein Gullvag Holter, Voldemar Kolga, Irina Novikova, and Carmine Ventimiglia. *The European Research Network on Men in Europe: The Social Problem and Societal Problematisation of Men and Masculinities. Volumes 1 and 2.* (Brussels: European Commission, 2004).

Hearn, Jeff, Irina Novikova, Keith Pringle, Iva Šmídová, Gunilla Bjerén, Marjut Jyrkinen, LeeAnn Iovanni, Fátima Arranz, Harry Ferguson, Voldemar Kolga, Ursula Müller, Elżbieta H. Oleksy, Dag Balkmar, Cornelia Helfferich, Ilse Lenz, Marek M. Wojtaszek, Elizabete Pièukâne, and Victoria Rosa. *Methodological Framework Report* (Helsinki: Hanken, Swedish School of Economics, 2006).

Hearn, Jeff, and Keith Pringle, 'Studying Men in Europe' in Jeff Hearn and Keith Pringle (eds.), *European Perspectives on Men and Masculinities: National and Transnational Approaches* (Basingstoke: Palgrave, 2006), pp. 1–19.

Heartfield, James, 'There is no Masculinity Crisis', *Genders* 35 (2002). Retrieved from http://www.genders.org/g35/g35_heartfield.html.

Heasley, Robert, 'Queer Masculinities of Straight Men: A Typology', *Men and Masculinities* 7. 3 (2005): 310–20.

Heelas, Paul, and Linda Woodhead, *The Spiritual Revolution: Why Religion Is Giving Way to Spirituality* (Oxford: Blackwell, 2005).

Hennen, Peter, 'Fae Spirits and Gender Trouble: Resistance and Compliance among the Radical Faeries', *Journal of Contemporary Ethnography*, 33.5 (2004): 499–533.

_____ 'Bear Bodies, Bear Masculinity: Recuperation, Resistance, or Retreat?', *Gender & Society*, 19.1 (2005): 20–45.

Heron, John, *Participatory Spirituality: A Farewell to Authoritarian Religion* (Morrisville, NC: Lulu Press, 2006).

Hicks, Robert, *The Masculine Journey: Understanding the Six Stages of Manhood* (Colorado Springs, CO: Navpress, 1993).

Hilliard, David, 'UnEnglish and Unmanly: Anglo-Catholicism and Homosexuality', *Victorian Studies* 25. 2 (1982): 181–210.

Hoffman, Shirl J., 'Evangelicalism and the Revitalization of Religious Ritual in Sport' in Shirl J. Hoffman (ed.), *Sport and Religion* (Champaign, IL: Human Kinetics Books, 1992a), pp. 111–25.

_____ 'Nimrod, Nephilim, Athletae Dei' in Shirl J. Hoffman (ed.), *Sport and Religion*, (Champaign, IL: Human Kinetics Books, 1992b), pp. 275–85.

Holmlund, Christine, 'The Lesbian, the Mother, the Heterosexual Lover: Irigaray's Recodings of Difference', *Feminist Studies* 17. 2 (1991): 283–309.

Hopcke, Robert H., *Jung, Jungians, and Homosexuality* (Boston: Shambhala Publications, 1989).

Horgan, John, *Rational Mysticism: Dispatches from the Border between Science and Spirituality* (Boston: Houghton Mifflin, 2003).

Horrocks, Roger, *Masculinity in Crisis: Myths, Fantasies, and Realities* (New York: St. Martin's Press, 1994).

Irigaray, Luce, *An Ethics of Sexual Difference* (Ithaca, NY: Cornell University Press, 1993a).

_____ *Sexes and Genealogies* (New York: Columbia University Press, 1993b).

_____ *Key Writings* (London: Continuum, 2004).

Irwin, Alexander, *Eros Toward the World: Paul Tillich and the Theology of the Erotic* (Minneapolis: Fortress Press, 1991).

Jagose, Annamarie, *Lesbian Utopics* (New York: Routledge, 1994).

Jameson, Fredric, *Postmodernism; or, the Cultural Logic of Late Capitalism* (London: Verso, 1991).

Janssen, A.I., and Larry K. Weeden (eds.), *The Seven Promises of a Promise Keeper* (Colorado Springs, CO: Focus on the Family, 1994).

Johnson, Stephen D., 'Who Supports the Promise Keepers?' in Rhys H. Williams (ed.), *Promise Keepers and the New Masculinity: Private Lives and Public Morality* (Lanham, MD: Lexington Books, 2001), pp. 93–104.

Johnson, Toby, *Gay Spirituality: The Role of Gay Identity in the Transformation of Human Consciousness* (Los Angeles: Alyson Books, 2000).

Jones, Adam (ed.), *Men of the Global South: A Reader* (London: Zed Books, 2006).

Jordan, Mark, *The Silence of Sodom: Homosexuality in Modern Catholicism* (Chicago: University of Chicago Press, 2000).

Joy, Morny, *Divine Love: Luce Irigaray, Women, Gender and Religion* (Manchester: Manchester University Press, 2006).

Kauffman, Christopher J., *Faith and Fraternalism: The History of the Knights of Columbus, 1882–1982* (New York: Harper & Row, 1982).

Keen, Sam, *Fire in the Belly: On Being a Man* (New York: Bantam Books, 1991).

Kimmel, Michael, S., 'The Contemporary "Crisis" of Masculinity in Historical Perspective' in Harry Brod (ed.), *The Making of Masculinities: The New Men's Studies* (Boston, MA: Allen & Unwin, 1987), pp. 121–53.

_____ 'Born to Run': Nineteenth-Century Fantasies of Masculine Retreat and Re-Creation (or the Historical Rust on Iron John)' in Michael. S. Kimmel (ed.), *The Politics of Manhood: Profeminist Men Respond to the Mythopoetic Men's Movement (and the Mythopoetic Leaders Answer)* (Philadelphia, PA: Temple University Press, 1995a), pp. 115–50.

_____ 'Introduction' in Michael. S. Kimmel (ed.), *The Politics of Manhood: Profeminist Men Respond to the Mythopoetic Men's Movement (and the Mythopoetic Leaders Answer)* (Philadelphia, PA: Temple University Press, 1995b), pp. 1–11.

_____ (ed.), *The Politics of Manhood: Profeminist Men Respond to the Mythopoetic Men's Movement (and the Mythopoetic Leaders Answer)* (Philadelphia, PA: Temple University Press, 1995c).

_____ 'Globalization and its Mal(e)Contents: The Gendered Moral and Political Economy of Terrorism', *International Sociology* 18. 3 (2003): 603–20.

Kimmel, Michael S., and Michael Kaufman, 'Weekend Warriors: The New Men's Movement' in Michael S. Kimmel (ed.), *The Politics of Manhood: Profeminist Men Respond to the Mythopoetic Men's Movement (and the Mythopoetic Leaders Answer)* (Philadelphia, PA: Temple University Press, 1995), pp. 15–43.

Kintz, Linda, *Between Jesus and the Market: The Emotions That Matter in Right-Wing America* (Durham, NC: Duke University Press, 1997).

Kipnis, Aaron, 'The Blessing of the Green Man' in Christopher Harding (ed.), *Wingspan: Inside the Men's Movement* (New York: St Martin's Press, 1992), pp. 161–65.

_____ 'The Postfeminist Men's Movement' in Michael S. Kimmel (ed.), *The Politics of Manhood: Profeminist Men Respond to the Mythopoetic Men's Movement (and the Mythopoetic Leaders Answer)* (Philadelphia: Temple University Press, 1995), pp. 275–86.

Kolodny, Annette, *The Lay of the Land: Metaphor as Experience and History in American Life and Letters* (Chapel Hill, NC: University of North Carolina Press, 1975).

Krattenmaker, Tom, 'Going Long for Jesus', *Salon* (2006). Retrieved from http:// www.salon.com/news/feature/2006/05/10/ministries/print.html.

Krondorfer, Björn (ed.), *Men's Bodies, Men's Gods: Male Identities in a (Post-) Christian Culture* (New York: New York University Press, 1996).

_____ 'Who's Afraid of Gay Theology? Men's Studies, Gay Scholars, and Heterosexual Silence', *Theology and Sexuality* 13. 3 (2007): 257–74.

Küpers, Wendelin, 'Phenomenology and Integral Pheno-Practice of Embodied Well-Be(com)Ing in Organisations', *Culture and Organization* 11. 3 (2005): 221–32.

Ladd, Tony, and James A. Mathisen, *Muscular Christianity: Evangelical Protestants and the Development of American Sport* (Grand Rapids, MI: Baker Books, 1999).

LaHaye, Tim F., *Left Behind: A Novel of the Earth's Last Days* (Wheaton, IL: Tyndale House Publishers, 1995).

Lakoff, George, and Mark Johnson, *Metaphors We Live By* (Chicago: University of Chicago Press, 2003, 2nd edn.).

Landrum, Nancy E., and Carolyn L. Gardner, 'Using Integral Theory to Effect Strategic Change', *Journal of Organizational Change Management* 18. 3 (2005): 247–58.

Laqueur, Thomas Walter, *Solitary Sex: A Cultural History of Masturbation* (New York: Zone Books, 2003).

Lefebvre, Henri, *The Production of Space* (Donald Nicholson-Smith trans; Oxford: Blackwell, 1991).

Lewis, C.S., *The Screwtape Letters* (London: G. Bles, 1942).

Lewis, Robert, *Raising a Modern-Day Knight: A Father's Role in Guiding His Son to Authentic Manhood* (Colorado Springs, CO: Focus on the Family, 1997).

Lienesch, Michael, 'Anxious Patriarchs: Authority and the Meaning of Masculinity in Christian Conservative Social Thought', *Journal of American Culture* 13. 4 (1990): 47–55.

Lindsay, D. Michael, 'Is the National Prayer Breakfast Surrounded by A "Christian Mafia"? Religious Publicity and Secrecy within the Corridors of Power', *Journal of the American Academy of Religion* 74. 2 (2006): 390–419.

Livingston, David J., 'Overcoming Heterosexual Anxiety before Gay Theology', *Theology & Sexuality* 14. 1 (2007): 81–88.

Locander, William B., Frank Hamilton, Daniel Ladik, and James Stuart, 'Developing a Leadership-Rich Culture: The Missing Link to Creating a Market-Focused Organization', *Journal of Market-Focused Management* 5.2 (2002): 149–63.

Lockhart, William H., '"We Are One Life" But Not of One Gender Ideology: Unity, Ambiguity, and the Promise Keepers' in Rhys H. Williams (ed.), *Promise Keepers and the New Masculinity: Private Lives and Public Morality* (Lanham, MD: Lexington Books, 2001), pp. 73–92.

Long, Ronald E., *Men, Homosexuality, and the Gods: An Exploration into the Religious Significance of Male Homosexuality in World Perspective* (New York: Harrington Park Press, 2004).

Longwood, W. Merle, 'Response to Björn Krondorfer's "Who's Afraid of Gay Theology? Men's Studies, Gay Scholars, and Heterosexual Silence"', *Theology & Sexuality* 14. 1 (2007): 100–05.

Louden, Stephen H., and Leslie J. Francis, 'The Personality Profile of Roman Catholic Parochial Secular Priests in England and Wales', *Review of Religious Research* 41. 1 (1999): 65–79.

Maddox, Marion, '"Nor Ever Chast Except You Ravish Mee": Sexual Politics and Protestant Pieties' in Morny Joy and Penelope Magee (eds.), *Claiming Our Rites: Studies in Religion by Australian Women Scholars* (Adelaide: Australian Association for the Study of Religions, 1994), pp. 37–56.

Madhubuti, Haki R., and Maulana Karenga (eds.), *Million Man March/Day of Absence: A Commemorative Anthology* (Los Angeles, CA: University of Sankore Press, 1996).

Magnuson, Eric, *Changing Men, Transforming Culture: Inside the Men's Movement* (Boulder, CO: Paradigm Publishers, 2007).

Mahalik, James R., and Hugh D. Lagan, 'Examining Masculine Gender Role Conflict and Stress in Relation to Religious Orientation and Spiritual Well-Being', *Psychology of Men & Masculinity* 1. 1 (2001): 24–33.

Malebranche, Jack, *Androphilia: Rejecting Gay Identity, Reclaiming Masculinity* (Baltimore, MD: Scapegoat Publishing, 2006).

Mansfield, Harvey C., *Manliness* (New Haven: Yale University Press, 2006).

Marcus, Sharon, 'Queer Theory for Everyone: A Review Essay', *Signs* 31.1 (2005): 191–218.

Massey, Doreen, *Space, Place, and Gender* (Cambridge: Polity Press, 1994).

Mazis, Glen, *The Trickster, Magician & Grieving Man: Reconnecting Men with Earth* (Santa Fe, NM: Bear & Co, 1993).

McCleary, Rollan, *A Special Illumination: Authority, Inspiration and Heresy in Gay Spirituality* (London: Equinox Publishing, 2004).

McDougall, Joyce, *The Many Faces of Eros: A Psychoanalytic Exploration of Human Sexuality* (New York: W.W. Norton, 1995).

McGrath, Tom, 'Is Men's Spirituality out of the Woods?', *US Catholic* (2002, April). Retrieved from http://uscatholic.claretians.org/site/News2?page=NewsArticle& id=6147&news_iv_ctrl=1283&abbr=usc_&JServSessionIdr007=zl1qxyi4f2.app43a.

McIntyre, John, 'Book Review. Sex, Ecology, Spirituality: The Spirit of Evolution', *Tricycle Buddhist Review* 5. 2 (1995): 117–19.

McManus, Erwin Raphael, *The Barbarian Way: Unleash the Untamed Faith Within* (Nashville, TN: Nelson Books, 2005).

McNeill, John J., *The Church and the Homosexual* (Kansas City, KS: Sheed Andrews and McMeel, 1976).

_____ *Freedom, Glorious Freedom: The Spiritual Journey to the Fullness of Life for Gays, Lesbians, and Everybody Else* (Boston, MA: Beacon Press, 1995).

_____ *Taking a Chance on God: Liberating Theology for Gays, Lesbians, and Their Lovers, Families, and Friends* (Boston, MA: Beacon Press, 1988).

McQuillan, Julia, and Myra Marx Ferree, 'The Importance of Variation among Men and the Benefits of Feminism for Families' in Alan Booth and Ann Crouter (eds.), *Men in Families: When Do They Get Involved? What Difference Does It Make?* (Mahwah: NJ: Erlbaum, 1998), pp. 213–26.

Meachum, Brandon, 'Muscle Ministry', *Denver Post* (2006). Retrieved from http://www.denverpost.com/sports/ci_4144610.

Meade, Michael, *Men and the Water of Life: Initiation and the Tempering of Men* (San Francisco: HarperCollins, 1993).

Messner, Michael A., *Politics of Masculinities: Men in Movements* (Thousand Oaks, CA: Sage Publications, 1997).

_____ *Power at Play: Sports and the Problem of Masculinity* (Boston: Beacon Press, 1992).

Mills, Sara, *Gender and Colonial Space* (Manchester: Manchester University Press, 2005).

Monick, Eugene, *Phallos: Sacred Images of the Masculine* (Toronto: Inner City Books, 1987).

Moore, Henrietta L., *Feminism and Anthropology* (Minneapolis, MN: University of Minnesota Press, 1988).

Moore, Robert, and Douglas Gillette, *King, Warrior, Magician, Lover: Rediscovering the Archetypes of the Mature Masculine* (New York: HarperCollins, 1990).

_____ *The King Within: Accessing the King in the Male Psyche* (New York: William Morrow, 1992a).

_____ *The Warrior Within: Accessing the Knight in the Male Psyche* (New York: William Morrow & Co., 1992b).

_____ *The Lover Within: Accessing the Lover in the Male Psyche* (New York: William Morrow & Co., 1993a).

_____ *The Magician Within: Accessing the Shaman in the Male Psyche* (New York: William Morrow & Co., 1993b).

_____ 'Initiation and the Male Spiritual Quest' in Stephen B. Boyd, W. Merle Longwood and Mark W. Meusse (eds.), *Redeeming Men: Religion and Masculinities* (Louisville KY: Westminster John Knox Press, 1996), pp. 187–96.

Morley, Patrick, 'Building the Lives of Men' in Phil Downer (ed.), *Effective Men's Ministry: The Indispensable Toolkit for Your Church* (Grand Rapids, MI: Zondervan, 2001), pp. 9–14.

_____ 'The Next Christian Men's Movement', *Christianity Today* (2000). Retrieved from http://www.christianitytoday.com/ct/2000/010/6.84.html.

Morrell, Robert (ed.), *Changing Men in Southern Africa* (London: Zed Books, 2001).

Muesse, Mark, 'Don't Just Do Something, Sit There: Spiritual Practice and Men's Wholeness' in Philip Culbertson (ed.), *The Spirituality of Men: Sixteen Christians Write About Their Faith* (Minneapolis, MN: Fortress Press, 2002), pp. 3–17.

Murray, Gordon, 'Homophobia in Bly's Iron John' in Michael S. Kimmel (ed.), *The Politics of Manhood: Profeminist Men Respond to the Mythopoetic Men's Movement (and the Mythopoetic Leaders Answer)* (Philadelphia, PA: Temple University Press, 1995), pp. 207–12.

Murray, Jacqueline, 'Masculinizing Religious Life: Sexual Prowess, the Battle for Chastity and Monastic Identity' in P. H. Cullum and Katherine J. Lewis (eds.), *Holiness and Masculinity in the Middle Ages* (Cardiff: University of Wales Press, 2004), pp. 24–42.

Murrow, David, *Why Men Hate Going to Church* (Nashville: Nelson Books, 2005).

Musskopf, André S., '"Who Is Not Afraid of Gay Theology?" Comments to Björn Krondorfer', *Theology & Sexuality* 14. 1 (2007): 89–94.

Nash, Roderick, *Wilderness and the American Mind* (New Haven, CT: Yale University Press, 2001, 4th edn.).

Nash, Ronald H., *Poverty and Wealth: The Christian Debate over Capitalism* (Westchester, IL: Crossway Books, 1986).

Nelson, James, *The Intimate Connection: Male Sexuality, Masculine Spirituality* (Philadelphia, PA: Westminster Press, 1988).

Newton, Judith, *From Panthers to Promise Keepers: Rethinking the Men's Movement* (Lanham, MD: Rowman & Littlefield, 2005).

Nicolosi, Joseph, and Linda Nicolosi, *A Parent's Guide to Preventing Homosexuality* (Downers Grove, IL: InterVarsity Press, 2002).

Noble, Jean Bobby, *Masculinities without Men? Female Masculinity in Twentieth-Century Fictions* (Vancouver: UBC Press, 2004).

Nonn, Timothy, 'Renewal as Retreat: The Battle for Men's Souls' in Michael S. Kimmel (ed.), *The Politics of Manhood: Profeminist Men Respond to the Mythopoetic Men's Movement (and the Mythopoetic Leaders Answer)*, (Philadelphia, PA: Temple University Press, 1995), pp. 173–212.

Novak, Michael, *The Catholic Ethic and the Spirit of Capitalism* (New York: Free Press, 1993).

O'Reilly, Sean, *How to Manage Your Dick: Destructive Impulses with Cyber-Kinetics: Redirect Sexual Energy and Discover Your More Spiritually Enlightened, Evolved Self* (Maryland, VA: Auriga Publications Group, 2001).

O'Brien, Mary, *The Politics of Reproduction* (London: Routledge & Kegan Paul, 1981).

O'Malley, William J., 'The Grail Quest: Male Spirituality', *America* 166, no. 16 (1992): 402–07.

_____ *Soul of a Christian Man: A Scriptural Look at Spirituality* (Chicago: Thomas More Association, 1999).

Otto, Rudolph, *The Idea of the Holy: An Inquiry into the Non-Rational Factor in the Idea of the Divine and Its Relation to the Rational* (John W. Harvey trans; Oxford: Oxford University Press, 1958).

Ouzgane, Lahoucine (ed.), *Islamic Masculinities* (London: Zed Books, 2006).

Ouzgane, Lahoucine, and Robert Morrell (eds.), *African Masculinities: Men in Africa from the Late Nineteenth Century to the Present* (New York: Palgrave Macmillan, 2005).

Pable, Martin W., *The Quest for the Male Soul: In Search of Something More* (Notre Dame, IN: Ave Maria Press, 1996).

_____ *A Man and His God: Contemporary Male Spirituality* (Notre Dame, IN: Ave Maria Press, 1998).

Pascal, Eugene, *Jung to Live By* (New York: Warner Books, 1992).

Paulson, Daryl S., *Competitive Business, Caring Business: An Integral Business Perspective for the 21st Century* (New York: Paraview Press, 2002).

Payne, Leanne, *Crisis in Masculinity* (Westchester, IL: Crossway Books, 1985).

Pease, Bob, and Keith Pringle (eds.), *A Man's World? Changing Men's Practices in a Globalized World* (London: Zed Books, 2006).

Pflugfelder, Gregory M., *Cartographies of Desire: Male-Male Sexuality in Japanese Discourse, 1600–1950* (Berkeley: University of California Press, 1999).

Phillips, Richard, *Mapping Men and Empire: A Geography of Adventure* (London: Routledge, 1997).

Phillips, Shawn, *ABSolution: The Practical Solution for Building Your Best Abs* (Golden, CO: High Point Media, 2002).

Piazza, Michael S., *Holy Homosexuals: The Truth About Being Gay or Lesbian and Christian* (Dallas, TX: Sources of Hope Publications, 1997, rev. edn.).

Pielstick, C. Dean, 'Teaching Spiritual Synchronicity in a Business Leadership Class', *Journal of Management Education* 29.1 (2005): 153–68.

Pleck, Joseph H., 'The Theory of Male Sex-Role Identity: Its Rise and Fall, 1936 to the Present' in Harry Brod (ed.), *The Making of Masculinities: The New Men's Studies* (Boston: Allen & Unwin, 1987), pp. 21–38.

Plumwood, Val, *Feminism and the Mastery of Nature* (London: Routledge, 1993).

Poling, James N., and Evelyn A. Kirkley, 'Phallic Spirituality: Masculinities in Promise Keepers, the Million Man March and Sex Panic', *Theology & Sexuality* 12. 6 (2000): 9–25.

Pollock, Griselda, 'Thinking the Feminine: Aesthetic Practice as Introduction to Bracha Ettinger and the Concepts of Matrix and Metramorphosis', *Theory, Culture & Society* 11. 1 (2004): 5–65.

Putney, Clifford, *Muscular Christianity: Manhood and Sports in Protestant America, 1880–1920* (Cambridge, MA: Harvard University Press, 2003).

Queen, Carol, and Lawrence Schimel, 'Introduction' in Carol Queen and Lawrence Schimel (eds.), *Pomosexuals: Challenging Assumptions About Gender and Sexuality* (San Francisco: Cleis Press, 1997), pp. 19–28.

Reuman, Ann E., 'Coming into Play: An Interview with Gloria Anzaldúa', *MELUS* 25. 2 (2000): 3–45.

Rinehart, Stacy T., 'Upside-Down Leadership' in Phil Downer (ed.), *Effective Men's Ministry: The Indispensable Toolkit for Your Church* (Grand Rapids, MI: Zondervan, 2001), pp. 98–106.

Robertson, Ross, 'Igniting the Flame of Intensity: The Spiritual Journey of a New Kind of Bodybuilder', *What Is Enlightenment?* (2005, March–May). Retrieved from http://www.wie.org/j28/phillips.asp.

Robinson, Paul, *Queer Wars: The New Gay Right and its Critics* (Chicago: University of Chicago Press, 2005).

Rodgers, William, 'The Radical Faerie Movement: A Queer Spirit Pathway', *Social Alternatives* 14. 4 (1995): 34–37.

Rohr, Richard, *Quest for the Grail* (New York: Crossroad, 1994).

_____ *Adam's Return: The Five Promises of Male Initiation* (New York: Crossroad, 2004).

Rohr, Richard, and Joseph Martos, *The Wild Man's Journey: Reflections on Male Spirituality* (Cincinnati, OH: Saint Anthony Messenger Press, 1992).

Rosaldo, Michelle Zimbalist, 'Woman, Culture, and Society: A Theoretical Overview' in Michelle Zimbalist Rosaldo and Louise Lamphere (eds.), *Woman, Culture, and Society* (Stanford, CA: Stanford University Press, 1974), pp. 17–42.

Roscoe, Will, *The Zuni Man-Woman* (Albuquerque, NM: University of New Mexico Press, 1991).

_____ *Changing Ones: Third and Fourth Genders in Native North America* (New York: St. Martin's Press, 1998).

Rosenthal, Bernard, *City of Nature: Journeys to Nature in the Age of American Romanticism* (Newark, DE: University of Delaware Press, 1980).

Ross, Andrew, 'Wet, Dark, and Low, Eco-Man Evolves from Eco-Woman', *boundary 2* 19. 2 (1992): 205–32.

Row, Jess, 'Remembering Iron John', *Slate* (2006). Retrieved from http://www.slate.com/id/2147359/.

Rowan, John, *The Horned God: Feminism and Men as Wounding and Healing* (London & New York: Routledge & Kegan Paul, 1987).

_____ *Subpersonalities: The People Inside Us* (New York: Routledge, 1990).

_____ *Healing the Male Psyche: Therapy as Initiation* (New York: Routledge, 1997).

_____ 'Ascent and Descent in Maslow's Theory', *Journal of Humanistic Psychology* 39. 3 (1999): 125–33.

_____ 'The Self, the Field and the Either-Or', *International Journal of Psychotherapy* 5. 3 (2000): 219–26.

Ruether, Rosemary Radford, 'Patriarchy and the Men's Movement: Part of the Problem or Part of the Solution?' in Kay Leigh Hagan (ed.), *Women Respond to the Men's Movement: A Feminist Collection* (San Francisco: HarperCollins, 1992), pp. 13–18.

_____ *Christianity and the Making of the Modern Family* (Boston: Beacon Press, 2000).

Rupp, Leila J., and Verta Taylor, *Drag Queens at the 801 Cabaret* (Chicago: University of Chicago Press, 2003).

Sadler, Kim Martin (ed.), *Atonement: The Million Man March* (Cleveland, OH: The Pilgrim Press, 1996).

Salzman, Marian L., Ira Matathia, and Ann O'Reilly (eds.), *The Future of Men* (New York: Palgrave Macmillan, 2005).

Sandy, P. R., *Female Power and Male Dominance: On the Origins of Sexual Inequality* (Cambridge: Cambridge University Press 1981).

Schacht, Steven P., 'Four Renditions of Doing Female Drag: Feminine Appearing Conceptual Variations of a Masculine Theme', *Gendered Sexualities* 6 (2002): 157–80.

Schacht, Steven P., and Lisa Underwood (eds.), *The Drag Queen Anthology: The Absolutely Fabulous but Flawless Customary World of Female Impersonators* (New York: Harrington Park Press, 2004).

Schaffer, Dan, 'The Mark of Leadership' in Phil Downer (ed.), *Effective Men's Ministry: The Indispensable Toolkit for Your Church* (Grand Rapids, MI: Zondervan, 2001), pp. 116–21.

Schlamm, Leon, 'Ken Wilber's Spectrum Model: Identifying Alternative Soteriological Perspectives', *Religion* 31.1 (2001): 19–39.

Schlichter, Annette, 'Queer at Last? Straight Intellectuals and the Desire for Transgression', *GLQ* 10. 4 (2004): 543–64.

Schneider, David, Tensho, *Street Zen: The Life and Work of Issan Dorsey* (Boston, MA: Shambhala, 1993)

Schneiders, Sandra, 'Spirituality in the Academy', *Theological Studies* 50.4 (1989): 676–97.

Schutte, Ofelia, 'A Critique of Normative Heterosexuality: Identity, Embodiment, and Sexual Difference in Beauvoir and Irigaray', *Hypatia* 12.1 (1997): 40–62.

Schwalbe, Michael, *Unlocking the Iron Cage: The Men's Movement, Gender Politics, and American Culture* (Oxford: Oxford University Press, 1996).

Schwartz, Tony, *What Really Matters: Searching for Wisdom in America* (New York: Bantam Books, 1995).

Seidler, Victor J., *Young Men and Masculinities: Global Cultures and Intimate Lives* (London: Zed Books, 2006).

Serna, J. Patrick, 'Fathers, Sons, and Hunting', *Catholic Men's Quarterly* (2005, Fall). Retrieved from http://www.houseonthemoor.com/Fall-Winter0506/Hunting.html.
_____ 'A Son Becomes a Father', *Catholic Men's Quarterly* (2006, Spring/Summer). Retrieved from http://www.houseonthemoor.com/Spring-Summer06/FrTodd.html.

Shand-Tucci, Douglas, *Boston Bohemia, 1881–1900: Ralph Adams Cram: Life and Architecture* (Amherst, MA: University of Massachusetts Press, 1996).

Shea, Mark P., 'Masculine and Feminine, Evangelical and Catholic', *This Rock* (2002, March). Retrieved from http://www.catholic.com/thisrock/2002/0203fea2.asp.

Simpson, Mark, 'Iron Clint: Queer Weddings in Robert Bly's Iron John and Clint Eastwood's Unforgiven' in Michael S. Kimmel (ed.), *The Politics of Manhood: Profeminist Men Respond to the Mythopoetic Men's Movement (and the Mythopoetic Leaders Answer)* (Philadelphia, PA: Temple University Press, 1995), pp. 257–68.

Singleton, Andrew, 'Good Advice for Godly Men: Oppressed Men in Christian Men's Self-Help Literature', *Journal of Gender Studies* 13. 2 (2004): 153–64.

Sogyal, Rinpoche, Patrick Gaffney, and Andrew Harvey (eds.), *The Tibetan Book of Living and Dying* (San Francisco, CA: Harper SanFrancisco, 1992).

Sonderman, Steve, 'What is Men's Ministry?' in Phil Downer (ed.), *Effective Men's Ministry: The Indispensable Toolkit for Your Church* (Grand Rapids, MI: Zondervan, 2001), pp. 25–35.

Spain, Daphne, *Gendered Spaces* (Chapel Hill, NC: The University of North Carolina Press, 1992).

St. Aubyn, Edward, *On the Edge* (London: Chatto & Windus, 1998).

Stanistreet, D., C. Bambra, and A. Scott-Samuel, 'Is Patriarchy the Source of Men's Higher Mortality?', *Journal of Epidemiology and Community Health*, no. 59 (2005): 873–76.

Starhawk, 'A Men's Movement I Can Trust' in Kay Leigh Hagan (ed.), *Women Respond to the Men's Movement: A Feminist Collection* (San Francisco: HarperCollins, 1992), pp. 27–37.

Stark, Rodney, 'Physiology and Faith: Addressing The 'Universal' Gender Difference in Religious Commitment', *Journal for the Scientific Study of Religion* 41. 3 (2002): 495–507.

Stecker, Chuck, 'Foundations of Christian Leadership' in Phil Downer (ed.), *Effective Men's Ministry: The Indispensable Toolkit for Your Church* (Grand Rapids, MI: Zondervan, 2001), pp. 107–15.

Steingard, David S., 'Spiritually-Informed Management Theory', *Journal of Management Inquiry* 14. 3 (2005): 227–41.

Stemmeler, Michael. L., 'Empowerment: The Construction of Gay Religious Identity' in Björn Krondorfer (ed.), *Men's Bodies, Men's Gods: Male Identities in a (Post-) Christian Culture* (New York: New York University Press, 1996), pp. 94–107.

Stone, Alison, *Luce Irigaray and the Philosophy of Sexual Difference* (Cambridge: Cambridge University Press, 2006).

Stowe, John R., *Gay Spirit Warrior: An Empowerment Workbook for Men Who Love Men* (Tallahassee, FL: Findhorn Press, 1999).

Stuart, Elizabeth, *Gay and Lesbian Theologies: Repetitions with Critical Difference* (Aldershot: Ashgate, 2003).

Sullivan, Nikki, *A Critical Introduction to Queer Theory* (New York: New York University Press, 2003).

Szyszkiewicz, Thomas A., 'Gathering His Sons Together', *Our Sunday Visitor* (2005, July). Retrieved from http://www.thecall.org/coverage.htm.

Tacey, David, *Remaking Men: Jung, Spirituality and Social Change* (London: Routledge, 1997).

Tarnas, Richard, *The Passion of the Western Mind: Understanding the Ideas That Have Shaped Our World View* (New York: Harmony Books, 1991).

Teilhard de Chardin, Pierre, *The Phenomenon of Man* (Bernard Wall trans; New York: Harper, 1959).

Thacker, Paul. D., 'Fighting a Distortion of Research', *Inside Higher Education* (2006). Retrieved from http://www.insidehighereducation.com/news/2006/12/19/gilligan.

Thomas, Calvin, 'Straight with a Twist: Queer Theory and the Subject of Heterosexuality' in Calvin Thomas (ed.), *Straight with a Twist: Queer Theory and the Subject of Heterosexuality* (Urbana, IL: University of Illinois Press, 2000a), pp. 11–44.

_____ (ed.), *Straight with a Twist: Queer Theory and the Subject of Heterosexuality* (Urbana, IL: University of Illinois Press, 2000b).

Thompson, Edward H., and Kathryn R. Remmes, 'Does Masculinity Thwart Being Religious? An Examination of Older Men's Religiousness', *Journal for the Scientific Study of Religion* 41. 3 (2002): 521–32.

Thompson, Keith (ed.), *To Be a Man: In Search of the Deep Masculine* (Los Angeles: J. P. Tarcher, 1991).

Thompson, Mark, *Gay Body: A Journey through Shadow to Self* (New York: St. Martin's Press, 1999).

_____ *Gay Soul: Finding the Heart of Gay Spirit and Nature with Sixteen Writers, Healers, Teachers, and Visionaries* (San Francisco: HarperSanFrancisco, 1994).

Thompson, William G., 'Men and the Gospels', *The Catholic World* 235, no. 1407 (1992): 104–11.

Thompson, William Irwin, *Coming into Being: Artifacts and Texts in the Evolution of Consciousness* (New York: St. Martin's Press, 1996).

Timmons, Stuart, *The Trouble with Harry Hay: Founder of the Modern Gay Movement* (Boston, MA: Alyson, 1990).

Tolkien, J.R.R., *The Return of the King* (New York: Ballantine Books, 1955).

United States Conference of Catholic Bishops, *Hearing Christ's Call: A Resource for the Formation and Spirituality of Catholic Men* (Washington, DC: United States Conference of Catholic Bishops, 2002).

Upton, Charles, *Hammering Hot Iron: A Spiritual Critique of Bly's Iron John* (Wheaton, IL: Quest Books, 1993).

van Leeuwen, Mary Stewart, 'Servanthood or Soft Patriarchy? A Christian Feminist Looks at the Promise Keepers Movement', *Journal of Men's Studies* 5. 3 (1997): 233–61.

van Marrewijk, Marcel, 'Concepts and Definitions of CSR and Corporate Sustainability: Between Agency and Communion', *Journal of Business Ethics* 44, no. 2–3 (2003): 95–105.

van Marrewijk, Marcel, and Teun W. Hardjono, 'European Corporate Sustainability Framework for Managing Complexity and Corporate Transformation', *Journal of Business Ethics* 44, no. 2–3 (2003): 121–32.

Vernadsky, Vladimir Ivanovich, 'The Biosphere and the Noosphere', *Scientific American* 33, no. 1 (1945): 1–12.

Visser, Frank, *Ken Wilber: Thought as Passion* (Albany, NY: State University of New York Press, 2003).

Volckmann, Russ, 'Assessing Executive Leadership: An Integral Approach', *Journal of Organizational Change Management* 18. 3 (2005): 289–302.

Walby, Sylvia, *Theorizing Patriarchy* (Oxford: Basil Blackwell, 1990).

Wall, John, 'Fatherhood, Childism and the Creation of Society', *Journal of the American Academy of Religion* 75. 1 (2007): 52–76.

Wallis, Jim, *God's Politics: Why the Right Gets It Wrong and the Left Doesn't Get It* (San Francisco, CA: HarperSanFrancisco, 2005).

Ward, Graham, 'Bodies: The Displaced Body of Jesus Christ' in John Milbank, Catherine Pickstock and Graham Ward (eds.), *Radical Orthodoxy* (London: Routledge, 1999), pp. 163–81.

Watkins, G. F., *G-Men: The Final Strategy* (Southlake, TX: Watercolor Books, 2001).

Waugh, Evelyn, *Brideshead Revisited* (London: Penguin, 1962).

Weber, Stu, *Tender Warrior: God's Intention for a Man* (Sisters, OR: Multnomah, 1993).

West, Michael O., 'Like a River: The Million Man March and the Black Nationalist Tradition in the United States', *Journal of Historical Sociology* 12. 1 (1999): 81–100.

Whitford, Margaret, 'Introduction' in Margaret Whitford (ed.), *The Irigaray Reader* (Oxford: Basil Blackwell, 1991), pp. 1–15.

Whyte, Frederick, *The Life of W.T. Stead* (London: Jonathan Cape, 1925, Vol. 2).

Wilber, Ken, *A Brief History of Everything* (Boston, MA: Shambhala, 1996b).

_____ 'A More Integral Approach', *ReVision* 19. 2 (1996a): 10–35.

_____ *One Taste: The Journals of Ken Wilber* (Boston, MA: Shambhala, 1999).

_____ *Sex, Ecology, Spirituality: The Spirit of Evolution* (Boston, MA: Shambhala, 2000a, 2nd edn.).

_____ A Theory of Everything: An Integral Vision for Business, Politics, Science, and Spirituality (Boston, MA: Shambhala, 2000b).

_____ Integral Spirituality: A Startling New Role for Religion in the Modern and Postmodern World (Boston: Integral Books, 2006).

Wilcox, W. Bradford, Soft Patriarchs, New Men: How Christianity Shapes Fathers and Husbands (Chicago: University of Chicago Press, 2004).

Williams, Rhys H. (ed.), Promise Keepers and the New Masculinity: Private Lives and Public Morality (Lanham, MD: Lexington Books, 2001).

Wood, Stephen, Christian Fatherhood: The Eight Commitments of St. Joseph's Covenant Keepers (Port Charlotte, FL: Family Life Center Publications, 1997).

Wright, Les K. (ed.), The Bear Book: Readings in the History and Evolution of a Gay Male Subculture (New York: Harrington Park Press, 1997).

_____ (ed.), The Bear Book: Further Readings in the History and Evolution of a Gay Male Subculture (New York: Harrington Park Press, 2001).

Wright, Peggy A., 'Bringing Women's Voices to Transpersonal Theory', ReVision 17. 3 (1995): 3–11.

_____ 'Gender Issues in Ken Wilber's Transpersonal Theory', ReVision 18. 4 (1996): 25–37.

Wulff, David M., Psychology of Religion: Classic and Contemporary (New York: John Wiley & Sons, 1997, 2nd edn.).

Zipes, Jack, 'Spreading Myths About Fairy Tales: A Critical Commentary on Robert Bly's Iron John', New German Critique 55, Winter (1992): 3–19.

INDEX